T0254607

BlitzMax for Absolute Beginners

Games Programming for the Absolute Beginner

Sloan Kelly

Apress®

BlitzMax for Absolute Beginners: Games Programming for the Absolute Beginner

Sloan Kelly
Niagara Falls, Ontario, Canada

ISBN-13 (pbk): 978-1-4842-2522-6   ISBN-13 (electronic): 978-1-4842-2523-3
DOI 10.1007/978-1-4842-2523-3

Library of Congress Control Number: 2016961342

Copyright © 2016 by Sloan Kelly

This work is subject to copyright. All rights are reserved by the Publisher, whether the whole or part of the material is concerned, specifically the rights of translation, reprinting, reuse of illustrations, recitation, broadcasting, reproduction on microfilms or in any other physical way, and transmission or information storage and retrieval, electronic adaptation, computer software, or by similar or dissimilar methodology now known or hereafter developed.

Trademarked names, logos, and images may appear in this book. Rather than use a trademark symbol with every occurrence of a trademarked name, logo, or image, we use the names, logos, and images only in an editorial fashion and to the benefit of the trademark owner, with no intention of infringement of the trademark.

The use in this publication of trade names, trademarks, service marks, and similar terms, even if they are not identified as such, is not to be taken as an expression of opinion as to whether or not they are subject to proprietary rights.

While the advice and information in this book are believed to be true and accurate at the date of publication, neither the author nor the editors nor the publisher can accept any legal responsibility for any errors or omissions that may be made. The publisher makes no warranty, express or implied, with respect to the material contained herein.

Managing Director: Welmoed Spahr
Lead Editor: Steve Anglin
Technical Reviewer: Massimo Nardone
Editorial Board: Steve Anglin, Pramila Balan, Laura Berendson, Aaron Black, Louise Corrigan, Jonathan Gennick, Robert Hutchinson, Celestin Suresh John, Nikhil Karkal, James Markham, Susan McDermott, Matthew Moodie, Natalie Pao, Gwenan Spearing
Coordinating Editor: Mark Powers
Copy Editor: Michael G. Laraque
Compositor: SPi Global
Indexer: SPi Global
Artist: SPi Global
Cover image designed by Freepik

Distributed to the book trade worldwide by Springer Science+Business Media New York, 233 Spring Street, 6th Floor, New York, NY 10013. Phone 1-800-SPRINGER, fax (201) 348-4505, e-mail orders-ny@springer-sbm.com, or visit www.springeronline.com. Apress Media, LLC is a California LLC and the sole member (owner) is Springer Science + Business Media Finance Inc (SSBM Finance Inc). SSBM Finance Inc is a Delaware corporation.

For information on translations, please e-mail rights@apress.com, or visit www.apress.com.

Apress and friends of ED books may be purchased in bulk for academic, corporate, or promotional use. eBook versions and licenses are also available for most titles. For more information, reference our Special Bulk Sales–eBook Licensing web page at www.apress.com/bulk-sales.

Any source code or other supplementary materials referenced by the author in this text are available to readers at www.apress.com. For detailed information about how to locate your book's source code, go to www.apress.com/source-code/. Readers can also access source code at SpringerLink in the Supplementary Material section for each chapter.

Printed on acid-free paper

Contents at a Glance

Contents

About the Author

Sloan Kelly has been programming computers since 1982. His first computer was a ZX Spectrum 16K where he learned Sinclair BASIC and soon moved onto Z80 machine code. At the end of the 8-bit era he progressed to the Commodore Amiga where he coded some small games in a language called Blitz.

After graduating college and spending nine years in traditional IT working in senior or lead positions, Sloan went back to school and was awarded a Masters in Informatics (Game Technology) to allow him to pursue a career in the games industry where he has remained for almost ten years. He is currently working for PixelNAUTS Games in the beautiful Niagara Region of Canada as senior programmer. Their debut game, LOST ORBIT, was released in 2015 to critical acclaim.

About the Technical Reviewer

Massimo Nardone has more than 22 years of experience in security, web/mobile development, cloud, and IT architecture. His true IT passions are security and Android.

He has been programming and teaching how to program with Android, Perl, PHP, Java, VB, Python, C/C++, and MySQL for more than 20 years.

He holds a master of science degree in computer science from the University of Salerno, Italy.

He has worked as a project manager, software engineer, research engineer, chief security architect, information security manager, PCI/SCADA auditor, and senior lead IT security/cloud/SCADA architect for many years.

He has technical proficiency in security, Android, cloud, Java, MySQL, Drupal, Cobol, Perl, web and mobile development, MongoDB, D3, Joomla, Couchbase, C/C++, WebGL, Python, Pro Rails, Django CMS, Jekyll, Scratch, among others.

He currently works as chief information security officer for Cargotec Oyj.

He was a visiting lecturer and supervisor for exercises at the Networking Laboratory of Helsinki University of Technology (Aalto University). He holds four international patents (in PKI, SIP, SAML, and Proxy areas).

Massimo has reviewed more than 40 IT books for various publishing companies, and he is the coauthor of *Pro Android Games* (Apress, 2015).

CHAPTER 1

■ ■ ■

Computer System

A "modern" computer system is a bit of a misnomer, as not much has really changed in more than 20 years! The basics of the system are described in this section.

As far as aesthetics are concerned, the machine in the following diagram (Figure 1-1) may look nothing like yours! Be assured, however, that the items described in the diagram are contained within your system. At the heart of any computer is the central processing unit, or CPU. This is sometimes referred to as the brains of the computer. It is, in actual fact, more like a mill spinning raw data into solutions, as there is no intrinsic intelligence in the machine. If you provided the computer with garbage, it would process it to garbage (Garbage In, Garbage Out—GIGO).

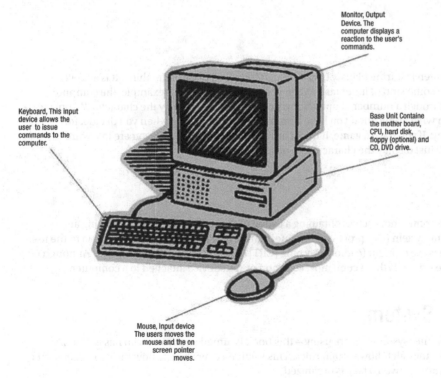

Monitor, Output Device. The computer displays a reaction to the user's commands.

Keyboard, This input device allows the user to issue commands to the computer.

Base Unit Containe the mother board, CPU, hard disk, floppy (optional) and CD, DVD drive.

Mouse, Input device The users moves the mouse and the on screen pointer moves.

Figure 1-1. *Diagram of a basic computer*

Electronic supplementary material The online version of this chapter (doi: 10.1007/978-1-4842-2523-3_1) contains supplementary material, which is available to authorized users.

In its simplest form, a computer takes input from some device, processes it, and generates output. This is shown in the following block diagram (Figure 1-2):

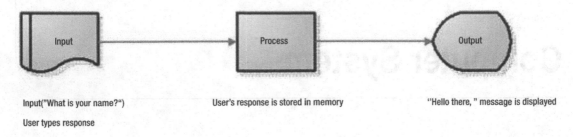

Input("What is your name?")   User's response is stored in memory   "Hello there, " message is displayed

User types response

Figure 1-2. *A computer takes input from some device, processes it, and generates output*

Input

When you think of an input device, you usually think of the keyboard or mouse. These are generally the two traditional means of accessing a computer. In addition, joysticks and game pads can be used to provide input and move player characters, such as Mario, around the screen.

Disk drive, CD-ROM, light pen, joystick, game pad, keyboard, mouse, and track ball are all types of input devices.

Process

Even when a computer screen is staring blankly back at you, it is, in fact, doing something. It is actually waiting for you to perform some kind of input task. When you press the A key, for example, the computer takes the key stroke and, through a number of operations, processes this to display the character "A" onscreen.

Processes depend on what application you have running on your machine when you decide, for instance, to press the A key. If you have a game, it might arm a weapon's array, or if you are in a word-processing package, it will just display the character "A" onscreen.

Output

Once the user has issued a command, such as obtaining a listing of the current directory or clicking an on-screen button, the operating system (OS) processes this information and displays the resulting data to the user. The most common device is the monitor (cathode ray tube [CRT] or liquid crystal display [LCD]). Although I will not cover its usage, the printer is the second most common output device attached to a computer.

The Computer System

Independent of what computer system you are using—this book is aimed at anyone who has either a Mac, PC, or Linux box, after all—they all follow certain rules. This section covers briefly how the computer system works and how the hardware/software stack is organized.

Inside each and every computer is a large sheet covered in electronics. This is called the motherboard. All the parts, apart from the fan attached to the CPU, are stationary. A motherboard looks like the following (Figure 1-3):

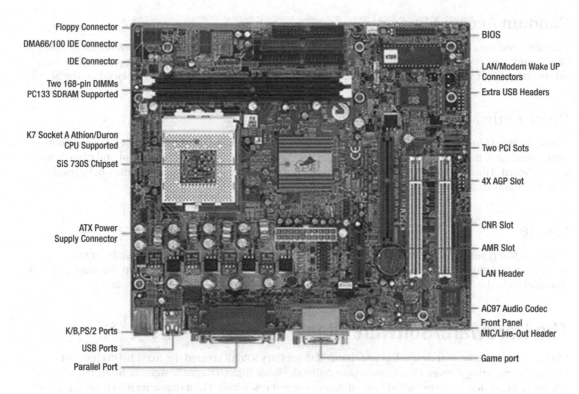

Floppy Connector
DMA66/100 IDE Connector
IDE Connector
Two 168-pin DIMMs
PC133 SDRAM Supported

K7 Socket A Athlon/Duron
CPU Supported
SiS 730S Chipset

ATX Power
Supply Connector

K/B,PS/2 Ports
USB Ports
Parallel Port

BIOS

LAN/Modem Wake UP
Connectors
Extra USB Headers

Two PCI Sots

4X AGP Slot

CNR Slot
AMR Slot
LAN Header

AC97 Audio Codec
Front Panel
MIC/Line-Out Header

Game port

Figure 1-3. *A motherboard and its components*

The socket for the CPU is the large white square at the middle left on the motherboard. The main memory fits into the sockets directly above—the long black lines running left to right. The ROM-BIOS is located at the top right of the motherboard. There are additional connectors to external systems, such as keyboard, mouse, floppy, and hard disks. The IDE (Integrated Drive Electronics) connectors to the top allow DVD-ROM, CD-ROM, and hard drives to be connected.

Computer Memory

When a computer is running, it stores its data and programs in memory. There are four types of computer memory: disk, random access memory (RAM), read-only memory (ROM), and cache.

Disk

The hard disk stores the operating system of all your major applications (such as word processors, spreadsheets, Internet browsers, and, of course, BlitzMax), even when the computer is turned off. This type of memory is sometimes referred to as permanent storage, because no matter how many times you power down/power up, the programs remain on disk.

CD-ROMs and DVDs are becoming more and more popular to store large amounts of data that can be transported easily from one system to another. For the most part, these types of disks are Write Once, Read Many, or WORM, for short. If you want to rewrite to them, you will have to purchase a device that has RW in the title, such as CD-ROM (RW) or DVD-RW.

Random Access Memory

Programs and data are not accessed directly from disk. They are, in fact, read into random access memory (RAM) and manipulated in there. Think of RAM as a dry marker board. You can store lots of ideas on a dry marker board, but sooner or later, the information can be erased, and new data can be placed on the board.

Read-Only Memory

The basic input/output system (BIOS) is stored in a chip on the motherboard and cannot be overwritten. This is read-only memory. The programs and data are encoded at a chip fabrication plant and placed on the motherboard. The chip allows data to be read from it but not written to it. It can, therefore, not be used to store programs or data.

Cache

There are two types of cache memory: Level 1 (L1) and Level 2 (L2). Both act as scratchpads for the CPU during computations. They differ in physical location, because the L1 cache is located on the same physical silicon chip as the CPU, whereas the L2 cache is located beside the CPU on the motherboard.

The Hardware/Software Stack

Modern computer system design has not changed since Gary Kildall created the ROM BIOS chip and changed computing forever. He created a chip called the Basic Input/Output System, or BIOS, that allowed his operating system to be ported to many different computers, without him requiring him to do much work. The problem is that as you move farther up the stack, the more difficult it is to port (copy) applications from one system to another. The full software stack is shown here (Figure 1-4):

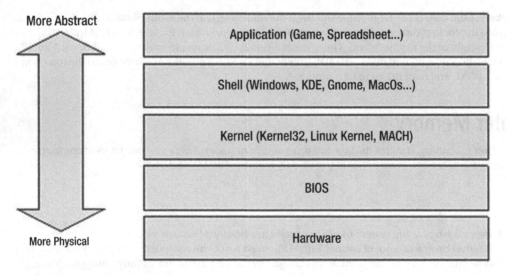

Figure 1-4. Diagram of the software stack

The hardware can read and write single bytes of data at a time to and from external devices. In a computer system, an external device is anything not attached to the motherboard. This includes the disk drives, CD-ROM, DVD, monitor, keyboard, and mouse.

The BIOS acts as an interface between the operating system's kernel and the hardware. The BIOS does this by exposing a number of functions to the kernel that call hardware functions multiple times. This allows for more complex actions to be undertaken, such as reading in large files from a disk drive with a single call.

The kernel is the core of the operating system. It handles all input/output requests and memory management. The kernel code is specific to the operating system that you are using. For example, a Windows kernel is not compatible with the Linux operating system. The kernel exposes a number of functions to the application's layer. These functions are collectively known as the application programming interface, or API, for short.

The shell is the interface to the operating system, from a user's perspective. It allows users to load and execute applications as well as perform file operations. All this is achieved using the function exposed by the kernel's API.

An application is any executable that is invoked by the shell or some call to the kernel. This means that the shell is also an application! For example, Explorer.exe is the shell for Windows. It is also the file manager application. The application uses the kernel's API to create windows, load files, and perform all the other input/output functions.

It should be noted that in the early days—not so much now—many application developers bypassed the kernel to call the BIOS, to make their programs run faster. This is because the kernel contains a lot of error trapping code that can slow down operations. Thankfully, modern kernel designs mean that the code is fully optimized and is just as fast as a call to the BIOS.

Keyboard

The keyboard is the main input device in a modern computer system. It is basically an alphanumeric keyboard with special and function keys. To the right are three examples of keyboards through the ages—the lower model is the one that most systems will have. It is an AT-style keyboard with approximately 102 keys. There may also be keys marked z, ?, q, or ?. These keys have special functions, depending on the operating system you are using.

Mouse

The mouse has been used in computers since the early 1980s. It took a while for the IBM PC and compatibles to get the device adopted, but with the advent of windowed operating systems, the mouse became the second input device for most PCs.

On a PC system, the mouse has a minimum of two buttons, sometimes more. Mac users are still getting frustrated because their new machines come with a single button mouse, although multiple mouse buttons are supported by the OS.

Screen

The screen or monitor is the primary output device for the computer system. As mentioned previously, there are two different types of screens: cathode ray tube (CRT) and liquid crystal display (LCD). The latter is becoming cheaper and, therefore, more popular, or is it cheaper because it is popular?

The computer outputs to the monitor at a given resolution. Resolution means "How many pixels along? How many pixels down?"

Physical screen resolution is measured in pixels. The word pixel is a shortened form of "Picture Element1." There are a variety of resolutions available on your PC, from 320×240 pixels (PC only) to 2560×1600 (Mac only).

A graphics card inside the computer works with the CPU to produce images on the monitor. With newer graphic cards, a graphics processing unit (GPU) is placed on the card to improve the 3D capabilities of the system, such as make games more realistic, by providing higher resolutions, special effects, and a better frame rate.

Resolution

Resolution defines how detailed your images will look on screen. The number of columns—the horizontal axis and the number of rows—the vertical axis define the number of pixels available to the application. In the following example, a 640×480 resolution screen map is shown (Figure 1-5). No matter what resolution your monitor is running at, the top-left corner will always have the coordinate (0,0).

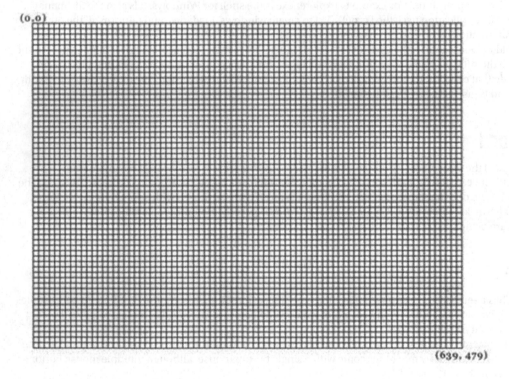

Figure 1-5. *A 640×480 pixel resolution screen map*

Coordinate numbers start from 0 (zero). Resolution works independently of the physical size of your monitor. So, if you have a large monitor and a low-resolution screen, you will easily see pixels, and the screen image will appear blocky (Figure 1-6).

Figure 1-6. *Diminishing resolution, from higher to lower (left to right)*

Essentially, the design of a modern computer system has not changed in more than 20 years. The system still has a keyboard, mouse, and monitor. It still has a CPU and some way to power the monitor, using either built-in graphics or a second-party graphics card.

Computers operate on a simple premise: input, process, and, finally, output. Information is gathered from sources such as the disk drive, network, keyboard, and mouse and run through a series of commands—*processed,* so to speak—resulting in changes to the visual display.

Number Systems

Computers cannot count in the same way that we can. We use the decimal system to perform calculations. This involves ten numbers: zero through nine, inclusive. Computers are built using electronics, which can be either on or off. This is a binary system—a system that can be in one of two states. This means that computers are, in fact, restricted to two numerical values: zero and one.

The Decimal System

In the decimal system, we count numbers from 0 to 9, then in 10s, 100s, 1000s, and so on. For example, the number 1,225 could be understood as the following (Table 1-1):

Table 1-1. *The Decimal System*

1000's	100's	10's	1's
1	2	2	5

which is $(1 * 1000) + (2 * 100) + (2 * 10) + (5 * 1) = 1,225$.

The boldface numbers in the preceding table are actually powers of 10. So, we could rewrite the table as in Table 1-2, that is, $(1 * 10^3) + (2 * 10^2) + (2 * 10^1) + (5 * 10^0)$.

Table 1-2. *Powers of Ten*

10^3	10^2	10^1	10^0
1	2	2	5

You should note that anything to the power 0 is 1.

The binary system follows a similar pattern, but instead of having ten numbers, binary systems must make do with only two.

The Binary System

As we have discovered, any numerical system can be represented in powers. The binary system uses two digits, and so the system uses powers of two to represent numbers (Table 1-3).

Table 1-3. *Powers of Two*

Powers of Two	2^7	2^6	2^5	2^4	2^3	2^2	2^1	2^0
Decimal Value	128	64	32	16	8	4	2	1
		Most significant bit				Least significant bit		

Bits are numbered from the right to the left, from 0 to 7. The "most significant bit" is the leftmost bit. So, the "most significant bit" is bit 7. The "least significant bit" is the rightmost bit. Bit 0 is the "least significant bit."

To represent numbers in this restrictive numbering system, we place a zero or a one in the appropriate box. Some examples follow:

The decimal 5 in binary can be expressed as in Table 1-4.

Table 1-4. *Decimal 5 in Binary*

Powers of Two	2^7	2^6	2^5	2^4	2^3	2^2	2^1	2^0
Decimal Value	128	64	32	16	8	4	2	1
	0	0	0	0	0	1	0	1

Because: 4 + 1 = 5, the decimal 26 in binary can be expressed as in Table 1-5.

Table 1-5. *Decimal 26 in Binary*

Powers of Two	2^7	2^6	2^5	2^4	2^3	2^2	2^1	2^0
Decimal Value	128	64	32	16	8	4	2	1
	0	0	0	1	1	0	1	0

This is because 16 + 8 + 2 = 26.

Note that for even-numbered values, the least-significant bit is zero.

Binary Numbering

To convert from decimal to binary, find the largest number equal to or below the one you are looking for. Then, if needed, add lower numbers to get that figure. For example, let's take the number 23. How would it be represented in binary?

The highest number before 23 is 16, so we remember 16. Now we have to see what number we have to add to 16 to get 23. The number below 16 is 8, but adding 16 to 8 would give us 24, so we ignore that and go to the next lowest number, 4. This gives us 20, which is perfect. So far, so good. Adding the next lowest number (2) gives us 22, and, finally, adding the last number (1) gives us the 23 we are looking for.

So, 23 in binary is 10011. Note that you can ignore the leading zeros in binary.

Groups of Binary Digits

To make things easier for the programmer, computers group binary digits together. The groups of digits are shown following.

1—Bit: A binary digit. Either a zero or a one. This is the lowest "grouping." There are two reasons why it's called "bit." The first is that it is a contraction of BInary and digIT to give you BIT. However, the one I am most fond of is when a dollar could be split into eight pieces. Each piece was called a "bit." Remember that old rhyme? Shave and a haircut—two bits? Well, two bits is 2 8ths, which is a quarter.

4—Nybble (also, nibble, nyble): This term is hardly ever used anymore, but it is included here on behalf of 8-bit programmers. A nybble is half a byte. As we'll see, it makes counting in hexadecimal a little easier.

8—Byte: This is the most common grouping of bits in a computer system. It represents a single memory location in the computer.

16—Word (also, halfword): In older machines, this represented an integer value. This is the equivalent of two bytes.

32—Long word (also, doubleword): Most modern machines use this as their current representation of an integer value. This is the equivalent of four bytes.

Groups of Bytes

When bits are too small to count, bytes are used and are represented by the following groupings:

1—Byte (B): This is the most common grouping of bits in a computer system. It represents a single memory location in the computer.

1,024—Kilobyte (KB) (roughly): One thousand bytes

1,048,576—Megabyte (MB) (roughly): One thousand kilobytes, or (roughly) one million bytes

1,073,741,824—Gigabyte (GB) (roughly): One thousand megabytes

1 Terabyte = 1,099,511,627,776 Bytes

Hexadecimal

Computer scientists—programmers—can also count in another numeric base: hexadecimal. As the name might suggest, this system uses 16 digits instead of just 10. So, where do we get the extra digits from? We use letters, of course! Table 1-6 shows the decimal, binary, hexadecimal, and English equivalents for each number.

Table 1-6. *Numerical Equivalents in Decimal, Hexadecimal, and Binary Systems*

Decimal	Hexadecimal	Binary
0	0	0000
1	1	0001
2	2	0010
3	3	0011
4	4	0100
5	5	0101
6	6	0110
7	7	0111
8	8	1000
9	9	1001
10	A	1010
11	B	1011
12	C	1100
13	D	1101
14	E	1110
15	F	1111

Let's look at some examples of hexadecimal numbers. The number 255 in base 10 in hexadecimal is FF. The binary number is 1111 1111.

Look at the binary and hexadecimal numbers closely? Do you see a pattern? In binary, the hexadecimal number F is written as 1111.

So, each hexadecimal digit from 0 to F can be represented by four bits. Knowing this can make calculations easier!

In the preceding example, the two 4-bit binary numbers are 1111 and 1111. To convert this to a hexadecimal number, we look up the preceding hexadecimal table to find the corresponding hex-digit. In this case, it is F. Both numbers are the same, so 255 is represented by FF. But how can we know for sure that FF_{16} equals 255_{10}?

As we did before with decimal and binary numbers, we can apply powers to our hexadecimal numbers, this time, in powers of 16.

So, our hexadecimal number is FF (Table 1-7).

Table 1-7. *Hexadecimal Number*

16^3	16^2	16^1	16^0
0	0	F	F

F is 15 in decimal, which means $(15 * 16^1) + (15 * 16^0) = 240 + 15 = 255$.

Now that we can use hexadecimal, binary addition can be so much easier. Let's try something else. The number 17 in decimal in hexadecimal is 11.

In binary it is 00010001.

Again, this means: (1 * 16) + (1 * 1) = 16 + 1 = 17.

The number 38 in decimal. In hexadecimal it is 26; in binary it is 0010 0110.

This means that the first 4-bit binary number is 0010, which is 2 in decimal. Because that's in our 16s column, we have to multiply it by 16. The second 4-bit binary number is 0110, which is 6, because it's in our 1s column: (2 * 16) + (6 * 1) = 32 + 3 = 38.

Larger Numbers

You will probably only encounter hexadecimal values with larger numbers, such as memory locations and colors. Those of you familiar with designing web pages may recognize the color red when you see #FF0000. Larger numbers are handled in the same way as smaller numbers. Take the number 8,000 in hexadecimal, for example.

When calculated out, it is as follows: 8 * 4096 + 0 * 256 + 0 * 16 + 0 * 1 = 32768.

For the curious, how would this be represented in binary? Answer: 1000000000000000. If we were to split that into 4-bit binary numbers, it would be as follows:

1000

0000

0000

0000

In summary, then, computers can only count using base 2 or *binary*. This consists of two digits, 0 and 1, to represent all numbers.

Hexadecimal can be used to group binary digits together, to make them easier for humans to read. Converting between hexadecimal and binary is relatively easy when you break down the hex number into 4-bit nybbles.

CHAPTER 2

■ ■ ■

How BlitzMax Works

When computers first began to be used, the only way to program them was to manually pull switches and rotate dials on the front. Nothing much improved in 30 years, and in 1975, when the world got its first personal computer, the MITS Altair, one still had to use switches to program the box.

And that was all it was—a box. There was no keyboard, no monitor, and no mouse. The only thing it had was a series of switches and small light-emitting diodes (LEDs). All this changed when third parties began supporting this new machine. Soon, teletypes—a keyboard-like device—were attached, along with displays, printers, etc. But still there was no actual way to program the machine until two Harvard men, Bill Gates and Paul Allen, created a version of the popular BASIC programming language for the new machine.

Computers Can't Read English

Computers can only understand binary data, and as I have previously discussed, this means that, as electronic devices, each binary digit can have a state of off or on.

The computer's central processing unit (CPU) is hard-coded with a list of commands. These commands are fired whenever the correct instruction is sent. This is part of what is called the fetch-execute cycle.

Translating English to Computerese (Machine Code)

The solution is to have some conversion between our language (I'll assume English) and the computer. Two professors, at Dartmouth College, John Kemeny and Thomas Kurtz, created the BASIC language. BASIC, or Basic, is an acronym that stands for "Beginner's All-purpose Symbolic Instruction Code." The two professors created Basic to include many English words, to ensure that those new to programming a computer would pick up the new language quickly. BlitzMax is an updated object-oriented version of this popular language.

The programs we write are called source code. Source code is translated by a program called a compiler. A compiler works like a translator at the United Nations. It takes source code written in one language and converts it to another. In this case, our BlitzMax code is converted to machine code. BlitzMax is even cleverer! If we take our source code from one system (say, Windows) to another (say, Mac OS X), we can re-compile the source code on that machine to generate Mac machine code. This means that BlitzMax is portable.

Portability is important in the games industry. In its basic sense, you are increasing your possible market by 200%, because you can write-once and compile-many on multiple systems. For example, so long as you have access to a Linux, Windows, and a Mac OS X box, you can write programs for all three systems! Think of the user base! And fixes to all three versions are simple: write it on one, and re-compile on the other two.

© Sloan Kelly 2016

S. Kelly, *BlitzMax for Absolute Beginners*, DOI 10.1007/978-1-4842-2523-3_2

Compilation Process

The following is a very simple program:

```
Print "This is a small program"
```

This will display the message "This is a small program" onscreen. When we run it, the output in the BlitzMax IDE will be:

```
Building SimpleProg
Compiling:SimpleProg.bmx
flat assembler version 1.51
3 passes, 2285 bytes.
Linking:SimpleProg.debug.exe
Executing:SimpleProg.debug.exe
This is a small program
Process Complete
```

Notice the size of the file is 2285 bytes. When we look at our source code, it only contains 31 characters. How did it get so big? The problem is that the operating system needs some code to initialize itself. Remember portability? Well, on the PC, the source code is compiled to Intel assembly language—the machine code equivalent of source code—and is then converted to machine code—zeros and ones. The assembly language is shown. Please note that it has been chopped for brevity:

```
        format      MS COFF
        extrn ___bb_basic_basic
        extrn ___bb_blitz_blitz
        :     :
        public      __bb_main
        section    "code" code
__bb_main:
        push  ebp
        mov   ebp,esp
        push  ebx
        cmp   dword [_19],0
        je    _20
        mov   eax,0
        pop   ebx
        pop   ebp
        ret
        :     :
        call  ___bb_blitz_blitz
        call  ___bb_appstub_appstub
        call  ___bb_basic_basic
        :     :
        push  _12
        call  _brl_standardio_Print
        :     :
_12:
        dd    _bbStringClass
        dd    2147483647
        dd    23
```

```
dw    84,104,105,115,32,105,115,32
dw    97,32,115,109,97,108,108,32
dw    112,114,111,103,114,97,109
```

You can see why it compiles to more than 2K worth of a program! There are several interesting lines in all of this, though.

```
push _12
call _brl_standardio_Print
```

This pushes the address of Label _12 onto the stack and calls the Print() function. Label _12 points to the memory location of our text ("This is a small program"). So, what this function does is print the text on the screen, using a standard function created by Blitz Research. Notice that it's kind of backwards, because the actual parameter comes first, before the command. This is a standard way of calling something in machine code. I only mention it to give you a greater understanding of what the compiler does! Now, when we look at Label _12, it contains the following information:

```
_12:
    dd    _bbStringClass
    dd    2147483647
    dd    23
    dw    84,104,105,115,32,105,115,32
    dw    97,32,115,109,97,108,108,32
    dw    112,114,111,103,114,97,109
```

What is interesting about this is that it defines the type of data (_bbStringClass), the length of the string (23), and the actual data. There are 23 characters in the string, and they are shown in Table 2-1.

Table 2-1. *The 23 Characters in the String*

T	H	I	S
84	104	105	115
	I	S	
32	105	115	32
A		S	M
97	32	115	109
A	L	L	
97	108	108	32
P	R	O	G
112	114	111	103
R	A	M	
114	97	109	

The values stored are actually ASCII (American Standard Code for Information Interchange) codes. See the appendixes of this book for a list of ASCII codes. I've included the ASCII byte values below each of the letters above them.

Q. What does all this mean?

A. We don't have to learn complex machine code to program a computer! We can do it all with one line and let the compiler do the hard work.

Application/Game/Program

These terms are all effectively interchangeable, and as you will see from this book, I interchange them all the time. The difference, if there is any, is that *application* is a new word for *program*, and a *game* is a type of application. I hope that clears things up!

But Why BlitzMax?

There are other frameworks out there like MonoGame and Gamemaker Studio to help you create games. But for someone just starting out coding though, BlitzMax is an excellent choice. BlitzMax is born from a long line of tools created by Blitz Research. I started using BlitzBASIC on an Amiga about twenty-odd years ago. There have been other iterations of the language through the years including Blitz3D and BlitzPlus. The key though is the simplicity of the language. It has that easy-to-get into quality of BASIC, but the power required for modern games.

The IDE, which was open sourced, is available on Windows, Mac and Linux distributions. So no matter what machine or OS you are running you're sure to find a version of BlitzMax for it. Not only that but because the language is hardware and Operating System agnostic, a simple recompile on a target platform means that your game can be shipped cross-platform. The program; the IDE and the compiler, tools and examples can be downloaded from `http://www.blitzmax.com/`.

CHAPTER 3

■ ■ ■

The BlitzMax IDE

BlitzMax (Figure 3-1) provides an out-of-the-box Integrated Development Environment, or IDE. This application offers the following components:

The Editor: Edits source code

The Compiler: Translates source code to machine language

The Debugger: Helps to fix your program when things go wrong

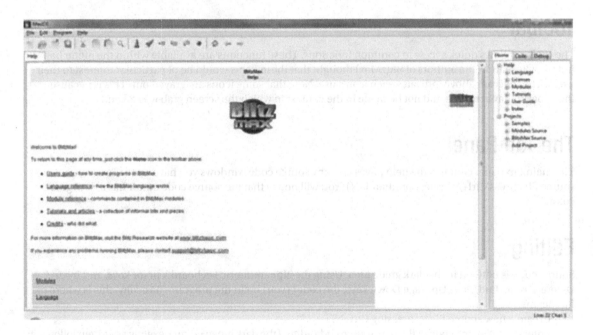

Figure 3-1. *BlitzMax screen*

Launching the IDE

Depending on your operating system, locate the BlitzMax program icon and launch it (in Windows, it's a single click from the start menu, on Mac and Linux, you will have to locate the icon in your Applications folder and double-click it). The IDE will launch.

© Sloan Kelly 2016

S. Kelly, *BlitzMax for Absolute Beginners*, DOI 10.1007/978-1-4842-2523-3_3

The IDE is split into a number of parts.

Menu bar: File, Edit…Help, as you would expect

Toolbar: Quick access to common functions, such as Open a file, Compile, etc.

Tab panel: For each help window source file open, a new tab is created.

Tree panel: This, too, is tabbed, to allow access to Help/Projects, Debug symbols, and code files.

Menu Bar

The menu bar contains four items:

File: Access to file operations (open, close, save, etc.)

Edit: Access to clipboard operations (copy, delete, paste, etc.)

Program: Access to compilation operations (build, debug, etc.)

Help: Access to online help

Toolbar

The toolbar allows quick access to common functions. These functions are available within the menu bar, but Blitz Research (the authors of BlitzMax) thought that these items would be of particular interest to their users. The diagram above indicates each icon's use. Note that some icons are grayed out. This is because those particular actions could not be made in the context in which the screen grab was taken.

The Tab Panel

The main tab panel contains the help pages and any source code windows you have open. To create a new source file, press Ctrl+N (Mac: Command+N). You will notice that the source code editor has a dark green color.

Editing

Source code is entered in the dark green area. Using the alphanumeric keyboard, cursor keys, and Insert/Delete/Home/End/Page Up/Page Down keys, the coder (you) build the program. Basically, this is where the fun begins!

Create a new source file by pressing Ctrl+N.

Enter the following code in the new source code editor (the dark green editor), exactly as written following:

```
Graphics 640, 480, 16
While Not KeyHit(KEY_ESCAPE)
    Cls
Flip
Wend
```

Make sure you have checked the code and that it matches exactly that preceding.

To run the program, press the F5 key or, on the Mac, Command+R. The output panel will appear and contain text similar to the following:

```
Building untitlied1
Compiling:untitlied1.bmx
flat assembler version 1.51
3 passes, 2719 bytes.
Linking:untitlied1.debug.exe
Executing:untitlied1.debug.exe
```

The screen will then go black and...nothing. Our program doesn't do anything. Well, it's actually doing quite a lot, but we can't see it! To quit the application, press the Escape key.

Insert

We have already inserted text into the source code editor one line at a time, but as with word processing packages, we can go back and re-edit the code to change its meaning or, perhaps, fix a bug.

With the previous program still in the source code editor, use the cursor keys to position the cursor on the flashing (|) character after the CLS, as shown following:

```
...
While Not KeyHit(KEY_ESCAPE)
Cls |
...
```

The ... represents the rest of the program. I've used it here for brevity. Press the Return key. (Notice how the line stays indented? This is a nice feature of the BlitzMax editor.) Enter the following text, again, exactly as written:

```
DrawText("BlitzMax!", 284, 240)
Our program now looks like this:
Graphics 640, 480, 16

While Not KeyHit(KEY_ESCAPE)
    Cls
    DrawText("BlitzMax!", 284, 240)
    Flip
Wend
```

Run the program again (F5/Command+R) and see what happens. Did it work? If it did, the screen should go blank, and the exclamation *BlitzMax!* appears at the center.

File Operations

As this is a relatively small program, we could stand to lose it. After all, we could type it in again. But to save us the time and effort required, we can save the file to our disk.

In your operating system of choice (please consult relevant manuals, etc.), create a subfolder in your Documents folder called BlitzSource. This will be our root folder for all the sample code that will be written throughout this book. Within this folder, create another subfolder called IDE.

Save

To save our source file, we can press the Save toolbar button, press Ctrl/Apple+S, or Choose File ➤ Save from the menu bar.

Save the source file by pressing Ctrl/Command+S and locate the BlitzSource/IDE folder. Save the file in this folder, using the name FirstProgram. BlitzMax will add the .bmx extension automatically when you click the OK/Save button.

Close

When we have finished with a file, we can close the panel associated with its editor. To do this, select the panel by clicking it, as follows:

Press Ctrl/Command+W to close the window, or press the Close Window tool bar button.

Close the FirstProgram.bmx editor panel.

Open

Now that we have safely stored our next gaming masterpiece, it's time to bring it back, so that we can do some more editing. To do this, we use the File ➤ Open menu item or Ctrl/Command+O, or click the Open File toolbar button.

Open the FirstProgram.bmx file. BlitzMax remembers where you last performed a file open/save and displays the folder. For the paranoid among us, feel free to run it, to ensure that it still works.

Clipboard

The edit functions allow us to copy one or more lines of source code from one area to another. The lines we copy do not have to be in the same source file.

We are going to copy the line DrawText... in this example. Position the cursor at the start of the DrawText line.

```
|DrawText("BlitzMax!", 284, 240)
```

Hold down the Shift key and click after the) character on the same line. The whole line should be highlighted, as follows:

```
DrawText("BlitzMax!", 284, 240)
```

Press Ctrl/Command+C. This copies the selected text to the clipboard. We can then paste this information to another location. With the mouse, click just after the) character on the same line and press Return. This inserts a blank line. The cursor moves to this new line and waits for us to type something. In this case, we are going to insert text from the clipboard. Press Ctrl/Command+V to insert. The source code will now look like this:

```
While Not KeyHit(KEY_ESCAPE)
    Cls
    DrawText("BlitzMax!", 284, 240)
    DrawText("BlitzMax!", 284, 240)
    Flip
Wend
```

On running the program, you will, of course, notice that it does not make any difference to the previous code. This is because the new text is drawn on top of the other. To rectify this situation, we'll offset the first line.

Change the first DrawText line to

```
DrawText("BlitzMax!", 285, 241)
```

Save and run the program.

It must be noted at this time that BlitzMax draws from the back of the monitor to the front. So, anything that is drawn first is drawn at the back, and subsequent items are drawn on top. This will become apparent when we add some color. To add color to our program, we use the SetColor() function.

Change the preceding program to the following:

```
Graphics 640, 480, 16
While Not KeyHit(KEY_ESCAPE)
    Cls
    SetColor(128, 128, 128)
    DrawText("BlitzMax!", 285, 241)
    SetColor(255, 255, 255)
    DrawText("BlitzMax!", 284, 240)
    Flip
Wend
```

Save and run the program. You will now see a small shadow behind the text. You can make it more pronounced if you want, by changing the values for SetColor(). The three numbers represent the strength of the red, green, and blue colors in a pixel. Each number can be between 0 and 255, inclusive.

Change the shadow color to bright red (255, 0, 0) and the text color to blue (0, 0, 192). Save and run the application. Now try green or yellow (yellow is a mix of green and red) or purple (red/blue).

Cut

Occasionally, we have to completely remove code from one section and put it into another. We can achieve this goal by using the clipboard Cut operation.

We are going to invert the colors in this code:

```
Graphics 640, 480, 16


While Not KeyHit(KEY_ESCAPE)
    Cls
    SetColor(192, 0, 0)
    DrawText("BlitzMax!", 285, 241)
    SetColor(0, 0, 192)
    DrawText("BlitzMax!", 284, 240)
    Flip
Wend
Highlight the "SetColor(192..." line:
Graphics 640, 480, 16
```

```
While Not KeyHit(KEY_ESCAPE)
     Cls
     SetColor(192, 0, 0)
     DrawText("BlitzMax!", 285, 241)
     SetColor(0, 0, 192)
     DrawText("BlitzMax!", 284, 240)
     Flip
Wend
```

Press Ctrl/Command+X. This cuts the line from the editor and places it on the clipboard. Now, position the cursor at the end of the DrawText(... 285, 244) line and press Return. This creates a blank line. Press Ctrl/Command+V to paste the new line into position. You will now have the following code:

```
While Not KeyHit(KEY_ESCAPE)
     Cls

     DrawText("BlitzMax!", 285, 241)
     SetColor(192, 0, 0)
SetColor(0, 0, 192)
     DrawText("BlitzMax!", 284, 240)
     Flip
Wend
```

Cut the SetColor(0, 0, 192) line and paste this into the blank line under the Cls keyword and tidy up the code, as follows:

```
While Not KeyHit(KEY_ESCAPE)
     Cls
SetColor(0, 0, 192)
     DrawText("BlitzMax!", 285, 241)
     SetColor(192, 0, 0)
     DrawText("BlitzMax!", 284, 240)
     Flip
Wend
```

Save and run the program. We now have red text on a blue shadow.

Undo

Occasionally, we will make a mistake and have to put back the code we broke. In this case, we used the Undo function. This allows us to retrace our steps to where we were before everything went wrong. To undo, press Ctrl/Command+Z. If we make a mistake undoing (!), we can press Shift+Ctrl/Command+Z to redo.

Use the Undo function (Ctrl/Command+Z) to return the red/blue text to blue/red.

Now, perform the reverse, change the blue/red text to the red/blue text, using the Redo function (Shift+Ctrl/Command+Z).

Getting Help

BlitzMax contains an online reference to all its keywords. To access this help, click the Help tab in the editor panels. This shows a welcome screen and a tree view. Expanding the nodes on the tree view shows more detail for a particular topic.

Using the tree view, access help on SetColor(). Hint: Expand Help, Modules, and Index. Then scan down the alphabetic list for SetColor(). Now try the same for DrawText().

If you are stuck on a problem, head over to the BlitzMax forums. The beginners forum http://www.blitzbasic.com/Community/topics.php?forum=101 contains lots of tips for people just starting BlitzMax programming. If you are looking for tutorials, http://www.blitzbasic.com/Community/topics.php?forum=112 contains advise from seasoned BlitzMax coders.

CHAPTER 4

■■■

Literals, Constants, and Variables

There are three different ways to store data in BlitzMax: Literals, Constants and Variables. After a quick visit to dictionary.com, I came up with the following descriptions:

Literal: Word for word; verbatim

Constant: Unchanging in nature, value, or extent; invariable

Variable: Likely to change or vary; subject to variation; changeable. Inconstant; fickle

In terms of computer programming

A literal is a string of characters enclosed in quotation marks or a number placed in the source code.

A constant is declared at the start of the source code and is not changed.

A variable is a temporary storage area used by the program at runtime.

When BlitzMax compiles the source code into an executable, the only values it is sure of are the literals and constants. The variables will change during the execution of the program, depending on input from the user or other random events.

Literals and constants are hard-coded values in the source code of your program and cannot be changed. However, there is a very subtle difference between the two that will be discussed later.

Variables

A variable is like a box inside your computer that holds some item. That item can be a whole number, a real number, a line of text, pretty much anything. You can define as many variables as you require, because BlitzMax does not restrict you in any way. But don't forget that you are restricted by the amount of memory that you have available to you.

It is good practice to declare your variables before using them. You can enforce this in all your programs by placing the keyword Strict at the top of the source code, before any other line. When defining a variable, it is possible to give it an initial value.

There are a number of phrases associated with variables.

Declaration: When you first write about a variable in the source code of your program

Assignment: When you give a value to a variable

Type: The type of data that can be stored inside the variable

© Sloan Kelly 2016
S. Kelly, *BlitzMax for Absolute Beginners*, DOI 10.1007/978-1-4842-2523-3_4

You can declare variables in a number of ways. Here are three examples:

```
Local x
Local y:Int = 5
Global radius:Float
```

Variables declared without a type identifier are defaulted to Integer, or Int, for short. Any variable not assigned an initial value is assigned the value Null at runtime.

Multiple variables can be declared in one statement, using commas to separate each variable declaration. For example:

```
Local x:Int, y:Int, score:Int
Local energy:Int=100, lives:Int=5
```

Data Types

The following data types (Table 4-1) are used in BlitzMax. Your variables should be assigned a data type. This tells the compiler what information you're going to use your variable to store. If you *don't* specify a data type, Int (integer) will be assumed.

Table 4-1. *Data Types Used in BlitzMax*

Description	Keyword	Minimum Value	Maximum Value
8-bit unsigned integer	Byte	0	255
16-bit unsigned integer	Short	0	65535
32-bit signed integer	Int	-2^{31}	$+2^{31}-1$
64-bit signed integer	Long	-2^{63}	$-2^{63}-1$
32-bit floating point	Float	???	???
64-bit floating point	Double	???	???
16-bit Unicode string	String	n/a	n/a

Variables have certain attributes associated with them. These are:

Each variable has a name.

Each variable has a type associated with it.

Each variable contains a value.

Variable Names

Each variable must be given a unique name that can be referenced later in the code.

Variable Types

All variables are associated with a type. This data type describes the kind of information that can be assigned to the variable. By default, variables are declared as type Int—or Integer—if they are not explicitly defined as any other variable type.

Variable Values

Variables can be assigned values at declaration or later by assignment. When declaring variables, it is best to give them a default value. If an initial value is not specified, the variable is assigned a null value. *Null* is a special computer word that means "no value."

Why Do We Use Variables?

We use variables to keep track or monitor the changes of objects in our program. For example, the location of the player onscreen, how many lives they have, or how many bullets they have left. Take the following one-line program as an example:

```
Print "Total cost for a bundle of apples is " + 8
* 12 + "c"
```

Create a new blank editor window, then enter the program and run it.

```
Print "Total cost for a bundle of apples is " + 8
* 12 + "c"
```

You will see the following message in the Output tab of the IDE:

```
Total cost for a bundle of applies is 96c
```

The answer is correct, but the method of achieving this result is incorrect. The problem we have is that the values 8 and 12 are literal values. A literal is a string of text enclosed in quotation marks or a number placed within the source code. This method is called hard-coding values. Because the 8 and 12 values don't have labels, we don't know what is what. Is it 8 apples per bundle at 12c?

The next example replaces the literal values with variables.

```
Local apple:Int = 8 ' eight cents per apple
Local bundle:Int = 12 ' twelve apples in a bundle
Local totalcost:Int = apple * bundle ' total cost  for a bundle
Print "Total cost for a bundle of apples is " +  totalcost + "c"
```

Three variables are declared: apple, bundle, and totalcost. Each is assigned a value. Remember that at declaration, the programmer can add an optional initial value. The first two variables (apple and bundle) are assigned literal integer values: 8 and 12. The totalcost variable is assigned an initial value of apple * bundle.

When the program is run, the output is not too dissimilar to the previous one-liner. However, the underlying code is a better design. Whereas we used literal values in the first example, the second uses variables that can be changed with program flow. For example:

```
Local apple:Int = 8 ' eight cents per apple
Local bundle:Int = 12 ' twelve apples in a bundle  Local totalcost:Int = apple * bundle '
total cost for a bundle
Print "Total cost for a bundle of apples is " + totalcost + "c"

apple = 9 ' new cost for an applie is nine cents
totalcost = apple * bundle ' re-calculate cost of bundle
Print "New cost for a bundle of apples is " + totalcost + "c"
```

The preceding code builds on the second example. Now, we add an additional three lines that change the cost of one apple to nine (cents). We then recalculate the cost of a bundle of apples and display the information to the user.

Variable Scope

There are three kinds of variables: local, global, and field or type level. This is commonly referred to as variable scope. Think of variable scope as putting your variables (boxes) in different rooms in your house. Although you may have two identical boxes in separate rooms, they may or may not contain the same items.

Local

Local variables are available only within the current block of code. A block of code is defined as

The body of a function or loop

The body of an if...then...else statement

The body of a case or default statement

The following example shows the difference between local and global variables:

```
Global x:Int = 5
Function PrintX()
    Local x:Int = 10
    Print "Local x = " + x
End Function
PrintX()
Print "Global x = " + x
```

As I have not yet discussed functions, I will briefly explain that a function is a block of code that allows you to extend the built-in functions of the BlitzMax language. In the preceding example, we are creating a command called PrintX. Enter the program exactly as written and run it. The output will be as follows:

```
"C:/BlitzMax/tmp/localglobal.debug"
Local x = 10
Global x = 5
Process complete
```

Global

Global variables are available to any program block, following its declaration. The caveat to this is that if a local variable has been declared, the local variable is used, and not the global, as shown in the preceding local variable example.

Global variables cannot be declared after they are first used. Take this example:

```
Print integer
Global integer:Int = 5
Print integer
```

This will result in an error, specifically "Duplicate Identifier," because we effectively created the variable integer on the fly (remember, we can do this) and then tried to re-declare it as a global.

There is also a further complication when global variables are used, as we can see in the next example:

```
Function PrintInteger()
Print integer
End Function

PrintInteger()
Global integer:Int = 5
Print integer
```

This is where it gets complicated! You might possibly expect that the local variable inside the function would be used, resulting in 0 (zero) being displayed. This is not the case!

When compiling, BlitzMax does multiple passes to get all the declarations and calls organized. In the preceding example, the global variables are processed before any functions, resulting in two 5's being drawn on screen.

Field

The third type of variable is called field. I will discuss field variables in detail in Chapter 9, on object-oriented programming.

Literals

When you take something literally, you take it at face value. In BlitzMax terms, anything that is hard-coded in the source file is a literal value. For example:

```
Print "Game Over"
```

The string Game Over is a literal value, because it cannot be changed and cannot be reused. This means, that if we wanted to print the string Game Over anywhere else in the code, we would have to type in this line again. This means that at compile time, the game will contain multiple versions of the string Game Over.

Constants

A constant is declared in the same fashion as a variable and cannot be altered, as with a literal. However, because it is a variable, it can be reused anywhere in the program. This means that unlike a literal value, a constant is defined once and is referenced throughout the code. Therefore, at compile time, the game only contains one instance of the value. For example:

```
Const C_GAMEOVER:String = "Game Over"
Print C_GAMEOVER
Print C_GAMEOVER + " Press Any Key"
```

Changing Variables

A developer uses operators on the contents of variables to manipulate the outcome of the game. The following mathematical operators (Table 4-2) are available in BlitzMax.

Table 4-2. *Mathematical Operators*

	Plus	Minus	Multiply	Divide	Modulo
Operator	+	-	*	/	Mod

In addition to mathematic operators, BlitzMax also allows Boolean bitwise operators (Table 4-3).

Table 4-3. *Booleaan Bitwise Operators*

	And	Or	Xor	Shift Left	Shift Right	Arithmetic Shift Right
Operator	&	|	~	Shl	Shr	Sar

Arithmetic Operators

The standard arithmetic operators are used in the same way as you would on a calculator. In fact, with BlitzMax, you can create a very powerful calculator, if you so wish.

I will use variables in the following example (Table 4-4). Remember: When you are using variables, it is the contents of the variable that you are using. The name is merely a nice label that the programmer uses. In the first example (the plus operator), I use three variables: x, y, and total. The contents of these variables is used.

Table 4-4. *Provide Table Caption*

Source Code	Mathematically
x = 5	The value 5 is stored in x.
y = 5	The value 5 is stored in y.
Total = 0	The value 0 is stored in Total.
Total = x + y	The value 5 + 5 is stored in Total; therefore, 10 is stored in Total.

The Plus Operator

The plus operator (+) adds two numbers together. For example:

```
Local x:Int = 5
Local y:Int = 5
Local total:Int = 0
Total = x + y
Print "Total is " + total
```

The answer shown will be "Total is 10". Did you notice that the plus symbol is used in the print statement? The plus symbol is an example of an overridden operator. There is only one in BlitzMax.

The plus symbol can also be used to add two strings together. This is called string concatenation.

String Concatenation

In the preceding example, the variable Total is converted to a string before the concatenation takes place. No arithmetic addition can occur after a string concatenation has been performed on the same line of source code.

The Minus Operator

The minus operator (-) subtracts the second number from the first. For example:

```
Local x:Int = 15
Local y:Int = 5
Local total:Int = 0
Total = x - y
Print "Total is " + total
```

The answer shown will be "Total is 10".

The Multiplication Operator

The multiplication operator (*) multiplies two numbers together. For example:

```
Local x:Int = 5
Local y:Int = 5
Local total:Int = 0
Total = x * y
Print "Total is " + total
```

The answer shown will be "Total is 25".

The Divide Operator

The divide operator (/) divides the first number by the second number. For example:

```
Local x:Int = 10
Local y:Int = 5
Local total:Int = 0
Total = x / y
Print "Total is " + total
```

The answer shown will be "Total is 2".

The Modulo Operator

The modulo operator (Mod) returns the remainder of the first number, divided by the second. For example:

```
Local x:Int = 7
Local y:Int = 5
Local modval:Int = 0
```

```
Total = x Mod y
Print "Mod is " + modval
```

The answer shown will be "Mod is 2", because 7 / 5 = 1 r 2, that is, five goes into seven once, with a remainder of two.

Using the Colon

It is possible to shorthand some of the mathematical operators using the colon (:). The following pairs (Table 4-5) are shown as an example.

Table 4-5. *Examples of Some Mathematical Operators Using the Colon*

n = n + 1	n:+1
y = y / 2	y:/2
p = p * 5	p:*5
i = i - 1	i:-1

The following program will prompt the user for a weight in pounds and return the value in stones and pounds. Type in the code exactly as written.

```
Rem
     Pounds -> Stone and Pounds
End Rem
Local pounds:Int = Input("Enter a value in pounds ?:").ToInt()
Local stone:Int = pounds / 14
Local poundout = pounds Mod 14
Print "Answer is " + stone + "st. " + poundout + "lbs"
```

Run the program and type in a number. There are 14 pounds in 1 stone. The Input line is a little tricky, in that there is a .ToInt() at the end. BlitzMax is an object-oriented language, and, as such, strings are handled as objects. This method converts whatever is in the string that the user gives to an integer value. I cover object-oriented programming in a later chapter.

Boolean Mathematics

This branch of mathematics derives its name from George Boole, a mathematician from Lincoln, England. He discovered a branch of mathematics using binary (two) states, on and off, and the ability to combine the two states using a number of operations, namely, AND, OR, and NOT. There is also a fourth: exclusive OR (XOR).

Boolean logic has had a profound impact on the world, mostly because computers wouldn't be here without it. Remember, from the "Computer Memory" section in Chapter 1, that memory is stored in collections of bits? Because bits have two states, set or not set, they are ideal candidates to use with Boolean logic.

The AND Operator

The AND operator (&) is obtained by pressing Shift+7 on most keyboards. The output from this is 1 only when both A and B are 1. All other combinations result in an output of 0 (Table 4-6).

Table 4-6. *Output of the* AND *Operator for Hypothetical A and B*

A	B	Output
0	0	0
0	1	0
1	0	0
1	1	1

The OR Operator

The OR operator is a single pipe (|). This symbol is located to the left of the Z key on most keyboards. The output from this is 1 when either A is 1, B is 1, or both are 1. Only when A=0 and B=0 does the output equal zero (Table 4-7).

Table 4-7. *Output from the* OR *Operator for Hypothetical A and B*

A	B	Output
0	0	0
0	1	1
1	0	1
1	1	1

The NOT Operator

The NOT operator (!) is obtained by pressing Shift+1 on most keyboards. This is a unary operator in that it only requires one input. This is used to reverse the contents of A. For example, if A=0, then the output would be 1 (Table 4-8).

Table 4-8. *Output of the* NOT *Operator If A Equals 0*

A	Output
0	1
1	0

The Exclusive OR Operator

The exclusive OR operator (~, to the left of the Enter key on most keyboards) produces an output of 1 only when A=1, B="0" OR when A=0, B="1." The output is 0 in all other instances (Table 4-9).

Table 4-9. *Output of* OR *Operator for Hypothetical A and B*

A	B	Output
0	0	0
0	1	1
1	0	1
1	1	0

String Methods

Strings in BlitzMax are more complex than characters, integers, and floating point numbers. They are a collection of printable characters and are actually complex *objects*. As an object, they can have methods associated with them. The String object has the following methods:

Find

FindLast

Trim

Replace

StartsWith

EndsWith

Contains

Join

Split

ToLower

ToUpper

ToInt

ToLong

ToFloat

ToDouble

ToCString

ToWString

FromInt

FromLong

FromFloat

FromDouble

FromCString

FromWString

FromBytes

FromShorts

These methods operate on the contents of string literals, constants, and variables. They allow programmers to search through and find the first occurrence of a phrase or convert a string to a different type.

Strings are arrays of characters, and BlitzMax supports both ASCII (8 bits per character) and Unicode (16 bits per character).

Find

Find returns the index of the first occurrence of the substring. The method will return -1 if no matching occurrence is found. You can pass in a starting index value as well. The following program displays a list of index values where the character "i" is located in the string:

```
blitzMax:String = "This is BlitzMax!"
pos:Int = blitzMax.Find("i")
While(pos > 0)
Print pos
pos = blitzMax.Find("i", pos + 1)
Wend
```

FindLast

FindLast returns the index of the last occurrence of the substring. The method will return -1 if no matching occurrence is found. Like Find(), a starting index value can be passed in. The following program displays the index value of the "Max" word in the string:

```
blitzMax:String = "This is BlitzMax!"
pos:Int = blitzMax.Find("Max")
Print "Max is located at element " + pos
```

Trim

Trim removes all nonprintable characters from the string. In the following example, the text is bloated with space characters that are removed using Trim:

```
bloatedString:String = "           TOO MANY SPACES"
Print "<" + bloatedString + ">"
Print "<" + bloatedString.Trim() + ">"
Print "<" + bloatedString + ">"
```

Note that bloatedString is *not* altered. Trim() returns the altered string but keeps the original intact.

CHAPTER 4 ■ LITERALS, CONSTANTS, AND VARIABLES

Replace

Replace replaces all the occurrences in a string. For example, if you wanted to replace all the occurrences of "ca" with "dog," you would do the following:

```
animals:String = "Cats are much smarter pets. Cats are so loving"
Print animals.Replace("Cat", "Dog")
Print animals
```

Again, the original text is not altered. Replace() returns the altered text.

StartsWith

StartsWith returns true if the string starts with the given value.

```
author:String = "Wells, Herbert George"
Print author.StartsWith("Wells")
Print author.StartsWith("WELLS")
```

Note that WELLS is not the same as Wells. Strings are case-sensitive.

EndsWith

EndsWith returns true if the string ends with the given value.

```
bookTitle:String = "BlitzMax"
Print bookTitle.EndsWith("Max")
```

Contains

Contains works in a similar way to Find but does not allow for a starting offset and will only return true if the substring is contained within the larger string.

```
simplePhrase:String = "Bill Gates is a founder member of Microsoft"
Print simplePhrase.Contains("founder member")
```

Join

Join concatenates arrays of strings together. If you are coming from another language such as Java or C#, you will be familiar with this construct, but it has been slightly tipped on its head, as you will see from the example. This is handy, if you want to output data to a CSV or JSON, for example.

```
Local listOfNames:String[] = ["Fred", "Barney", "Wilma", "Betty"]
Print ",".Join(listOfNames)
```

Split

Split is the opposite of Join. It takes a list of strings and separates them, using the given character delimiter. In this example, we will reuse our join from before:

```
Local listOfNames:String[] = ["Fred", "Barney", "Wilma", "Betty"]
Local joinedNames:String = ",".Join(listOfNames)

Local namesArray:String[] = joinedNames.Split(",")
For s:String = EachIn namesArray
    Print s
Next
```

ToLower

ToLower converts all the alphabetic characters in the string to lowercase. In this example, we are running the method on a string constant:

```
Print "THIS IS SHOUTY TEXT".ToLower()
```

ToUpper

ToUpper converts all the alphabetic characters in the string to uppercase:

```
Print "Apples! 6 for $2!".ToUpper()
```

ToInt, ToLong, ToFloat, ToDouble

These methods all convert strings to their respective data types:

```
one:Int = "1".ToInt()
two:Long = "2".ToLong()
three:Float = "3".ToFloat()
four:Double = "4".ToDouble()
Print one
Print two
Print three
Print four
```

ToCString

The ToCString method converts the string to a zero- (null-) terminated string that can be used by C programs. This method is outside the scope of this book, because we are not going to be doing any low-level operating system calls, for example. However, for completeness, here is an example:

```
Local memLoc:Byte Ptr = "This is a string".ToCString()
Local i:Int = 0
While memLoc[i] <> 0
    Print Chr$(memLoc[i])
    i:+1
Wend
```

ToWString

The ToWString method converts the string to a zero- (null-) terminated Unicode string. This method is outside the scope of the book, because we are not going to be doing any low-level operating system calls, for example. However, for completeness, here is an example:

```
Local memLoc:Byte Ptr = "This is a string".ToWString()
Local i:Int = 0
While memLoc[i] <> 0
     Print Chr$(memLoc[i])
     i:+2
Wend
MemFree(memLoc)
```

Note that because the Unicode character set is represented by two bytes per character, we must increment the index value by two.

When using ToCString and ToWString, always free your memory using MemFree().

FromInt, FromLong, FromFloat, FromDouble,

As with their corresponding ToXXX methods, these convert from a given data type to a string. For example:

```
one:Int = "1".ToInt()
two:Long = "2".ToLong()
three:Float = "3".ToFloat()
four:Double = "4".ToDouble()

Print String.FromInt(one).Length
Print String.FromLong(two).Length
Print String.FromFloat(three).Length
Print String.FromDouble(four).Length
```

FromBytes

FromBytes takes a zero- (null-) terminated string and its length and converts it to a BlitzMax-compatible string. This is the opposite of ToCString() but allows greater control, in that you can specify the number of bytes to return.

```
Local stream:Byte Ptr = "The cake is a lie.".ToCString()
Local cake:String = String.FromBytes(stream, 4) Print cake
```

FromCString

FromCString takes a zero- (null-) terminated string, and its length and converts it to a BlitzMax-compatible string. This is the opposite of ToCString() and returns the entire string.

```
Local stream:Byte Ptr = "The cake is a lie.".ToCString()
Local cake:String = String.FromCString(stream) Print cake
```

FromShorts

FromShorts takes a zero- (null-) terminated Unicode string and its length and converts it to a BlitzMax-compatible string. This is the opposite of ToWString() but allows greater control, in that you can specify the number of bytes to return.

```
Local stream:Short Ptr = "The cake is a lie.".ToWString()
Local cake:String = String.FromShorts(stream, 4) Print cake
```

FromWString

FromWString takes a zero- (null-) terminated Unicode string and its length and converts it to a BlitzMax-compatible string. This is the opposite of ToWString() but allows greater control, in that you can specify the number of bytes to return.

```
Local stream:Short Ptr = "The cake is a lie.".ToWString()
Local cake:String = String.FromWString(stream) Print cake
```

Length of String

You can also get the length of a string, using the read-only Length field.

```
cat:String = "Cat"
Print cat + " is " + cat.Length + " characters long"
```

To summarize what we have looked at so far, in addition to standard arithmetic operators such as add, subtract, multiply, and divide, BlitzMax also offers the F and Boolean operators AND, OR, and NOT. Strings can be added (concatenated) together using the plus operator (+). The product of arithmetic operations can be reassigned to the same or other variables. Boolean operators can be used as part of IF and WHILE statements. You will see more of that in following section, "Going with the Flow."

Going with the Flow

Computers step through each program line by line until there are no more lines to run. In this chapter, we discover that we can control what lines the computer reads and, more important, the order in which we want them read.

Simple Decisions

We can make simple decisions in computing, as we do in life, such as: If it's raining, I will take my umbrella to work. In computing terms this can be written as follows:

```
Local isRaining:Int = True
If isRaining
    Print "I will take my umbrella to work today."
End If
```

Line 1 declares an integer value, isRaining, which we give an initial value of True. Line 3 causes the program to make a decision based on the contents of the isRaining variable.

IF Conditions Always Equate to One of Two Values: TRUE or FALSE

The equals character (=) is used to test for equality. Previously, we used the equals character to assign values. In the preceding example, we are not assigning the value; we are determining if the isRaining variable contains that value. Line 4 will only execute if isRaining is true. Line 5 ends the IF block.

We can also place more than one line between the IF and END IF lines, as shown in the following example:

```
Local isSunny:Int = True
If isSunny
     Print "It is sunny outside"
     Print "I won't need my umbrella"
End If
```

Both lines inside the IF...END IF block are executed only if isSunny is True.

What if we wanted to display something if isRaining wasn't true? Could we do the following?

```
Local isRaining:Int = True

If isRaining
     Print "I will take my umbrella to work today."
End If
Print "It is nice and sunny"
```

If we ran this code, we would get the following output:

```
I will take my umbrella to work today.
It is nice and sunny
```

This is not an ideal situation, because we were only looking for one line to be output. The second line is always going to be executed, because, as we know, programs run blindly step-by-step through a program until they get to the end, and there are no more lines to process. What we need to do is the following:

```
Local isRaining:Int = True
If isRaining
     Print "I will take my umbrella to work today."
Else
     Print "It is nice and sunny"
End If
```

Note the extra keyword Else. This allows us to better control what we expect to do if isRaining turns out to be false. The Else portion is optional.

Testing for Equality

As with previous versions of BASIC, BlitzMax allows the programmer to test for equality. We have seen this in so far as we were testing that a particular variable is equal to true. We know that IF conditions have to equate to one of two values: TRUE or Y, so how can we test for equality? We use one of the following operators (Table 4-10).

Table 4-10. *Operators That Can Test for Equality*

Operator	Description
=	Equals
<	Less than
>	Greater than
<=	Less than or equal to
>=	Greater than or equal to
<>	Not equal to

These are mathematical symbols. For those of you unfamiliar with them, especially the less than and greater than symbols, the small end is the lesser. You cannot use these operators against variables that contain Boolean True or False. Equality operators can only work against numbers or character strings.

The following program prompts the user to enter two string values and then checks which string is greater. I'll cover the finer details in just a second, but the program does have some shortcomings. Can you see what they are?

```
Print "This program takes in two strings and decides which one is greater"
Local first$ = Input("Enter the first string : ")
Local second$ = Input("Enter the second string : ")

If first$ > second$
    Print "The first string was greater than the second string"
Else
    Print "The second string was greater than the first string"
End If
```

The first line displays a message indicating what the program will do. The next two lines prompt the user to enter two separate string values and place them in first$ and second$ variables. The IF statement condition is

```
If first$ > second$
```

This checks to see if the first string is greater than the second. If it is, the message "The first string was greater than the second string" is displayed. On ANY OTHER EVENT the ELSE block is executed.

Type in the preceding program and run it. Enter the following values (Table 4-11).

Table 4-11. *Values to Enter to Run the Preceding Program*

Run # of Program	First$	Second$
1	Lowercase "a"	Uppercase "A"
2	Aaa	Zzz
3	9	100

What do you notice about the results? Were you expecting that?

The problem with our little example is that unless first$ is absolutely greater than second$, the ELSE block is executed. We can remedy this by changing the program to the following:

```
Print "This program takes in two strings and decides which one is greater"

Local first$ = Input("Enter the first string : ")
Local second$ = Input("Enter the second string : ")

If first$ > second$
    Print "The first string was greater than the second string"
Else If first$ < second$
    Print "The second string was greater than the first string"
Else
    Print "The two strings were equal"
End If
```

Change the preceding program to use an equals sign in the second IF. Will you have to change the text of the PRINT statements? If so, what would you change them to?

More commonly, you will be testing for equality with numbers. Say, for example, we wanted to check whether the player's character was within a certain boundary on the screen. We could use this code:

```
Local playerX:Int = 50
Local playerY:Int = 50

If playerX > 0 And playerX < 250
    Print "Player is within the boundary"
End If
```

Using Boolean Logic

As we saw in Chapter 3, computers use Boolean logic for any question, as long as it warrants a TRUE or FALSE answer. The following Boolean keywords can be used to make more complex IF conditions:

```
        And

        Or

        Not
```

For example:

```
Local isRaining:Int = True
Local isSunny:Int = True

If isRaining And isSunny
    Print "Sun showers"
End If
```

In the context of a game, you might have a condition to test whether the player has a key, then hits a door, and opens the door.

```
If playerHasKey And playerHitDoor
    OpenTheDoor()
    RemoveKeyFromInventory()
End If
```

The two methods `OpenTheDoor()` and `RemoveKeyFromInventory()` are programmer-made; they're not part of BlitzMax. We'll learn about how to make user-defined functions in a later chapter.

Nesting IFs

When we have to make complex decisions based on a number of facts, we can do what is called "nesting." This means placing a block of code inside another block of code, for example:

```
Local isRaining:Int = True
Local isCloudy:Int = True

If isRaining
    Print "I will take my umbrella to work today."
Else If isCloudy
        Print "It looks like it will rain, I'll take my umbrella incase."
Else
    Print "It is sunny. I will wear jeans and a T-shirt."
End If
```

The truth table for this (Table 4-12) is shown below to make the above example clearer.

Table 4-12. *Truth Table for Our Nesting Example*

IsRaining	IsCloudy	Output
True	True	I will take my umbrella to work today
True	False	I will take my umbrella to work today
False	True	It looks like it will rain, I'll take my umbrella in case
False	False	It is sunny. I will read jeans and a T-shirt

The format of an IF statement is shown in the following:

```
IF condition [THEN]
    Action
[ELSE
    Action]
[ELSE IF condition
Action]
END IF
```

Select Case

There are a number of occasions on which the humble and yet powerful IF statement is a little simplistic for our needs. For example, if we had a menu-driven application, we could write code as shown following:

```
If menuSelected = 1
    Print "Menu 1"
Else If menuSelected = 2
    Print "Menu 2"
Else If menuSelected = 3
    Print "Menu 3"
Else If menuSelected = 4
    Print "Menu 4"
Else
    Print "No such option"
End If
```

This is a perfectly valid code block, but it has two downsides. First of all, it takes longer to write. Second, it will be difficult to maintain or read later. Don't forget that one of a programmer's goals is to be able to reuse her code. How can we reuse code if we can't read it? What we need is some kind of in-built menu command. The SELECT CASE block is a perfect replacement.

```
Local menuSelected:Int = 3
Select menuSelected
    Case 1
        Print "Menu 1"
    Case 2
        Print "Menu 2"
    Case 3
        Print "Menu 3"
    Case 4
        Print "Menu 4"
    Default
        Print "Sorry - I did not understand that menu item"
End Select
```

Line 1 declares the menuSelected variable that we are using in this example. Line 3 starts the SELECT block. The select statement starts with the SELECT keyword and the variable we want to test. This is *not* the same as the IF statement, in that what follows the SELECT keyword is *not* conditional. So, the following is not a valid SELECT line:

```
Select menuSelected = 5
```

The last line marks the end of the SELECT block with the keywords END SELECT. The Case keyword is used to check the value of the control variable.

```
Print "This program will prompt the user " + ..
    "For a letter of the alphabet" + ..
    "and then convert that to the number " + ..
    "it would appear on a mobile" + ..
    "phone. It's case-insensitive -- A = a...
    " Local letter$ = Input("Enter a letter : ") letter$ = Upper(letter$)
```

```
Select letter$
    Case "A", "B", "C"
        Print "2"
    Case "D", "E", "F"
        Print "3"
    Case "G", "H", "I"
        Print "4"
    Case "J", "K", "L"
        Print "5"
    Case "M", "N", "O"
        Print "6"
    Case "P", "Q", "R", "S"
        Print "7"
    Case "T", "U", "V"
        Print "8"
    Case "W", "X", "Y"
        Print "9"
    Default
        Print "Not a valid letter"
End Select
```

The .. at the end of the line means "continue this line on the next line."

Iteration—Making the Computer Repeat Itself

A video game repeats the action until all the player's lives have gone or the end of the game has been reached. So far, we have only written programs that run through a sequence of commands and then terminate. With the use of certain BlitzMax keywords, we can get the computer to repeat a block of code, when required, either using conditions or for a set number of times.

The for Loop

The for loop is the simplest type of iteration in computing. The computer is told how many times the block of code is repeated. The format of a For...Next loop is shown following:

```
FOR control_variable = start TO end [STEP interval]
    {block}
NEXT
```

For example:

```
For n:Int = 1 To 5
    Print "This message will be displayed five times"
Next
```

will display

```
This message will be displayed five times
This message will be displayed five times
```

```
This message will be displayed five times
This message will be displayed five times
This message will be displayed five times
```

Note two things: first, you can assign the variable type to the control variable, and second, the step keyword is not used. We could have written the program as

```
For n:Int = 1 To 5 Step 1
    Print "This message will be displayed five times"
Next
```

This would have had the same effect. What would happen if we changed the line so that it ends in Step 2? It is also possible to count down, as follows:

```
For countdown:Int = 10 to 0 Step -1
    Print countdown
Next
Print "Blast-off!"
```

This produces the following output:

```
10
9
8
7
6
5
4
3
2
1
Blast-off!
```

If the Step -1 is removed, the only thing written would be

```
Blast-off!
```

Why would this be the only thing written?

For EachIn…Next

There is an extension to the For...Next loop that is used to cycle through a collection of objects. The format of this form of the For...Next loop is

```
For temp_variable = EachIn collection_variable
...
Next
```

For example:

```
list:TList = CreateList()

list.AddLast("New Game")
list.AddLast("Options")
list.AddLast("Controls")
list.AddLast("Help")
list.AddLast("Exit")

For b:String = EachIn list
    Print b
Next
```

This displays the title menu of a game. You can put anything in TList. It's a system type that is more powerful than traditional arrays in a lot of ways. For example, it's easier to iterate (loop) through the values in TList.

While/Wend

Although For...Next loops are powerful and can be used for all sorts of reasons detailed above, they fall short in a number of ways. Some of which lead to spaghetti code and bad programming—The Dark Side, if you will. This is where the While...Wend block comes into play.

The format of a While...Wend block is

```
While boolean_condition
    ...
Wend
```

For example:

```
i:Int = 0
While i < 5
    i = i + 1
    Print i
Wend
```

will display

```
1
2
3
4
5
```

i is incremented with each iteration (every time the code within the block is looped) and is displayed. When I is incremented to 6, the While...Wend block exits. This is the loop that the majority of developers use when looping through a block based on a Boolean condition, for example, to detect if a player has any lives/energy left. It should be noted that a While...Wend block does not guarantee that it will execute. Let's look again at the previous example.

```
i:Int = 5
While i < 5
    i = i + 1
    Print i
Wend
```

This will display nothing, because the value held in I as it enters the loop is not less than 5. This is a good property of the While...Wend loop, because it means that the loop will only be entered when the Boolean condition is true.

Let's take a look at another example.

```
answer:String = ""
While answer<>"Y" And answer<>"y"
    answer = Input("Do you want to exit?")
Wend
```

The initial value of answer is a blank string. So, answer contains neither "Y" or "y". This means that the loop will execute. When this program is run, you are presented with a prompt Do you want to exit? A sample session might be

```
Compiling:untitled2.bmx
Linking:untitled2.debug
Executing:untitled2.debug
Do you want to exit?no
Do you want to exit?no
Do you want to exit?y
Done.
```

Repeat...Until

Repeat...Until is very similar to the While...Wend block. The format of Repeat...Until is as follows:

```
Repeat
    ...
Until boolean_condition
```

Take our earlier example of counting to 5.

```
i:Int = 0
Repeat
    i = i + 1
    Print i
Until i >= 5
```

The Boolean condition in the preceding Until line is "greater than OR equal to." Running the preceding code produces the following output:

```
1
2
3
4
5
```

But, what if we changed the initial value of i, as we did in the While...Wend example?

```
i:Int = 5
Repeat
    i = i + 1
    Print i
Until i >= 5
```

The following will be displayed when the program is run:

```
6
```

Why? This is because the Repeat...Until loop executes the block at least once. This can be necessary if you know that you will be performing an action at least once. For example, in a game loop you know that the player will take control of the spaceship, say, at least once...then lose a life and start again. This is a good situation in which the Repeat...Until loop can be used.

Repeat...Forever

Repeat...Forever is a variation on Repeat...Until. The format is

```
Repeat
    ...
Forever
```

This is the same as the following Repeat...Until loop:

```
Repeat
    ...
Until False
```

A sample usage of this (in this author's opinion) useless construct would be the following:

```
Repeat
    Print i+" Ctrl-C to End!"
    i = i+1
Forever
```

I believe that this construct is a little redundant, because, as previously noted, the Repeat...Until False construct would work just as well!

Exit

The Exit keyword is used to step out of a Repeat, While, or Select block. For example:

```
Repeat
    Print n
    n = n+1
    If n="5" Exit
Forever
```

Continue

The Continue keyword is used to step out of a For...Next loop. For example,

```
For i:Int="0" To 50
    If i > 30
        Continue
    Else
        Print i
    End If
Next
Print "Out at 30!"
```

would display:

```
1
2
:
:
29
30
Out at 30!
```

A Note on Exit and Continue

Exit and Continue are used to short-circuit your code and perform what's called an "early out." For example, say you have a list of 10,000 items. To search for a particular item, you use a for loop. You test each value, in turn, to see if there is a match. On the 1,000th item, you find your match. At that point, you should exit the for loop and continue execution. There is little point in checking the other 9,000 entries on the list, if you've found your match.

■ ■ ■

CHAPTER 5

The Great Escape

For our first project, we are going to build a simple bat-and-ball game. I think that everyone should be familiar with the concept of this game. Basically, we are going to create a play area with a bat and a ball. The ball hits off our bat and the sidewalls, until we drop it. At that point, we lose a life. Every time we successfully defect the bat, we score 1 point.

The game is loosely based upon a scene in *The Great Escape* with Steve McQueen. He's sent to the cooler and passes the time by throwing his baseball at the wall—a kind of one-player catch. This is the game we are re-creating in our world. Let's get started then!

Create within BlitzMaxSource a folder called Escape.

Game Elements

Every game has to define the world in which it is played. In our game, we have certain elements that define a bat-and-ball game:

A bat

A ball

There are some elements that we could do without but that make the screen look nice—not to mention better define our gaming world to the player:

Scorecard

Lives remaining

Amiga-style gradient

For those of you not in the know, Amiga was a home computer from the 1980s to 1990 that employed a number of techniques to prettify games. One of these was to create a gradient fill as the background.

Creating the Graphic Elements

You will need a graphics package to create the game elements for The Great Escape. There are a number of good programs out there.

Windows

Paint.Net (www.getpaint.net/)

Photoshop Elements (www.adobe.com/products/photoshopel/)

© Sloan Kelly 2016

S. Kelly, *BlitzMax for Absolute Beginners*, DOI 10.1007/978-1-4842-2523-3_5

Mac

iPaint (http://ipaint.sourceforge.net/)

Photoshop Elements (www.adobe.com/products/photoshopel/)

Seashore (http://seashore.sourceforge.net/The_Seashore_Project/About.html)

Pixen (http://opensword.org/pixen/)

All Platforms

The GIMP (www.gimp.org/)

Photoshop Elements isn't free; it's about US$100 and probably overkill, if you want to have it just for sprite work. If you're using Windows, I recommend Paint.Net. For all other OSs, I'd go with GIMP.

Once you choose your art package of choice, you'll have to create the images for the bat and the ball.

The bat image is 128×24 pixels in size. Save the image as bat.png.

The ball image is 24×24 pixels in size. Save the image as ball.png. The images should be saved in the Escape folder.

Splitting Up the Tasks

Our game will be split into three sections. It's always a good idea to break down the problem into lots of smaller, more manageable problems. We'll see this done in greater detail later in the book. For now, though, we'll split our game into the following:

Initial setup

Main loop

Gradient fill

Initial Setup

The purpose of the initial setup is to

Put the computer into graphics mode

Load the images we will use

Initialize any variables we have to use

Don't worry if you don't understand this in detail just now. I will cover these topics in a later section. Our code to set up The Great Escape is shown following. The sections below all the code sections explain the steps. Code sections are set in a distinctive font.

```
Graphics 640, 480
```

The Graphics keyword puts the computer into graphics mode. In this case, we are asking the computer to give us a resolution of 640×480. This will show our game in a window. If you want to show the game in full-screen mode, you will have to add an additional ,16 to the end of that line, to put the display into full-screen 16-bit color mode.

```
bat:TImage = LoadImage("bat.png")
ball:TImage = LoadImage("ball.png")
```

There are two images in our program (see above for how to create them). The images are loaded into variables called bat and ball, respectively. Variables are temporary locations inside the computer's memory that we use to store information that we need during program execution.

```
px:Int = (640 - 128) / 2
py:Int = 400
lives:Int = 3
```

These three variables will set the player's position (px and py) and the number of lives. Notice that the width of the bat is taken into consideration when we set the x coordinate of the player. The player's x coordinate will be determined by the position of the mouse.

```
bx:Int = 0
by:Int = 0
sx:Int = 0
sy:Int = 0
```

The four variables bx, by, sx, and sy control the ball's position and speed. These variables will be updated by code that we write later.

```
HideMouse
```

This keyword hides the mouse pointer. After all, we don't have mouse pointers in our world!

If you haven't already, enter the code written in this font exactly as written above, and save it to your BlitzMaxSource\Escape folder as GreatEscape.bmx.

The Main Loop

Every game contains a main loop. Computer programs run through each command until they run out of commands. When they run out of commands, they return to the operating system. To stop that from happening, and to keep people in our game, we loop around.

Much like a racing car circuit, a computer program contains a loop. A computer program performs certain tasks specified by the programmer (you) and then repeats those tasks until some event occurs.

Our loop will follow these steps:

1. Clear the screen

2. Draw the gradient (this will be covered later)

3. Draw the ball

4. Draw the bat

5. Update the player

6. Update the ball

7. Flip the screen

BlitzMax, as you will discover later, uses a technique known as double buffering. Basically, nothing is drawn to the screen. In effect, what happens is all the images are drawn to an area of memory that the player is not viewing, and the graphics card then points to this new screen when BlitzMax flips the screen. It's explained in the Graphics section later.

Our main loop is the following:

```
While Not KeyHit(KEY_ESCAPE)
```

This line, coupled with the Wend at the end, is the key to the main loop. This says "do everything between While...Wend, until the user hits the Escape key."

```
Cls
DrawImage(ball, bx, by)
DrawImage(bat, px, py)
```

This section draws all the graphics on the screen. Note that we don't have a gradient yet. The screen is cleared, and the ball is drawn, then the bat is drawn.

```
px = MouseX()
```

The variable px is updated to contain the x coordinate of the mouse. So, when the user moves the mouse, the information is stored in the px variable. We then have to check that the user's bat is within the boundaries of our world—our 640×480 screen.

```
If px < 0
    px = 0
End If
```

This checks to see if the player's bat is off the leftmost edge of the screen, and if it is, it sets the position to the leftmost pixel position: zero.

```
If px > 640 - 128
    px = 640 - 128
End If
```

This checks to see if the player's bat is off the rightmost edge of the screen. Note that the width of the bat (128 pixels) is used again here. We could have allowed the user to move the bat outside our world, but we want the screen boundary to be our world's boundary.

```
bx = bx + sx
by = by + sy
```

The player's position is determined by user input, but for the ball's movement, we code is required. This is done in the preceding lines. The x coordinate of the ball is incremented by the speed along the x axis, and the y coordinate of the ball is incremented by the speed along the y axis.

```
If bx < 0 Or bx > 640 - 24
    sx = sx * -1
End If
If by < 0 Then
    by = 0
    sy = sy * -1
End If
```

Again, our world is contained within a 640×480 screen, and this means that when the ball hits the edges of the screen, it should bounce back. This task is achieved by reversing the speed of either the x or y axis—x axis if the left or right edges have been hit, the y axis if the top of the world has been hit.

```
If by > py
    lives = lives - 1
    bx = 0
    by = 0
    sx = 0
    sy = 0
End If
```

This section deals with what happens when the player misses the ball and it goes past her. One life is removed, and the ball's position and speed are reset to 0.

```
If ImagesCollide(bat, px, py, 0, ball, bx, by, 0)
    by = by - 1
    sy = sy * -1
    score = score + 1
End If
```

It's not a bat-and-ball game if the ball can't collide with the bat. We have to test if the ball image touches the bat image, and if so, reflect the ball back up the playing field. To do this, we use the built-in ImageCollide function. When the player successfully hits the ball with his bat, we add one to his score.

```
Flip
```

The Flip keyword tells the graphics card which screen to look at. Remember: We have two areas we can work with. The graphics card only flicks a switch to show the next scene. It works kind of like a ViewMaster.

```
Wend
```

This keyword matches with the While line at the top. This will loop back to the stop and perform all the lines in between this and the While again, until the condition is met, i.e., when the user presses the Escape key.

```
ShowMouse
```

The final keyword in our program shows the mouse again. Remember that we hid it earlier on using HideMouse?

Add the previous code, exactly as written, to the GreatEscape.bmx file. Save the file and run the application. You should have a screenshot similar to that shown in Figure 5-1.

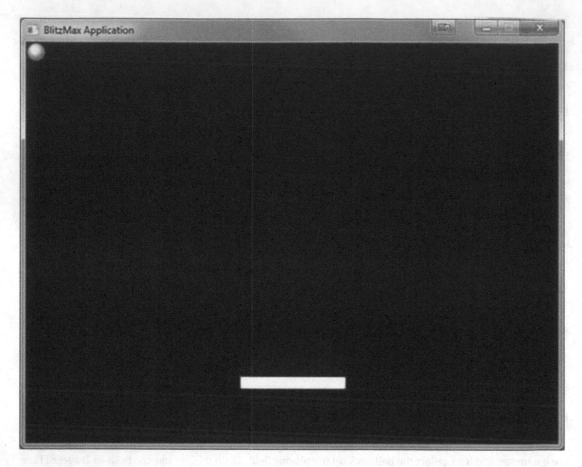

Figure 5-1. *Provide a caption*

But the ball is not moving. We have to get the ball in motion for this game to be any kind of fun. To do this, we must add a little bit more code. To add more code, we have to go back to the editor. Press the Escape key and click the "GreatEscape.bmx" tab.

Starting the Game

To start the game, we'll get the player to press the spacebar. This has the effect of serving the ball. To achieve this, we will add the following lines of code after the px = MouseX( ) line:

```
If KeyHit(KEY_SPACE) And sx = 0
    sx = 4
    sy = 4
End If
```

This code checks to see if the user has pressed the spacebar, but it also checks whether the ball is stationary. If both conditions are met, the ball's x axis and y axis speeds are set.

Now our game is starting to take shape, but we have no feedback information for the user. We'll fix that next.

If you haven't already, add to the `GreatEscape.bmx` file the code after the `px = MouseX()` line, exactly as written previously. Save the file and run the application. Hit the spacebar when you want to serve and play. Don't forget to hit Escape when you're finished. There is still work to be done! Did you miss the ball three times? If you did, what happened?

Clearly, that's a bug, and we should fix it. Change the `While` statement at the top to

```
While lives > 0
```

The game ends a bit abruptly now, but at least we won't have negative lives left. What could you add to make the end of the game a little more pleasant for the player?

Giving the Player Feedback

As with every other game, we have to inform the user as to what is happening in the world. We do this by showing the user graphics representing the player and the objects in the game world, but we can also aid the users by showing them information (attributes) about their game-world player, such as lives left and score. To achieve this, we're going to add a few more lines to the game.

```
m:String = ""
```

This line is added between the `While` and `Cls` lines. It creates a variable called `m`. This variable will be used to display all the messages. I've created this variable because we are going to use a function called `TextWidth()` to center the text on the screen.

```
If sx = 0
    m = "Press SPACE to serve ball"
    DrawText(m, (640 - TextWidth(m))/2, 240)
    m = "You have " + lives + " lives left!"
    DrawText(m, (640 - TextWidth(m))/2, 254)
End If

m:String = "Score <" + score + "> Lives <" + lives
+ ">"
DrawText(m, (640 - TextWidth(m))/2, 0)
```

Add these lines after the `DrawImage()` lines.

And now our game is done. Congratulations! You have just taken the first step into a larger world!

Add all the lines as shown in the areas described. Save and run the game. You should now have some feedback!

The Linear Gradient

Add the following function, exactly as written, just below the `sy:Int = 0` line. Remember to give yourself a couple of blank lines, by hitting Enter a couple of times.

```
Function DrawGradient(increment:Int)
    y:Int = 0

    While y < 480
        blueshade:Float = Float(y) / 480
        blue = (192 * blueshade)
```

```
        SetColor(0, 0, blue)
        DrawRect(0, y, 640, increment)
    y = y + increment
    Wend
' reset to white for next operation
SetColor(255, 255, 255)
End Function
```

Next, add the following line in the main loop, just before the image of the ball is drawn:

```
DrawGradient(24)
```

Save the program and run. You should now have a lovely Amiga-style gradient (Figure 5-2).

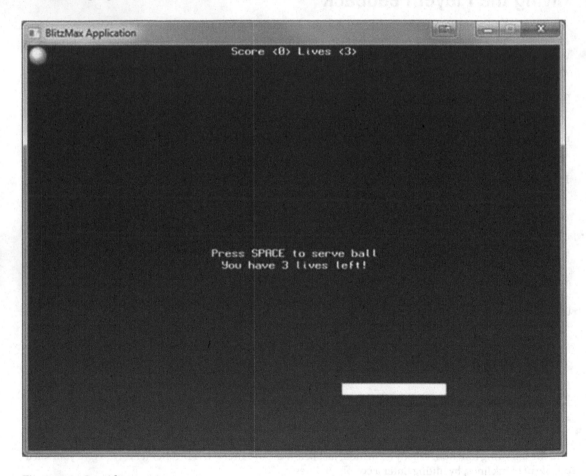

Figure 5-2. *Provide a caption*

Remember that the game ends a bit abruptly when you lose all your lives? When the player dies, it would be nice to let her have another chance to play. To allow players to play again, add the following line just before the While line:

```
#mainloop
```

This is a label that we will use later to "jump" to it. Now, between the `Wend` and the `HideMouse` lines add

```
While Not KeyHit(KEY_ESCAPE)
```

This works the same way as the previous `While` line. We're going to keep doing what's between the `While` and `Wend` lines until the condition has been met.

```
If KeyHit(KEY_P)
    lives = 3
    bx = 0
    by = 0
    sx = 0
    sy = 0
    score = 0
    Goto mainloop
End If
```

This is the interesting bit. If the user presses the P key, the game resets itself and jumps back to our main loop. Goto can lead to what is called "spaghetti code" and should be used in moderation. At this stage, all we want is a simple callback to our first loop, so this is a fairly acceptable use.

```
Cls
m = "Game Over"
DrawText(m, (640 - TextWidth(m))/2, 240)
m = "Press ESCAPE to return to OS"
DrawText(m, (640 - TextWidth(m))/2, 254)
m = "Press 'P' to play again"
DrawText(m, (640 - TextWidth(m))/2, 272)
```

The user is informed that his game is over, and he can return to the OS, if he wishes, by pressing the Escape key, or he can play again by pressing the P key.

```
    Flip
Wend
```

What things do you think could improve this game? Don't forget, games programming is not just about hacking code. It's about being creative! You can revisit this game later, when more topics have been covered, to flesh it out and make it better.

As we have discovered, variables are used to store information employed by your game at runtime. Variables are only used for one thing: to monitor change. And who exacts change on the objects within the game? The user interacts with the application, some random number generator or pattern decides how an alien will move, but, really, it comes down to the developer. Write down as many things as you can think of that would change the contents of a variable. For example, moving a player would require some additional arithmetic.

Debugging Your Code

During the course of writing a program, it may be required to stop the execution, to view the contents of variables at a particular point. If we have a calculation that is wrong, and we can't immediately see from just looking at the code what is wrong, we can step through it line-by-line. This is called debugging. A bug is a small glitch in a program's code that is unintentionally put there—usually owing to lack of sleep! The following built-in commands are available to help us debug our code; DebugStop, DebugLog, RuntimeError, Assert. For now we will explore DebugStop and DebugLog in detail.

Stopping Execution

To stop the execution of a program in mid-flow, we use the DebugStop keyword. This returns control to the integrated development environment (IDE), where the developer can step through the code, examine the contents of variables, and such. DebugStop is ignored when no debugger is present, i.e. when you package up your game for final distribution.

Enter the following code into a new editor panel:

```
Local i:Float = 30
Local k:Float = 15

Local b:Float = i - k
Local t:Float = 5 / b
DebugStop
Print t
```

Run the program. The IDE will pop up after execution, and the DebugStop line is highlighted. Click the Debug panel on the right-hand pane. There is a tree view with the name of your program, for example, untitled3.bmx (see Figure 5-3). Expand that node, and you will see all your variables.

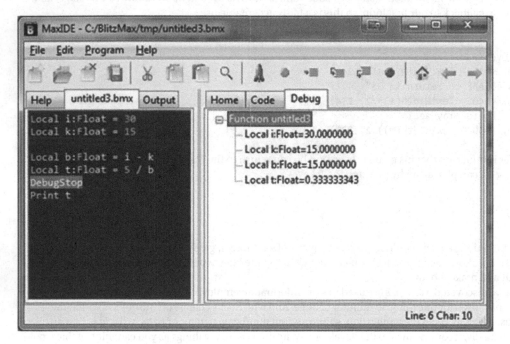

Figure 5-3. *Provide a caption*

Press Alt ➤ Option+X to stop the program.

Move the DebugStop between the Local b... and the Local t... lines. Run the program. Now what do you see when you debug? Why do you think this is the case?

You should probably have noticed that the variable t contains 0.00000. This is because it has not been initialized. BlitzMax knows that it exists, it just has not had a value assigned to it. Remember: Non-initialized variables are assigned a default value. In the case of numeric types, that value is zero.

Now that we have stopped the execution of the program, we can step through line-by-line to see the path of execution.

You should have the following program in the editor:

```
Local i:Float = 30
Local k:Float = 15

Local b:Float = i - k
DebugStop
Local t:Float = 5 / b
Print t
```

Run the program, and the control will return to the IDE. At this point, we can step line-by-line through what each part of the code does. To do this, press the F9 key. Keep looking at the variable t in the Debug panel. Note when we execute that line that its value changes from 0 to 0.33333343.

Printing Output

Sometimes, all we want to do is display the contents of a variable, but allow the program to keep running. This is most true in graphic applications such as games, in which we don't want to keep flicking in and out of graphics mode. To capture information and display it on the console window and not the screen, we use DebugLog. As with DebugStop, DebugLog is not executed when there is no debugger present.

Type the following program into a new editor panel. Run the program and observe the dot moving about the screen. Press the Escape key when you are finished. Look at the output window.

```
Graphics 640, 480

Local x:Int = 0
Local y:Int = 0

Local xs:Int = 8
Local ys:Int = 8

While Not KeyHit(KEY_ESCAPE)
    Cls
    Plot x, y

    x:+xs
    'y:+ys
    y:+(ys * Sin(x))
    If x <= 0 Or x >= 640
        xs:*-1
        DebugLog "Ouch! Hit the sides!"
    End If
    If y <= 0 Or y >= 480
        ys:*-1
        DebugLog "Ouch! Hit the top / bottom"
    End If
    Flip
Wend
```

When you run the program, you should get an output similar to the one shown following:

```
Building 001_DebugLog
Compiling:001_DebugLog.bmx
flat assembler version 1.51
3 passes, 4066 bytes.
Linking:001_DebugLog.debug.exe
Executing:001_DebugLog.debug.exe
Ouch! Hit the top / bottom
Ouch! Hit the top / bottom
Ouch! Hit the sides!
Ouch! Hit the top / bottom
Ouch! Hit the top / bottom
Ouch! Hit the top / bottom
Ouch! Hit the top / bottom
Ouch! Hit the sides!
Ouch! Hit the sides!
Ouch! Hit the top / bottom
Ouch! Hit the top / bottom
```

Other Debug Methods

As previously mentioned, if you are working in graphics mode, it is difficult to display debug information without flicking to the standard output of the console. However, there is an alternative way that I have used as a temporary measure: DrawText.

Rewrite the preceding program with the bouncing pixel and remove the DebugLog lines. Add the following lines after Plot():

```
DrawText("X = " + x, 0, 0)
DrawText("Y = " + y, 0, 12)
```

CHAPTER 6

Reusing Code with Functions

Games programmers are no different than normal computer programmers, in that they strive to reuse code wherever possible. So far, we have looked at linear programs that cannot be reused in their current state. The programs perform a specific number of tasks and end. What we have to do is create almost mini-programs that are independent of the main code. These mini-programs are called functions.

Functions allow you, the programmer, to virtually extend the keywords in BlitzMax with your own routines. These routines can then be shared with your other programs or, indeed, other programmers. Functions also allow multiple programmers to work on the same larger project without tripping over each other.

Where Would I Use a Function?

Any task that is repetitive in nature, such as displaying the lives a player has left, his or her score, drawing the characters onscreen... I think you will agree, pretty much anything can be declared repetitive in a computer game!

Declaring a Simple Function

The general format for a function declaration is:

```
Function function_name : ReturnType (Parameters)
     {block}
End Function
```

{block} represents where you will put your code, to perform each time the function name is called. We use function names in BlitzMax just as we would a registered keyword.

Drawing a Line

To draw a line in BlitzMax, we use the Line keyword. The following function draws a line from the top left of the window to the bottom right.

```
Graphics 640, 480

Function Line()
    DrawLine(0, 0, 640, 480)
End Function
```

© Sloan Kelly 2016
S. Kelly, *BlitzMax for Absolute Beginners*, DOI 10.1007/978-1-4842-2523-3_6

```
While Not KeyHit(KEY_ESCAPE)
    Cls
    Line()
    Flip
Wend
```

The is achieved by calling our new function, Line, which draws a line across the top of the screen.

Write another routine, called OppositeLine, that draws a vertical line down the other diagonal. Hint: The DrawLine keyword requires four parameters: start-x, start-y, end-x, and end-y. To draw a diagonal line, you must pass 640, 0, 0, 480 to the DrawLine keyword.

But what if we wanted to specify how far along the line is drawn? How could we do that? Much like the built-in keywords in BlitzMax, you can specify parameters.

Specifying Parameters

To allow people to pass parameters to your functions, you must specify what parameters are required when you declare that function. The format of a function that requires parameters is

```
Function function_name(param1:ParamType [,
param2:ParamType ...])
    {block}
End Function
```

You can have as many parameters as you like, but good sense says that anything more than 10 is a little on the excessive side. For example:

```
Graphics 640, 480

Function Line(;
While Not KeyHit(KEY_ESCAPE)
    Cls
    Line(640)
    Flip
Wend
```

Change the value passed to the Line function. Choose any value between 0 and 640. Run the program and see what happens. What happens when you choose a value greater than 640? What did you expect to happen?

Optional Parameters

Sometimes an optional parameter is required to pass in default information to a function. This can be achieved by using the following function declaration:

```
Function function_name(param1:ParamType = value [,
param2:ParamType ...])
    {block}
End Function
```

ParamType is any valid BlitzMax data type, class, or UDP-based Data Transfer Protocol (UDT). See the "Object Oriented Programming" section for more details on classes and UDTs.

In the following example, there are two optional parameters, x and c. Only the middle parameter is a required input to the function.

```
Function Defaults(x:Int = 24, y:Int, c:Int = 3)
    Print x
    Print y
    Print c
End Function

Print "Specifying X:"
Defaults(0, 4, 10)
Print "Missing out X:"
Defaults( , 4, 10)
```

To omit passing a parameter, enter a single comma in its place, as in the preceding example. If the last parameter is optional and you want to miss that out, do not add the additional comma. So, for example, to miss out the c parameter, use the following:

```
Defaults(1, 2)
```

It is valid because we have omitted the last comma. However,

```
Defaults(1, 2, )
```

is invalid because the last comma is still there. It is not possible to miss out the middle parameter, y, because it has no default value.

So, the following code is invalid:

```
Defaults(0, , 5)
```

Change the preceding line program to default the width parameter to 640, if no width is specified.

Extending Existing Keywords

As I have mentioned before, it is possible to extend existing keywords. For example, although BlitzMax has a DrawRect keyword to draw a filled-in box, it does not have one to draw an outlined box. We have to write our own. The following code does just that. It allows us to draw a box anywhere onscreen, based on the parameters passed to the function.

```
Rem
    Program to demonstrate the DrawBox function
    The program draws an outline using DrawBox
    and then a filled rectangle using DrawRect
End Rem

Graphics 640, 480

Function DrawBox(x:Int, y:Int, ;
```

```
While Not KeyHit(KEY_ESCAPE)
    DrawBox(50, 50, 100, 50)
    DrawRect(52, 52, 97, 47)
    Flip
    Cls
Wend
```

This example employs extended use of the DrawLine keyword to draw an outlined box in the declaration for the DrawBox function. It takes in parameters similar to the DrawRect function's start x and y coordinates, the width and height, and uses these to draw lines on the screen. The lines are drawn, and a box forms.

Place a WaitKey keyword between each of the DrawLine lines, to see the rectangle slowly build up. Now re-read the code and see what the comments on each line say.

Returning Values from Functions

For the most part, functions are used to return values to the calling routine, which can be the main program or, indeed, another function. To return an integer value from a function, the programmer need not do anything; however, it is good practice to specify the return value data type in the function declaration. In the following example, a function GetSquare is declared. It requires one parameter, x, and returns an integer based on the product of x multiplied by x.

```
Function GetSquare:Int(x:Int)
    Return x * x
End Function
Print GetSquare(5)
```

Notice the :Int after the function name? This is the return data type. If none is specified, BlitzMax assumes that the return type is an Int. The Return keyword is used to send information back to the calling routine. Without the Return keyword, nothing is sent back—that's literally nothing. It could be a 0 or an empty string or a null object, depending on what data type is to be returned.

Recursion

There is a mathematical function called Factorial, and its formula is shown following:

```
n! = n * (n-1) * (n-2) * ... * 1
```

Basically, any number is multiplied by that number and all integers down to 1. So, for 5, it would be 5 * 4 * 3 * 2 * 1 = 120.

This is called recursion, and it is when you have a routine calling itself. Think of it as a snake eating its tail. The thing with recursion is that you have to be able to have an "out," or else the program loses control, gobbles up all the memory/processor, and crashes your machine, thereby causing the loss of hours of work!

The program below contains a function for factorial called Factorial. Pass in any integer value to it.

```
Rem
    Factorial example. This returns n!
End Rem
Function Factorial(x:Int)
```

```
    If x > 1
        x = x * Factorial(x-1)
    End If
    Return x
End Function
Print Factorial(5)
```

The "out" in the Factorial function is the If clause, which checks to make sure that x is greater than 1. It is only when x is greater than 1 that the Factorial function calls itself again.

Change the function call to Factorial to pass in 6, 10, 20.

Change the Factorial function to divide by each number instead of multiply. To make this change, you must change the parameters and output to Float.

Returning Multiple Values

When a value is passed to a function, only a copy of it is passed.

This type of parameter passing is known as by value. The example that follows best illustrates this point. When you pass in a parameter by value, it is unchanged.

```
Rem
    Passing By Value
End Rem
Function ByValue(x:Int)
    x = 5
End Function

Local x:Int = 10
ByValue(x)
Print x
```

The x:Int in the ByValue function is a local variable to the function that represents the variable passed to it by the calling routine. As soon as a variable goes out of scope, all information about it is lost.

We could change the preceding program to read:

```
Rem
    Passing By Value
End Rem
Function ByValue(x:Int)
    x = 5
    Return x
End Function

Local x:Int = 10
x = ByValue(x)
Print x
```

This change would allow us to capture the change in x. It is fairly straightforward and is suitable for returning one value. But what if we want to return more than one value? If we want to return multiple values from a single function, we must pass the parameters by reference.

To change a variable passed to a function, we add the keyword Var.

```
Rem
    Passing By Reference
End Rem
Function ByValue(x:Int)
    x = 5
End Function


Function ByReference(x:Int Var)
    x = 5
End Function


Local x:Int = 10
Print "x = " + x
ByValue(x)
Print "x after ByValue = " + x
ByReference(x)
Print "x after ByReference = " + x
```

In this example, the keyword Var has been added to the x:Int parameter of the ByReference function. This tells BlitzMax to pass the variable in by reference. This means that the variable is altered by the function. Here is an example of multiple values being returned. The SumProductDiv function takes five parameters, and x and y are two integers that will be manipulated by the function. The function performs three calculations: summation, product, and division on the two numbers and returns them to the user into the specified parameters, as follows:

```
Rem
     Multiple Values returned
End Rem
Function SumProductDiv(x:Int, y:Int, sum:Int Var,
..
    prod:Int Var, div:Int Var)
    sum = x + y
    prod = x * y
    If y > 0
            div = x / y
Else
    div = -1
End If
End Function


Local x:Int = 5
Local y:Int = 5
Local sum:Int = 0
Local prod:Int = 0
Local div:Int = 0

SumProductDiv(x, y, sum, prod, div)
Print "Sum=" + sum
Print "Product=" + prod
Print "Divide=" + div
```

In this example, the first two parameters (x and y) are passed by value. This means that they will remain unaltered, and, indeed, the code within the SumProductDiv function does not alter them.

Write a function called IsGreaterThan that takes in two floats. It returns a third parameter containing the larger of the two.

Write a function called Pythagoras that takes in one parameter called angle. It has to return three values for sine, cosine, and tangent. Hint: Use the Sin, Cos, and Tan functions to return these float values.

This activity shows how you can combine functions by getting them to call others. The following function draws a rectangle and a piece of text on the screen at a given location. Change the code to show a yellow outline, as follows:

```
Graphics 640, 480
Function DrawBoxText(x:Int, y:Int, text:String)

    SetColor(255, 255, 255)
    DrawRect(x, y, TextWidth(text) + 1,
TextHeight(text) + 1)
    SetColor(0, 0, 0)
    DrawText(text, x + 1, y + 1 )
End Function

While Not KeyHit(KEY_ESCAPE)
    DrawBoxText(50, 50, "Hello BlitzMax!")
    Flip
    Cls
Wend
```

Hint: You can use the function we created earlier (DrawBox) to draw an outline. Also, SetColor(255, 255, 0) changes the drawing color to yellow.

CHAPTER 7

■ ■ ■

Using the File System

BlitzMax allows almost unfettered access to the operating system, to read files and folders (directories) and their contents, as follows:

```
ChangeDir
CloseDir
CloseFile
CreateDir
CreateFile
CurrentDir
DeleteDir
DeleteFile
Eof
FileType
LoadDir
NextFile
OpenFile
ReadDir
ReadLine
WriteLine
```

In any application you will have to manipulate some files on the hard disk or CD-ROM drive. Your games hi-score table can be stored in a file and manipulated by your program, or you could load a cut-scene. But let's start with some basics first.

Reading a Directory

There are nine keywords used to manipulate directories:

```
CurrentDir
ChangeDir
```

© Sloan Kelly 2016

S. Kelly, *BlitzMax for Absolute Beginners*, DOI 10.1007/978-1-4842-2523-3_7

```
        ReadDir

        NextFile

        CloseDir

        LoadDir

        FileType

        CreateDir

        DeleteDir
```

CurrentDir

This keyword returns the current directory:

```
Print CurrentDir()
```

ChangeDir

This keyword changes the current directory. It returns a Boolean True, if successful.

```
If ChangeDir("C:\BlitzMax")
    Print "There is a BlitzMax folder"
Else
    Print "There is not a BlitzMax folder!"
End If
```

ReadDir, NextFile, and CloseDir

These three commands allow us to open a directory for reading, to traverse through the files contained within the directory, and to close it afterwards, as this example shows:

```
dir = ReadDir("C:\")
If Not dir
    Print "Can't open directory"
Else
    f:String = NextFile(dir)
    While f <> ""
            Print f
            f = NextFile(dir)
    Wend
End If
CloseDir(dir)
```

LoadDir

This is slightly more elegant than the ReadDir, NextFile, and CloseDir example above. It basically does the same thing but in one step: it reads all the names of the files and folders in the given directory. You can also pass in an optional Boolean parameter (true/false) to skip the current and parent directories (. and ..), respectively.

```
Local files:String[]
files = LoadDir("C:\")
For f:String = EachIn files
    Print f
Next
```

FileType

We can also examine the files that we find, to determine what type they are.

0: File does not exist

1: Standard file

2: Directory

In the following example, the root directory of the C: drive is examined, and any directories are surrounded in angle brackets.

```
Local files:String[]
files = LoadDir("C:\")
For f:String = EachIn files
    If(FileType("C:\" + f))="2"
        Print "<" + f + ">"
    Else
        Print f
    End If
Next
```

Graphical Representations of Directories

You can represent files and folders easily as graphics. After all, Windows/Finder/Gnome can do it! You will have to get two 16×16 pixel images to represent files and folders. You can download them from the web site (www.blitzmaxbook.com). Here is a simple GUI to list the files and folders in BlitzMax:

```
Graphics 800, 600

imgfile:TImage = LoadImage("file.png")
imgfolder:TImage = LoadImage("folder.png")
Local files:String[]
Local y:Int = 0
files = LoadDir("C:\")

While Not KeyHit(KEY_ESCAPE)
    Cls
    For f:String = EachIn files
        If FileType("C:\" + f) = 2
            DrawImage(imgfolder, 0, y)
```

```
            Else
                  DrawImage(imgfile, 0, y)
            End If
            DrawText(f, 24, y+1)
            y = y + 20
      Next

      y = 0
      Flip
Wend
```

Rewrite the preceding code to show only the folders first and then the files second. Hint: Use two for loops.

CreateDir

CreateDir creates a folder. It returns Boolean True, if folder creation is successful.

```
If CreateDir("C:\BlitzMax")
      Print "Created BlitzMax folder"
Else
      Print "Couldn't create the BlitzMax folder!"
End If
```

CreateDir() will return true even if the folder exists. It only fails when it can't access a path or drive.

DeleteDir

DeleteDir removes a directory from the file system.

```
If DeleteDir("C:\BlitzMaxTestFolder")
      Print "The BlitzMaxTestFolder folder is
gone!"
Else
      Print "Something stopped me from killing the
folder!"
End If
```

File Manipulation with OpenFile

OpenFile creates a handle to the file stored on the hard disk/CD-ROM/DVD. It is always a good idea to check to make sure that the file can be opened. After all, you don't want to start reading from something that doesn't exist!

OpenFile has three parameters:

Filename: The path to the file you want to open. This can be any valid URL.

Readable *(optional)*: Whether you want to read from the file; True by default

Writable *(optional)*: Whether you want to write to the file; True by default

The following displays the contents of a file:

```
file=OpenFile("http::www.blitzmaxbook.com/")
If Not file
     Print "could not open web page"
Else
     While Not Eof(file)
               Print ReadLine(file)
     Wend
     CloseStream file
End If
```

You will need an open Internet connection for this to work. If you don't have one, create a simple text file in the C:\ drive and change the text within OpenFile(). In the preceding example, we are opening a URL to a web page (http::www.blitzmaxbook.com, for example). Note that to do this, you prefix the web address with http::. This is the format that BlitzMax uses to reference external files.

Think about the possibilities. You could have online hi-score tables for your games, or check for updates automatically...The sky is the limit!

ReadLine

ReadLine reads in one line of the chosen file at a time. As in the previous example, a single line is printed onto the screen. The format of ReadLine is:

```
s:String = ReadLine(file)
```

Eof

Eof stands for "end-of-file" and is used in While statements to check that the end of the file has not been reached. If we were to go over the length of the file, an error would occur, so this is a good check to make!

CloseStream

CloseStream closes the file and allows it to be used by other programs and processes. This is an important keyword and must be used each time you are finished with a file, especially if writing to it—which brings us neatly to WriteLine.

WriteLine

WriteLine is used in conjunction with WriteFile. WriteFile works in much the same way as OpenFile, but allows us to write to the file, as follows:

```
file = WriteFile("C:\test.txt")
```

```
If Not file
     Print "Can't create file!"
```

```
Else
     WriteLine(file, "Line 1")
     WriteLine(file, "Line 2")
     CloseStream(file)
End If

file = OpenFile("C:\test.txt")
If Not file
     Print "Can't open file!"
Else
   · While Not Eof(file)
           Print ReadLine(file)
     Wend
     CloseStream(file)
End If
```

The preceding program writes two lines of text to a file and then reads the file back in, to display the lines onscreen.

The file system can be accessed with a few simple keywords. Files and directories and their contents can be easily examined. A file can be opened and written to in a few lines of code. Similar code can be used to read back those lines.

Just remember to close the file as soon as you can. It can cause all sorts of problems if you don't. This is especially true if you are writing to it. It can cause the file to be locked. This means that to unlock it, you'll have to reboot your computer.

CHAPTER 8

■ ■ ■

Tank Attack: The Second Game

Tank Attack is a game for two players that is loosely based on the Combat game found on the Atari 2600 console. The tanks can rotate and fire a single shot at a time. When a bullet hits another tank, the tank positions are reset, and the player who destroyed the tank gets a point (Figure 8-1). The round lasts for 99 seconds, with the player with the most hits after that time winning.

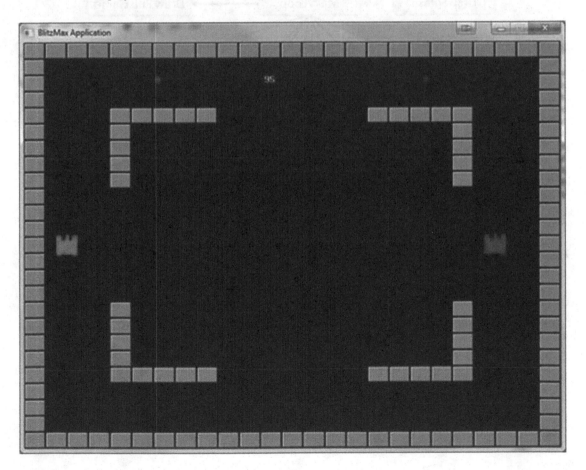

Figure 8-1. *Tank Attack*

© Sloan Kelly 2016
S. Kelly, *BlitzMax for Absolute Beginners*, DOI 10.1007/978-1-4842-2523-3_8

The game features three maps that we will load from disk. We'll be creating them in a somewhat unique way, with Google Docs spreadsheets, although you could use any spreadsheet program you want. Full graphics and source code are available on the web site www.blitzmaxbook.com.

The finished game code, including comments, comes in at more than 600 lines. That might seem like a lot, but we'll break the program into smaller chunks, to make things easier. Our smaller chunks, or *functions*, will make the program easier to read and to follow what's going on. To make it even easier, we're going to look at the structure chart of the program (Figure 8-2). It will show us where the information flows to and comes from within our program.

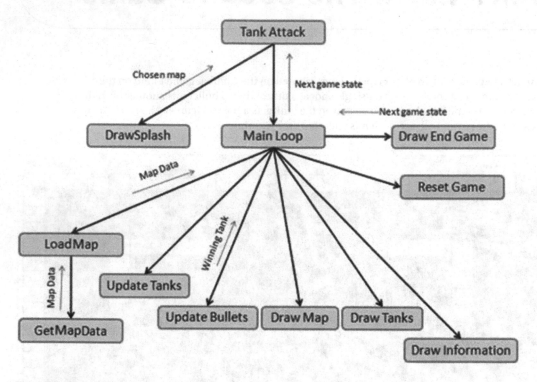

Figure 8-2. *Structure chart of the Tank Attack program*

The main entry point to the application is the "Tank Attack" block. It sets up the game state and starts the outer loop. The loop repeats until the player elects to quit the game. The game has three states:

1. Information/splash screen

2. Main game loop

3. Quit

Information/Splash Screen

The initial screen shown to the user is the splash screen. This page allows players to choose which map they want to play. The chosen map is returned to the main loop, and the state is changed to "play game." If players decide that they don't want to play, no map data is returned (we'll see how following), and the state is changed to "quit."

Main Game Loop

The main game loop handles all the updates and drawing of the items. It does it in a linear way. Updates are performed, then the screen is cleared, and the player, map, and information panel are drawn next.

Reset Game

The reset game method is called when a player's bullet connects with the tank of the opposing player. This function resets the players' positions to their starting locations and rotation.

Draw Endgame

The endgame screen shows which of the two players has won. The players are given a choice to play again or quit to the OS. This choice response is returned to the main game loop, which, in turn, passes it back to the main program, to alter the game state accordingly.

Remaining Functions

I will cover the remaining functions one at a time in due course, but first, we must generate some graphics and some data for our maps.

The Graphics

Our graphics are very simple, and there are only three of them. We reuse the graphics for each player, because we can recolor them when we draw them, so the first player is red, and the second is blue. The tank graphic looks like this (Figure 8-3):

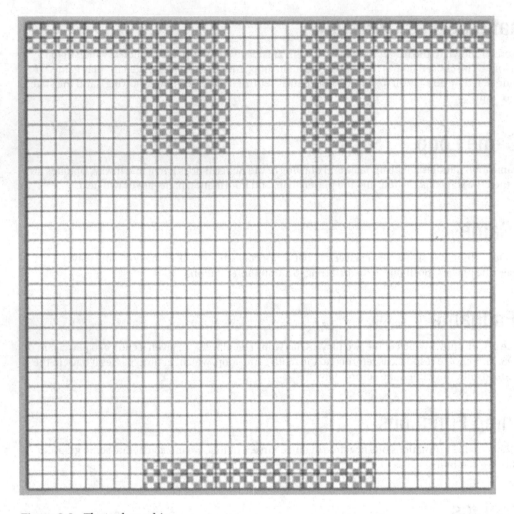

Figure 8-3. *The tank graphic*

The bullet is a 5×5 square (also white) with the corner pixels removed (Figure 8-4).

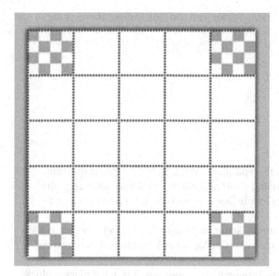

Figure 8-4. *Tank Attack bullet*

The block can be any color you want, but please ensure that it's 32×24 pixels. I made it a gray bas-relief brick (Figure 8-5).

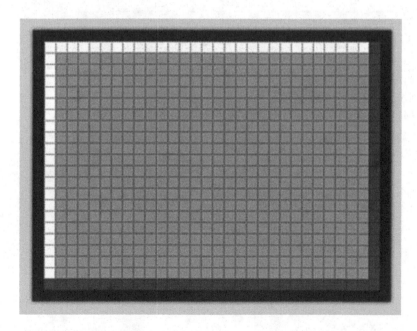

Figure 8-5. *Tank Attack game block*

Create a folder called TankAttack in your BlitzMax working folder and save the images there as the following names:

tank.png

bullet.png

brick.png

The Data

The data is created in a spreadsheet that can save files as tab-separated values. This isn't that important, but our code is assuming that it's in that format. If you're using another format, you'll have to change the GetMapData() function in the code listing. I suggest using Google Docs Spreadsheet. It's free to create a Google account, and, most important, it's free.

The files can be downloaded to your local hard drive as tab-separated value files (.tsv). These are just text files with each column's data separated by a tab character. The GetMapData() function shows how we parse that to get our game data.

Create a new blank spreadsheet and design your maps. Wherever an uppercase X is, we'll place a block in the game. The spreadsheet is 25 rows and has 25 columns (A–Y). This is how MapA looks in the web browser as a Google Docs spreadsheet (Figure 8-6):

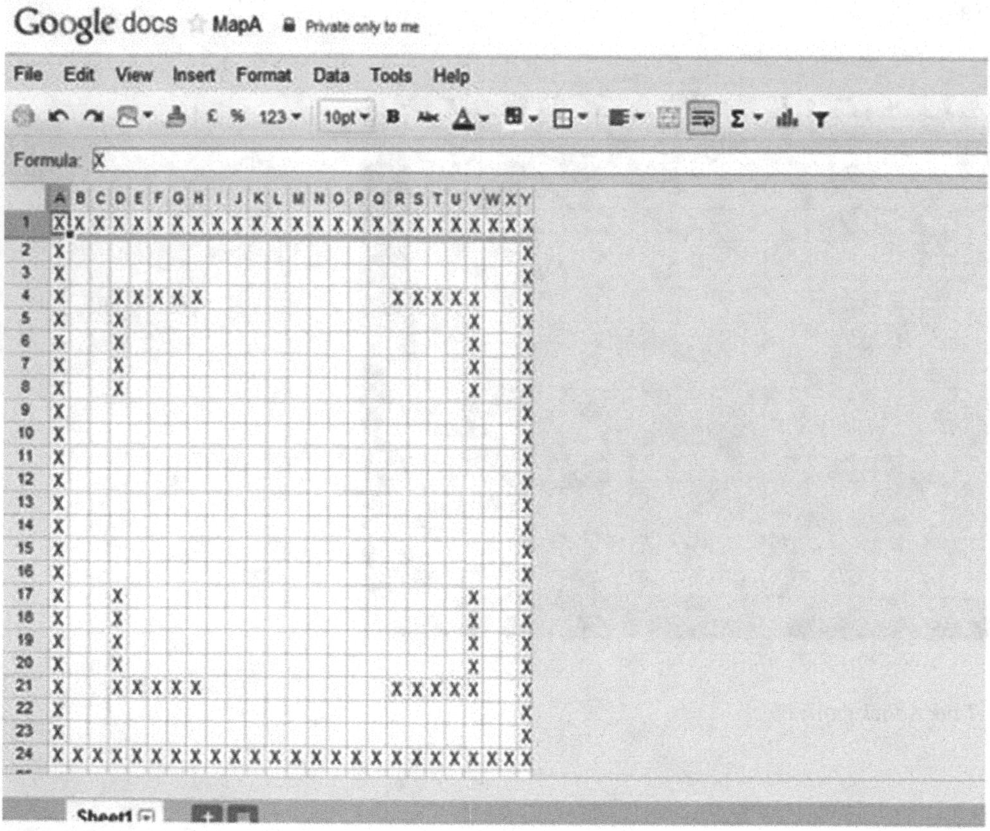

Figure 8-6. *How MapA looks in the web browser as a Google Docs spreadsheet*

You can make your own maps. There are three included with the source code on the web site. Make sure that they are named as follows:

    MapA.tsv

    MapB.tsv

    MapC.tsv

In addition, ensure that they have columns A–Y and rows 1–25. If you wanted to add more objects, you could add other letters/numbers, to create the map. For example, G for grass or W for water.

The Stub Code

If it isn't open already, start up BlitzMax and create a new file. Save this file in the same folder as the images, as TankAttack.bmx. The outline code is shown following. We will be filling this in as we go through this chapter. The outline will run, but it will not produce any output.

    Graphics 800, 600 Type TVector2

```
Graphics 800, 600
Type TVector2
End Type
Type TBullet
End Type
Type TTank
End Type
Function DrawNumber(x:Int, number:Int, offsetLeft:Int)
End Function
Function LoadMap:TList(mapID:Int)
    Local mapChar:String = Chr(65 + (mapID - 1))
    Local mapFilename:String = "Map" + mapChar +
".tsv"
    Return GetMapData(mapFilename)
End Function
Function GetMapData:TList(filename:String)
    Return Null
End Function
Function DrawInformation(tankList:TList,
countDown:Int)
End Function
Function PrintMessage(s:String, x:Int, y:Int, centre:Int = False)
End Function
Function UpdateCountDown:Int(roundTime:Int Var, countDown:Int)
    Local ms:Int = MilliSecs()
    If ms > roundTime + 1000
        roundTime = MilliSecs()
        countDown:-1
    End If
    Return countDown
End Function
Function DrawTanks(tankList:TList)
End Function
```

```
Function IsCrashWithBricks:Int(mapData:TList,
img:TImage, x:Float, y:Float)
    Return False
End Function
Function UpdateBullets:Int(mapData:TList, tankList:TList)
    Local currentTank:Int = 0
    Local tankVictor:Int = -1
    Return tankVictor
End Function
Function UpdateTanks(mapData:TList, tankList:TList)
End Function
Function DrawMap(mapData:TList)
End Function
Function ResetGame(tankList:TList, tankVictor:Int)
End Function
Function MainGameLoop:Int(currentLevel:Int)
    Return 2
End Function

Function DrawSplash:Int()
    Return 99
End Function
Function DrawEndGame:Int(p1:TTank, p2:TTank)
    Return 2
End Function
Local state:Int = 0
Local quit:Int = 0
Local currentLevel:Int = 0
While Not quit
    Select state
        Case 0
            currentLevel = DrawSplash()
            If currentLevel = 99
                quit = True
            Else
                state = 1
            End If
        Case 1
            state = MainGameLoop(currentLevel)
            If state = 2
                quit = True
            End If
    End Select
End While
```

There are a couple of new constructs that I'm introducing here that I'll explain in much more depth in the next chapter. The Type .. End Types at the start of the program listing are BlitzMax's interpretation of object-oriented programming and are called user-defined types, or UDTs. They allow data and algorithms (code) to exist together in a neat package. UDTs can be reused in any number of projects, not just this one.

Save and run the program. It won't do anything, but just make sure you don't get any errors when running it. We're going to start fleshing out the details now.

The Splash Screen

The splash screen introduces us to the game and gives the players a choice as to what map they want to play on. We will be updating the following functions in this section:

```
PrintMessage

DrawSplash
```

PrintMessage

BlitzMax allows us to draw text to the screen using DrawText. However, it is somewhat limited in its functionality. For this game, we want to center the text on a particular line, given the length of text. For our text, we'll write our own draw text method called PrintMessage. This will provide our functionality wrapped around the existing DrawText command. The PrintMessage looks like the following:

```
Function PrintMessage(s:String, x:Int, y:Int, centre:Int = False)
    If centre Then
        x = x - TextWidth(s) / 2
    End If
    DrawText s, x, y
End Function
```

We've kept the same format as the DrawText command, but we've added an optional parameter called centre. When you pass in True for that value, the text will be centered on the screen, on the specified y coordinate line, effectively ignoring the x coordinate specified.

DrawSplash

For the most part, there is nothing complicated in DrawSplash. It merely draws a series of text strings to the screen—using the PrintMessage function we just created—but it also contains some code to retrieve information from users, in particular, what map they want to play or whether they want to quit the game back to the OS. The DrawSplash function is shown following. Delete the Return 99 line and change the function to look like this:

```
Function DrawSplash:Int()
    Local retVal:Int = 0
    While retVal = 0
        Cls
            SetColor 255, 255, 255
            PrintMessage "Tank Attack", 400,
32, True
            SetColor 255, 192, 0
            PrintMessage "A GAME FOR TWO
PLAYERS", 400, 96, True
            SetColor 255, 255, 255
            PrintMessage "FIGHT TO THE DEATH
IN", 400, 228, True
            PrintMessage "NINETY-NINE
```

```
SECONDS", 400, 260, True
                SetColor 0, 255, 192
                PrintMessage "PLAYER WITH
HIGHEST", 400, 292, True
                PrintMessage "SCORE WINS", 400,
324, True
                SetColor 255, 0, 0
                PrintMessage "PRESS A B OR C FOR
MAP", 400, 492, True
                PrintMessage "ESCAPE TO QUIT TO
OS", 400, 524, True
            Flip
            If KeyDown(KEY_A)
                retVal = 1
            Else If KeyDown(KEY_B)
                retVal = 2
            Else If KeyDown(KEY_C)
                retVal = 3
            Else If KeyDown(KEY_ESCAPE)
                retVal = 99
            End If
        Wend
        FlushKeys
        Return retVal
End Function
```

Save and run the program. Now we have a splash screen! The game won't do anything beyond that. In fact, pressing a key will exit the program.

Loading and Drawing the Map

The main playing area is cell-based; that is each map clock represents one 32×24 area filling an 800×600 screen. In our map files, an X represents a block, and anything else is ignored. If you want to change that (please feel free), you will have to alter the GetMapData function. In this section, we will be updating the following:

> Loading images just under the Graphics command

> Adding fields to the TVector2 type

> GetMapData

> DrawMapData

> MainGameLoop

The Brick Graphic

To load the brick graphic, add the following line after the Graphics command:

```
Global brick:TImage = LoadImage("brick.png")
```

This will get used in the DrawMapData function.

Map Positions

The block positions are stored using the TVector2 type. T just means "type," and Vector is a position in space. See http://en.wikipedia.org/wiki/Vector_space for more details. The 2 just represents how many coordinates we have. Because this is a 2D (flat) game, we have two coordinates: x and y.

Change the TVector2 definition to

```
Type TVector2
    Field X:Float
    Field Y:Float
End Type
```

Type is short for "User Defined Type" and allows us to create a single record of information that we can pass around, rather than multiple variables. A trivial reason is that it makes parameter lists easier to read.

We'll see how types get created when we get the map data. It returns a list of positions in which each of the bricks is located onscreen.

Getting the Map Data

The map data is stored in a text file that contains blank spaces in which there are no blocks onscreen and an X wherein a block is to be placed. The spreadsheet this came from was 25 columns across by 25 rows. Our bricks are 32×24 pixels. This means that our playing field is 25 * 32 by 25 * 24 pixels, which is 800×600 pixels, which just so happens to be our screen size!

For this method, I've kept the comments in the code to make what's happening a little clearer. Breaking the code down, it does the following:

> Initializes some local variables used in the loop
>
> Opens the file
>
> Reads the file line by line
>
> Parses each line by splitting it up by tab character, and, if it's an X, it adds a cell to the list

When all lines have been parsed, the collection of brick positions are returned to the calling function.

The list of positions is actually made up of lists of TVector2 instances. The screen position is determined by multiplying the local x coordinate by 32 and the local y coordinate by 24, as follows:

```
Local vec:TVector2 = New TVector2
vec.X = x * 32
vec.Y = y * 24
```

Note that to create a user-defined type is slightly different than creating an instance of a simple type such as an integer or a floating point number. You must tell the BlitzMax complier that you are wanting to reserve some new memory for your type.

The full listing for GetMapData is shown following:

```
Function GetMapData:TList(filename:String)
    Local list:TList = CreateList()
    Local y:Int = 0
    Local x:Int = 0
    Local file:TStream = OpenFile(filename, True, False)
```

```
        While Not Eof(file)
                Rem
                        When we read in the string from the file, we need
                        to parse out the tab characters that are put in
                        by Google docs.
                EndRem
                Local line:String = ReadLine(file)
                Local cells:String[] = line.Split(Chr(9))

                Rem
                        Once that is done, it's a trivial matter of going
                        through each of the characters in turn and deciding
                        to put a block if the character contains an upper
                        case X.
                EndRem

                For Local x:Int = 0 To cells.Length - 1
                        Local c:String = cells[x]
                        If c = "X"
                                Local vec:TVector2 = New TVector2
                                vec.X = x * 32
                                vec.Y = y * 24
                                ListAddLast(list, vec)
                        End If
                Next
                y = y + 1
        Wend
        CloseFile(file)
        Return list
End Function
```

That was the hard part, now for the easy part. We've successfully transported the data in our file to an in-memory representation of the layout of the bricks. How do we display them? Well, we only have one brick shape, so displaying them is just a matter of going through each one and displaying it at the correct position onscreen. That's what the DrawMap function does.

```
Function DrawMap(mapData:TList)
        SetColor 255, 255, 255
        For Local vec:TVector2 = EachIn mapData
                DrawImage brick, vec.X, vec.Y
        Next
End Function
```

Because we only have one block, we need only store the position information. We can let the DrawMap decide how that block is drawn. In this case, we use the brick image that we loaded earlier and is available globally.

We're still not out of the woods yet. We still can't see the map when we choose it from the splash screen. To at least see something, we must add some code to MainGameLoop.

The Main Game Loop

The main game loop, as you remember from the structure diagram at the start of the chapter, calls LoadMap. It returns the loaded map data to the caller, in this case, the MainGameLoop. We'll add code that (for now) will at least get us to see the loaded map.

```
Function MainGameLoop:Int(currentLevel:Int)
    Local mapData:TList = LoadMap(currentLevel)
    While Not KeyHit(KEY_ESCAPE)
        Cls
        DrawMap(mapData)
        Flip
    Wend
    Return 2
End Function
```

You can now save and run the game. When you select a map, it will now appear onscreen. Pressing the Escape key will quit the game.

Let's add some combat to the game, by adding another player and a way to update fired bullets.

Adding Combat

Now that we have our world, we have to add conflict to it, and nothing says conflict more than red vs. blue. We are going to create two tanks: one colored red that starts on the left-hand side of the screen and a blue tank that starts on the right-hand side of the screen. The tanks are controlled by players, and their keys are listed in Table 8-1.

Table 8-1. *Keys Controlling Tank Movements and Their Meaning*

Key	Meaning
W	Move red tank forward
A	Rotate red tank left
D	Rotate red tank right
S	Fire red tank's gun
Up-Arrow	Move blue tank forward
Left-Arrow	Rotate blue tank left
Right-Arrow	Rotate blue tank right
M	Fire blue tank's gun

Because we are going to color the tanks when we draw them, we only have to bring in two new images: one for the tank shape and one for the bullet. Locate the following line in the source code:

```
Global brick:TImage = LoadImage("brick.png")
```

Add the following lines underneath:

```
Global tankImage:TImage = LoadImage("tank.png")
Global bulletImage:TImage =
LoadImage("bullet.png")
```

The tanks must rotate. If we left them as default, they would turn around the top-left corner of the image. Instead, we instruct BlitzMax to rotate and place them in the world using their center.

The bullets must align with the center of the tank, so we mid-handle that image too. So, after those two new lines to load the images, add these lines just underneath:

```
MidHandleImage(tankImage)
MidHandleImage(bulletImage)
```

We're going to use UDTs again, to store data. Our bullet class will hold the location, speed, and the "aliveness" (that's not a word!) of the bullet. Any "dead" bullet will be removed from the game. A "dead" bullet is one that hits a wall but misses a player. You could also add a time-out to that too, just to make the game a little harder. For now, though, our bullet UDT looks like this:

```
Type TBullet
    Field Location:TVector2
    Field Speed:TVector2
    Field IsAlive:Int

    Rem
        The init method sets the initial values for the bullet.
    EndRem
    Method Init(x:Float, y:Float, sx:Float, sy:Float)
        Location.X = x
        Location.Y = y
        Speed.X = sx
        Speed.Y = sy
        IsAlive = True
    End Method
End Type
```

The Init() method is used just to make our lives easier when we have to create bullets in the game. It sets up the fields of the bullet and sets its aliveness to True.

The tank is our most (at first glance, anyway) complex UDT. It contains lots of fields (values that will change when we run the program) and a Create function that is attached to the TTank UDT. This is a quick way for us to create a tank with some parameters, rather than setting each individual field itself.

```
Type TTank

    Field X:Float
    Field Y:Float

    Field R:Int
    Field G:Int
    Field B:Int

    Field Rotation:Float
```

```
    Field rotRightKey:Int
    Field rotLeftKey:Int
    Field forwardKey:Int
    Field fireKey:Int

    Field Bullet:TBullet

    Field Score:Int
    Function Create:TTank(x:Int, y:Int, r:Int,
g:Int, b:Int, rotLeft:Int, rotRight:Int,
forward:Int, fire:Int)
        Local tank:TTank = New TTank
        tank.X = x
        tank.Y = y

        tank.R = r
        tank.G = g
        tank.B = b

        tank.rotRightKey = rotRight
        tank.rotLeftKey = rotLeft
        tank.forwardKey = forward
        tank.fireKey = fire

        tank.Bullet = New TBullet
        tank.Bullet.IsAlive = False
        tank.Bullet.Location = New TVector2
        tank.Bullet.Speed = New TVector2
        tank.Bullet.Location.X = 0
        tank.Bullet.Location.Y = 0
        tank.Bullet.Speed.X = 0
        tank.Bullet.Speed.Y = 0

        Return tank

    End Function

End Type
```

I will get to the difference between a function and a method, with respect to UDTs, in the next chapter. For now, I'll just say that a method is run on an instance of a UDT, and a function runs on the UDT name itself, meaning that you don't have to create an instance of the type to run the code in the function.

Now that we have our images and data types set up, we must update the following functions in our bare-bones code:

```
    UpdateTanks

    UpdateBullets

    IsCrashWithBricks

    DrawTanks

    MainGameLoop
```

Updating the Tanks

The UpdateTanks method is the longest in the whole program listing. Don't let that put you off. The method doesn't contain any trick code and is straightforward enough:

```
For Each Tank:
        Update the tank's rotation based upon player input
        If the Fire button is down and no bullet is alive, create a bullet
                If the forward key is pressed
                        If the tank's new position would not crash into a wall
                                Update the tank's position
                        End For
                End If
        End If
End If
```

The full function is laid out next. It has some additional tests (for screen bounds), but those are not required, unless the map has no outside blocks. Note that at the end of the function, the rotation is set to 0 degrees, just to be on the safe side. It's good practice to tidy up the settings, such as rotation, coloring, and blending, when you've finished using them.

```
Function UpdateTanks(mapData:TList, tankList:TList)
    For Local t:TTank = EachIn tankList
        If KeyDown(t.rotLeftKey)
            t.Rotation = t.Rotation - 2.0
            If t.Rotation < 0
                t.Rotation = 360 - t.Rotation
            End If
        Else If KeyDown(t.rotRightKey)
            t.Rotation = t.Rotation + 2.0
            If t.Rotation > 360
                t.Rotation = t.Rotation - 360
            End If
        End If

        If KeyDown(t.fireKey) And Not
t.Bullet.IsAlive
            Local x:Float = t.X
            Local y:Float = t.Y

            x = x + (3.14/2.0 * Sin(t.Rotation))
            y = y - (3.14/2.0 * Cos(t.Rotation))
            Local dx:Float = x - t.X
            Local dy:Float = y - t.Y
            t.Bullet.Init(t.X, t.Y, dx * 2, dy * 2)
        End If
        If KeyDown(t.forwardKey)
            Local x:Float = t.X
            Local y:Float = t.Y
            x = x + (3.14/2.0 * Sin(t.Rotation))
            y = y - (3.14/2.0 * Cos(t.Rotation))
            If IsCrashWithBricks(mapData, tankImage, x, y)
```

```
                    Continue
                End If
                If x >= 32 And x <= 768
                    t.X = x
                End If
                If y >= 32 And y <= 568
                    t.Y = y
                End If
            End If
        Next
        SetRotation 0.0
End Function
```

At first glance, the bullet update function is also complex, but only because of its length. The function updates each tank's "alive" bullet in turn. Each time the function goes around, it remembers the "other" tank. We then use the IsCrashWithBricks and ImagesCollide functions (see under "Collision Detection"), to determine if the bullet has hit a wall or a tank.

If the bullet has hit a wall, it is marked as dead, by setting the IsAlive field to False. We use the Continue keyword to skip all the other instructions that follow and move on to the next tank. If a tank's bullet hits the other player, his index value (red is 0, blue is 1) is returned to the calling function. If no bullet hits a tank, -1 is returned. The tank that wins is stored locally in the function as tankVictor.

The full UpdateBullets function is shown following:

```
Function UpdateBullets:Int(mapData:TList, tankList:TList)
    Local currentTank:Int = 0
    Local tankVictor:Int = -1
    For Local t:TTank = EachIn tankList
        Local otherTank:TTank = Null
        If currentTank = 0
            otherTank = TTank(tankList.Last())
        Else
            otherTank = TTank(tankList.First())
        End If
        If t.Bullet.IsAlive
            Local nx:Float = t.Bullet.Location.X + t.Bullet.Speed.X
            Local ny:Float = t.Bullet.Location.Y + t.Bullet.Speed.Y
            If IsCrashWithBricks(mapData, bulletImage, nx, ny)
                t.Bullet.IsAlive = False
                Continue
            End If
            If ImagesCollide(bulletImage, nx, ny, 0, tankImage, otherTank.X, otherTank.Y, 0)
                tankVictor = currentTank
            End If
            t.Bullet.Location.X = nx
            t.Bullet.Location.Y = ny
            If t.Bullet.Location.X < 0 Or t.Bullet.Location.X > 800 Or t.Bullet.Location.Y <
0 Or t.Bullet.Location.Y > 600
                t.Bullet.IsAlive = False
            End If
        End If
        currentTank:+1
```

```
       Next
       Return tankVictor
End Function
```

Collision Detection

Collision detection for 2D graphics in BlitzMax is handled by the ImagesCollide function. It returns a true if the images overlap in any way. It's very accurate, as it uses per-pixel matching to determine collisions. Our IsCrashWithBricks uses the ImagesCollide function for both tank against wall and bullet against tank and bullet against wall. It does a very lazy check by looping through each brick in the map and testing the brick image against the supplied image and its coordinates.

There are a couple of drawbacks with this function that you can put right later. The first is that it does not take rotation into consideration. The second is that it loops through *all* the bricks in the level. You could partition the level into quadrants, for example, to reduce the amount of checks required. Here is the full listing for the IsCrashWithBricks as it stands now:

```
Function IsCrashWithBricks:Int(mapData:TList,
img:TImage, x:Float, y:Float)
    For Local vec:TVector2 = EachIn mapData
            If ImagesCollide(brick, vec.X, vec.Y,
0, img, x, y, 0)
                    Return True
            End If
    Next
Return False
End Function
```

Drawing the Tanks

The tanks use the same shape. As you've seen, we use this technique a lot in the code. Basically, we cycle through all the tanks in the given list and then set the appropriate color and rotation and then draw them. If they have an "alive" bullet, we draw that too. This means that if you have three, four, or four hundred tanks, all you would have to do is add them to the tankList and call the DrawTanks function, as follows:

```
Function DrawTanks(tankList:TList)
    For Local t:TTank = EachIn tankList
            SetColor t.R, t.G, t.B
            SetRotation t.Rotation
            DrawImage tankImage, t.X, t.Y
            SetRotation 0.0
            If t.Bullet.IsAlive
                    DrawImage bulletImage, t.Bullet.Location.X, t.Bullet.Location.Y
            End If
    Next
End Function
```

Main Game Loop

Our main game loop has to be rewritten. We want to add code that will

Update the tanks

Update the bullets

Draw the map

Draw the tanks

Our new main game loop now looks like this:

```
Function MainGameLoop:Int(currentLevel:Int)
    Local roundTime:Int = MilliSecs()
    Local countDown:Int = 99
    Local mapData:TList = LoadMap(currentLevel)
    Local tankList:TList = CreateList()
    Local player1:TTank = TTank.Create(64, 300, 255, 0, 0, KEY_A, KEY_D, KEY_W, KEY_S)
    Local player2:TTank = TTank.Create(704, 300, 0, 0, 255, KEY_LEFT, KEY_RIGHT,
    KEY_UP, KEY_M)
    ListAddLast(tankList, player1)
    ListAddLast(tankList, player2)
    While Not KeyHit(KEY_ESCAPE) And countDown > 0
        UpdateTanks(mapData, tankList)
        Local tankVictor:Int = UpdateBullets(mapData, tankList)
        If tankVictor > -1
            ResetGame(tankList, tankVictor)
        End If
        Cls
        DrawMap(mapData)
        DrawTanks(tankList)
        Flip
    Wend
    Return 2
End Function
```

We use the `Create` function of the `TTank` UDT to create our two player tanks. We use the `UpdateTanks` function to get the user input to determine the new location and rotation of the tanks. And, who could forget, to fire the bullet, we use the `tankList` again to `DrawTanks`.

Save and run the game. The tanks can now roll about the screen firing at each other. The next step is to build tension by adding a countdown and a heads-up display, to let players know what their scores are.

Adding Tension

We have a world, we have combat, but we also must build tension in our game. In this next section, we will add the following:

Countdown timer

Players' scores

Reset function

But first, we'll add methods that will draw information onto the screen:

DrawNumber

DrawInformation

Drawing Information

Drawing numbers onscreen is done using the DrawText built-in function. I have wrapped it in its own function, to allow an offset to the left to be set. This allows better positioning for the number on the screen. The DrawNumber function is in the code as a skeleton. Locate it in code and change it to the following:

```
Function DrawNumber(x:Int, number:Int, offsetLeft:Int)
    Local s:String = "" + number
    x = x - TextWidth(s) / 2
    x = x - offsetLeft
    DrawText s, x, 48
End Function
```

The heads-up display, or HUD for short (see http://en.wikipedia.org/wiki/HUD_(video_gaming)), allows players to see at a glance their status in the game. Our HUD will consist of three numbers. The red number is the number of times that the red player has hit the blue tank. The orange number is the countdown number for the round, and the blue number is the number of times the blue tank's bullets have hit the red tank.

Locate the DrawInformation function in the code and change it look like this:

```
Function DrawInformation(tankList:TList,
countDown:Int)
    Local firstTank:TTank =
TTank(tankList.First())
    Local secondTank:TTank =
TTank(tankList.Last())

    SetColor 255, 0, 0
    DrawNumber 200, firstTank.Score, True

    SetColor 255, 192, 0
    DrawNumber 366, countDown, False

    SetColor 0, 0, 255
    DrawNumber 600, secondTank.Score, False
End Function
```

Resetting the Game

When a player hits the other with a bullet, the game is reset. This means that we're going to return the players to their original starting positions and rotations. We remove all bullets from the game and increase the winning player's score.

Locate the ResetGame function in the code and change it as follows:

```
Function ResetGame(tankList:TList, tankVictor:Int)
    Local winningTank:TTank = Null
    If tankVictor = 0
        winningTank = TTank(tankList.First())
    Else
        winningTank = TTank(tankList.Last())
```

```
    End If
        winningTank.Score:+1
    Local i:Int = 0
    For Local t:TTank = EachIn tankList
        t.Bullet.IsAlive = False
        t.Rotation = 0
        If i = 0
            t.X = 64
            t.Y = 300
        Else
            t.X = 704
            t.Y = 300
        End If
        i:+1
    Next
End Function
```

Again, we're using the `For..EachIn` loop to reset the tanks. `If i = 0 .. Else .. End If` is used to reset the player to the right position. If it's the red player (`i = 0`), then its location is reset to the left-hand side of the screen, the opposite side from the blue player.

Decrementing the Counter

We already have code to decrement our counter. It's the `UpdateCountDown` function. We've just never called it. Until now. Locate the `MainGameLoop` function in the code and scroll down to the following line:

```
While Not KeyHit(KEY_ESCAPE) And countDown > 0
```

Below that line, enter the following text:

```
countDown = UpdateCountDown(roundTime, countdown)
```

Now locate the `DrawInformation` line in the same `While..Wend` block. Below that line add:

```
DrawInformation(tankList, countDown)
```

Save and run the game. We're almost there! We have tank movement and firing, the scores update, and the countdown...counts down.

The End Screen

Our final piece to the Tank Attack puzzle is the end screen. This screen tells the players who won and gives them an opportunity to cool down before the next round. They're given a choice to play again or return to the OS. There's also some housekeeping we want to perform here. Up until now, the game could be quit by pressing the Escape key at any time, to return to the OS, or, in our case, the BlitzMax IDE. We have to stop that from happening. So, locate the `MainGameLoop` function and this line within it:

```
While Not KeyHit(KEY_ESCAPE) And countDown > 0
Change that to:
While countDown > 0
```

This will stop the player from being able to hit the Escape key to break out of the game. After the Wend inside the MainGameLoop, add the following code. This will display the endgame and wait for the user to press the P key to play again, or escape to quit to the OS.

```
Local result:Int = 0
While result = 0
    result = DrawEndGame(player1, player2)
Wend
Return result
```

The result is returned to the loop at the bottom of the source code that uses the return value to determine the state of the application. Play again or quit to the OS.

The Endgame State

The endgame code doesn't exist yet. It currently looks like this:

```
Function DrawEndGame:Int(p1:TTank, p2:TTank)
    Return 2
End Function
```

This means that the game will always quit to the OS. If the user were to choose to play, this would return 1. In our endgame screen, we're going to establish what player won, or if both players drew, and tell the user what can happen next. We use FlushKeys because both players will probably be pressing the keyboard. This command resets all the keys and removes any pending characters in the queue.

The updated DrawEndGame is shown following:

```
Function DrawEndGame:Int(p1:TTank, p2:TTank)
    Local retVal:Int = 0
    FlushKeys
    While retVal = 0
        Cls
            SetColor 255, 255, 255
            PrintMessage "Tank Attack", 400, 32, True
            SetColor 255, 255, 255
            If p1.Score = p2.Score
                PrintMessage "IT WAS A DRAW", 400, 228, True
            Else If p1.Score > p2.Score
                PrintMessage "PLAYER ONE IS THE WINNER", 400, 228, True
            Else
                PrintMessage "PLAYER TWO IS THE WINNER", 400, 228, True
            End If
```

```
            SetColor 255, 0, 0
            PrintMessage "PRESS P TO PLAY AGAIN", 400, 492, True
            PrintMessage "ESCAPE TO QUIT TO OS", 400, 524, True
        Flip
        If KeyDown(KEY_P)
            retVal = 1
        Else If KeyDown(KEY_ESCAPE)
            retVal = 2
        End If
    Wend
    FlushKeys
    Return retVal
End Function
```

And that's it! Our tank game is complete. Now it's time to move on to learning more about UDTs and how they can help with your games.

CHAPTER 9

■■■

Object-Oriented Programming

Object-oriented programming (OOP) has been with us since the 1970s, but it has only really taken the software engineering world by storm in the last 20 years, even fewer for the games industry. There are a number of buzzwords associated with OOP that I have to clarify.

This is an introductory chapter to OOP. I will delve into it in more detail for our last project—Flood.

If you have never used an object-oriented language, you should understand the underlying concepts before you begin. By the end of this section, you should be able to answer the following questions:

What is an object? What is a class? What is an attribute? What is a method?

What is the difference between an object and a class? What is inheritance?

What is an interface?

What Is an Object?

An object is a software bundle of related variables and methods.

Software objects are often used to model real-world objects that you find in everyday life, such as a car, a person, or an animal.

What Is a Class?

A class is a blueprint or prototype that defines the attribute and the methods common to all objects of a certain kind.

What Is an Attribute?

An attribute describes an object, for example, its width, height, lives, power, gas level, etc.

What Is a Method?

A method is a special function that is only available to an object and performs some kind of action: move, draw, die, etc.

What Is the Difference Between an Object and a Class?

A class is the abstract of a physical object, a description. An object is an implementation or instance of that class. Much like the data type Int and the BlitzMax statement i:Int = 5. Int is an abstract concept, a whole number, whereas i:Int = 5 creates an instance of an Int and assigns a whole number value (in this case, 5) to it.

What Is Inheritance?

A class inherits state and behavior from its parent. Inheritance provides a powerful and natural mechanism for organizing and structuring software programs. For example, if you have a Player object, you could derive two new objects from it: OurHero and Baddie. Both would share common code (such as Move(), Draw(), Die()) but could be enhanced too. For example, Baddie could have a method SeekOurHero(). Inheritance is used to extend a parent class's attributes and methods.

What Is an Interface?

An interface is a contract in the form of a collection of method and constant declarations. When a class implements an interface, it promises to implement all of the methods declared in that interface.

Classes in BlitzMax

BlitzMax bases its implementation of OOP on its previous Type ... End Type construct. To this end, there is no "Class" keyword in BlitzMax. BlitzMax prefers to call classes "user-defined types" (UDTs).

Defining a User-Defined Type

The format to define a UDT is shown following:

```
Type type_name [Extends parent_type]
    [Fields]
    [Methods]
    [Functions]
End Type
```

The format of a Field is

```
Field attribute_name[:Type]
```

The format of Method is

```
Method method_name[:Type]([param-1[:Type], param-
2[:Type], ..., param-n[:Type]]) [Abstract]
    ...
End Method
```

The format of Function is

```
Function function_name[:Type]([param-1[:Type],
param-2[:Type], ..., param-n[:Type]])
    ...
End Function
```

As you can see, methods and functions are declared in almost the same way. The difference is in when and how each are called. I will discuss this at length below.

A Simple Class

The following is a simple class that contains three fields: X, Y, and Lives:

```
Type TSimplePlayer
    Field X:Int
    Field Y:Int
    Field Lives:Int
End Type
```

This is the BlitzMax version of a class. To create an object of this class, we have to create an instance.

```
Local simplePlayer:TSimplePlayer = New
TSimplePlayer
```

You can create instances of such types using the New operator. New takes one parameter—a user-defined type—and returns an instance of that type. Such instances are known as objects.

The preceding code line declares a variable simplePlayer to be of type TSimplePlayer. We then assign it a value New TSimplePlayer. Because it is an object, we must assign it an object. We cannot assign it a class, so we do the following:

```
Local simplePlayer:TSimplePlayer = TSimplePlayer
```

This line would result in a compilation error. This tries to set simplePlayer to be a class. The New keyword is used to create a new instance of the TSimplePlayer UDT.

Now that we have an instance of TSimplePlayer, we can assign values to its attributes or call its methods and functions.

```
simplePlayer.X = 320
simplePlayer.Y = 240
Print simplePlayer.X
Print simplePlayer.Y
Print simplePlayer.X / 2
```

It should be noted that the period character (.) is used to separate the instance of the UDT and its attribute/method/function. This is a standard that has been adopted throughout the OOP world. The general format is:

```
object_instance.[Attribute | Method | Function]
```

Within a user-defined type, you can declare the following:

Fields

Methods

Functions

Fields

Fields are variables associated with each instance of a user-defined type. Fields are declared in the same way as local or global variables using the Field keyword. To access the fields of an object, use the . operator.

Methods

Methods are function-like operations associated with each instance of a user-defined type. Methods are declared in the same way as functions, only using the Method keyword instead of Function. To access the methods of an object, use the . operator. Program code within a method can access other fields, methods, functions, consts, and globals within the same object, simply by referring to them by name.

Functions

These are declared in the same way as "normal" functions and can be accessed using the . operator. Unlike methods, functions within a type are not associated with instances of the type but with the type itself. This means such functions can be used regardless of whether any instances of the type have been created yet. Functions within a type can access other functions, consts, or globals within the same type, by referring to them by name. In OOP parlance, a function is the same as a static method.

Consts and Globals or Static Attributes

These are declared in the same way as "normal" consts and globals and can be accessed using the . operator. As with type functions, these are not associated with instances of the type but with the type itself.

Here is another example of a user-defined type:

```
Type TStar
    Global Count:Int
    Field X:Int
    Field Y:Int
    Field R:Int
    Field G:Int
    Field B:Int
    Method Draw()
        SetColor(R, G, B)
        Plot(X, Y)
        SetColor(255, 255, 255)
    End Method
    Function Create:TStar(nx:Int, ny:Int, nr:Int, ng:Int, nb:Int)
        TStar.Count:+1
        star:TStar = New TStar
        star.X = nx
        star.Y = ny
```

```
            star.R = nr
            star.G = ng
            star.B = nb
            Return star
        End Function
    End Type
```

In this example, the following attributes and functions are available to the class:

> Count attribute
>
> Create() function

The following attributes and methods are available to the object:

> X attribute
>
> Y attribute
>
> R attribute
>
> G attribute
>
> B attribute
>
> Draw() method

In object-oriented terms an attribute is something that describes an object. For example the colour of a pen would be an attribute. In BlitzMax, the keyword Field is used to denote an attribute. A field is like a variable but it can only be accessed from a class instance using the dot (.) operator. The following sample code is correct. It is assumed that star is an instance (object) of the TStar class and that BlitzMax is in graphics mode (using the Graphics keyword).

```
Local star:TStar = TStar.Create(50, 50, 255, 255,
255)
While Not KeyHit(KEY_ESCAPE)
     Cls
     star.Draw()
     Flip
Wend
```

The following sample code is incorrect. It is assumed that star is an instance (object) of the TStar class:

```
TStar.X
star.Create()
```

The full program listing follows:

```
Graphics 640, 480

Type TStar
     Global Count:Int
     Field X:Int
     Field Y:Int
     Field R:Int
     Field G:Int
     Field B:Int
```

```
    Method Draw()
        SetColor(R, G, B)
         Plot(X, Y)
         SetColor(255, 255, 255)
    End Method
    Function Create:TStar(nx:Int, ny:Int, nr:Int, ng:Int, nb:Int)
        TStar.Count:+1
        star:TStar = New TStar
        star.X = nx
        star.Y = ny
        star.R = nr
        star.G = ng
        star.B = nb
        Return star
    End Function

End Type
Local starfield:TList = CreateList()
While Not KeyHit(KEY_ESCAPE)
    If TStar.Count < 250
        star:TStar = TStar.Create(Rnd(640), Rnd(480), Rnd(255),Rnd(255), Rnd(255))
        starfield.AddLast(star)
    End If
    Cls
    For s:TStar = EachIn starfield
        s.Draw()
    Next
    DrawText("Star Count = " + TStar.Count, 0, 0)
    Flip
Wend
```

The object is created indirectly using the Create() function. This static method, if you will, creates a new instance of the class TStar, initializes the fields, increments the count of stars, and passes a reference back to the calling routine.

The Create() function is a technique that is used by the majority of BlitzMax programmers and will be employed within this book. It allows for complex initializations of an object before returning it to the calling routine.

Inheritance and Polymorphism

User-defined types can extend other user-defined types, using the Extends keyword. Extending a type means adding more functionality to an existing type. The type being extended is often referred to as the base type, and the resulting, extended type is often referred to as the derived type.

A Simple Object

In a game, we have a number of objects that share common features, such as player objects. In our game world, these objects inhabit a physical screen with x and y coordinates. These objects can be described using the following UDT declaration:

```
Type TSimplePlayer
    Field x:Int = 0
    Field y:Int = 0
End Type
```

Perhaps we want to create a player object that has additional attributes: Lives and Score. We could create an entirely new object, but because we are developers, we are into recycling and believe in reuse. So, we dust off our TSimplePlayer to create a new derived class, as follows:

```
Type TOurHero Extends TSimplePlayer
    Field lives:Int = 0
    Field score:Int = 0
End Type
```

This is called inheritance, because, like humans, we gain some of our attributes from our parents—our mother's eyes and our father's nose (but the rest belongs to you), for example. Likewise, the TOurHero UDT inherits the fields x and y, so the following is a perfectly valid program:

```
Type TSimplePlayer
    Field x:Int = 0
    Field y:Int = 0
End Type
Type TOurHero Extends TSimplePlayer
    Field lives:Int = 0
    Field score:Int = 0
End Type
hero:TOurHero = New TOurHero
hero.x = 5
hero.y = 50
hero.lives = 10
```

But the following is invalid:

```
Type TSimplePlayer
    Field x:Int = 0
    Field y:Int = 0
End Type

Type TOurHero Extends TSimplePlayer
    Field lives:Int = 0
    Field score:Int = 0
End Type

hero:TSimplePlayer = New TSimplePlayer
hero.x = 5
hero.y = 50
hero.lives = 10
```

This will fail because TSimplePlayer does not contain a definition of lives. But that is not all that inheritance can be used for. BlitzMax allows you to use a derived type anywhere a base-type object is expected. This is because a derived-type object is a base-type object with additional fields and methods.

107

For example, you can assign a derived-type object to a base-type variable or pass a derived-type object to a function expecting a base-type parameter.

The following program is perfectly valid. Type it in and run it.

```
Type TSimplePlayer
     Field x:Int = 0
     Field y:Int = 0
End Type
Type TOurHero Extends TSimplePlayer
     Field lives:Int = 0
     Field score:Int = 0
End Type

simple:TSimplePlayer = New TSimplePlayer
hero:TOurHero = New TOurHero
simple.x = 5
hero.x = 10
list:TList = CreateList()
list.AddLast(simple)
list.AddLast(hero)
For so:TSimplePlayer = EachIn list
     Print so.x
Next
```

So, you can see that all derived classes can be assumed to be base classes, but with extra attributes/methods/functions. In fact, we can take this one step forward with a new word: polymorphism.

Polymorphism

Dictionary.com defines polymorphism as "The occurrence of different forms, stages, or types in individual organisms or in organisms of the same species." In OOP, polymorphism allows us to rewrite methods, to adapt to our derived class's needs. This is often referred to as overriding.

Type in the following program and run it. You should see a circle and a rectangle on the screen. Press Escape to continue. The program code is broken up into sections. Each section is followed by a description.

```
Graphics 640, 480
Type TShape
     Field x:Int
     Field y:Int
     Method Draw()
          Plot x, y
          Plot x+1, y
          Plot x+1, y+1
          Plot x, y+1
     End Method
End Type
```

This is our base class. It contains the declaration of the x and y variables that define where the shape will be drawn onscreen. It also contains a rudimentary Draw() method that we will override in each of our derived classes.

```
Type TCircle Extends TShape
    Field r:Int
    Method Draw()
        DrawOval(x, y, r, r)
    End Method
End Type
```

The TCircle derived class contains an additional field, r, to allow a circle to be drawn—we need a radius. The Draw() method has been updated to draw an oval, as BlitzMax can only draw ellipses.

```
Type TRectangle Extends TShape
    Field w:Int
    Field h:Int
    Method Draw()
        DrawRect(x, y, w, h)
    End Method
End Type
```

As with TCircle, TRectangle extends the TShape class and provides two new fields, w and h, for the width of the rectangle and its height. The Draw method is overridden again to draw a rectangle.

```
s:TShape = New TShape
c:TCircle = New TCircle
r:TRectangle = New TRectangle
s.x = 50
s.y = 240
c.x = 200
c.y = 240
c.r = 50
r.x = 500
r.y = 240
r.w = 100
r.h = 50
```

Instances of the variables are created, and their fields are assigned values.

```
shapes:TList = CreateList()
shapes.AddLast(s)
shapes.AddLast(c)
shapes.AddLast(r)
All the shapes are added to the 'shapes' list.
While Not KeyHit(KEY_ESCAPE)
    Cls
    For shp:TShape = EachIn shapes
        shp.Draw()
    Next
    Flip
Wend
```

We use the same technique as before to loop through each of the contents of the list and, this time, call the Draw() method of each object. Because each object is either a TShape or derived from TShape, we can use this construct.

Save the program in your BlitzMaxSource\Objects folder. Remove the Draw() method from the TRectangle class. What happens?

When a method is not redefined in a derived class, the parent method is used. It's kind of like a biological throwback to an earlier time. After all, we didn't invent vision!

All the declarations for Draw have the same signature. This is required by the language. And, indeed, this definition for TCircle would be wrong.

```
Type TCircle Extends TShape
    Method Draw(r:Int)
        DrawOval(x, y, r, r)
    End Method
End Type
```

Self and Super

Code inside a method can access two special variables called Self and Super. These variables refer to the current class and its base class that it was derived from, respectively.

Enter the following program in a new editor panel and run it.

```
Graphics 640, 480, 16
Type TText
    Field x:Int
    Field y:Int
    Field txt:String
    Method Draw()
        DrawText(txt, x, y)
        DebugLog "TText"
    End Method
End Type
Type TBold Extends TText
    Method Draw()
        Super.Draw()
        DrawText(txt, x + 1, y)
        DebugLog "TBold"
    End Method
End Type
b:TBold = New TBold
b.x = 280
b.y = 234
b.txt = "BlitzMax Super!"
While Not KeyHit(KEY_ESCAPE)
    Cls
    b.Draw()
    Flip
Wend
```

When you run the program, wait a few seconds, then press Escape. The output from the DebugLog() lines will be shown, as follows:

```
Building 001_SuperSelf
Compiling:001_SuperSelf.bmx
flat assembler version 1.51
3 passes, 6207 bytes.
Linking:001_SuperSelf.debug.exe
Executing:001_SuperSelf.debug.exe
TText
TBold
TText
TBold
TText
TBold
:       :
TText
TBold
Process complete
```

Note that because we call the Draw() method of the derived class, it in turn calls the Draw() method of its base class, using the Super keyword.

New and Delete

User-defined types can optionally declare two special methods named New and Delete. Both methods must take no arguments, and any returned value is ignored.

The New method is called when an object is first created with the New operator. This allows you to perform extra initialization code.

The Delete method is called when an object is discarded by the memory manager—when you make an explicit call to Flushmem (see following code). Note that critical shutdown operations such as closing files, etc., should not be placed in the Delete method, as you are not always sure when Delete will be called.

The New and Delete methods are illustrated in the following code. Enter the code in a new editor panel.

```
Type TSimple
    Method New()
        DebugLog "New object created!"
    End Method
    Method Delete()
        DebugLog "Object deleted!"
    End Method
End Type
s = New TSimple
Release s
FlushMem
```

Note that Release only works with integer variables. Try changing the line s = New TSimple to s:TSimple = new TSimple, to see what happens. The compiler doesn't like it! This is because we have defined s as an instance of TSimple and not an integer pointer. Don't worry too much about this. We will always use strong type conventions in this book.

Abstract and Final

Abstraction allows us to create a user defined type that exposes an interface that acts as a contract for other UDTs. You cannot create an abstract class directly, but you can derive child classes from it. This contract, for example, stipulates that certain methods must be provided. Take the following class as an example:

```
Type IBurgerPlace Abstract
    Method MakeFries() Abstract
    Method MakeBurgers() Abstract
    Method MakeShake() Abstract
End Type
```

Much like a fast food franchisee signs a contract to deliver quality fast food, so, too, does our class. Using a drawing known as a class diagram, this class is represented by the diagram below.

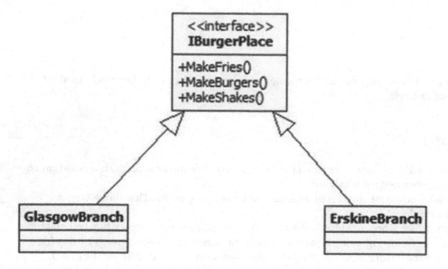

Figure 9-1. *Class diagram*

The rectangle is split into two areas. The top part is the name of the interface class. The capital *I* is used instead of capital *T* for the type name, because we are declaring an interface and not a type (as such). The bottom part lists the methods within the class that each derived object must expose.

The arrows represent the direction of the abstraction and should be read as "is a."

In BlitzMax, we would implement—code—the preceding diagram as

```
Type IBurgerPlace Abstract
    Method MakeFries() Abstract
    Method MakeBurgers() Abstract
    Method MakeShakes() Abstract
End Type
Type GlasgowBranch Extends IBurgerPlace
    Method MakeFries()
    End Method
    Method MakeBurgers()
    End Method
```

```
        Method MakeShakes()
        End Method
End Type
Type ErskineBranch Extends IBurgerPlace
        Method MakeFries()
        End Method
        Method MakeBurgers()
        End Method
        Method MakeShakes()
        End Method
End Type
```

We could create an object based on the GlasgowBranch class, using the following code:

```
gb:GlasgowBranch = New GlasgowBranch
```

Or we can use the abstract class.

```
gb:IBurgerPlace = New GlasgowBranch
```

This is much like the inheritance we have previously seen. Indeed, we can even add fully implemented methods, for example:

```
Type IBurgerPlace Abstract
        Method MakeFries() Abstract
        Method MakeBurgers() Abstract
        Method MakeShakes() Abstract
        Method CheeseFries()
                Print "Cheese Fries!"
        End Method
End Type
```

The CheeseFries() method can be overridden by developers who require more control over the making of cheese fries.

Differences Between Abstract and Inheritance

When an object is inherited, it obtains all the methods of the base class. The programmer can then override these methods, as he or she sees fit. The base class can be instantiated as an object. With abstraction, this is not the case.

When a class is defined as abstract, it can never be instantiated. It is designed to provide its child classes with a contract—methods they must provide. Not all methods in an abstract class need themselves be abstract. Indeed, as we have seen, it is possible to create an abstract class that contains implemented methods.

Inheritance **always** implements the base class's methods. Abstraction **must** implement the base class's methods.

And Finally...

If a user-defined type is declared as Final, it cannot be extended. If a method is declared as Final, it cannot be overridden. In our previous example, we had an implemented method in IBurgerPlace for CheeseFries(). GlasgowBranch could easily change this to the following:

```
Method CheeseFries()
     Print "Glasgow's Cheese Fries - Made from
Girders!"
End Method
```

But if we were to change the declaration of the CheeseFries() method in IBurgerPlace to Final, the following would result:

```
Method CheeseFries() Final
     Print "Cheese Fries!"
End Method
```

With the keyword Final after the method declaration, the following compilation error occurs:

```
---------------------------
BlitzMax Application
---------------------------
Compile Error
 Final methods cannot be overridden
---------------------------
OK
---------------------------
```

Use Final when you don't want people to change the code in a class or method.

Abstract types and methods are mostly used to create "template" types and methods that leave implementation details up to derived types. Final types and methods are mostly used to prevent modification to a type's behavior.

Summary

Object-oriented programming has been with us for a long time, but it was initially slow to take hold with developers. Whereas functions allowed us to reuse small bits of code, objects, or user-defined types, as they are called in BlitzMax, allow us to reuse entire data structures, or make component-based models, with ease.

CHAPTER 10

■ ■ ■

Project File Management

Correct file management is important in any project, but especially in game development, where it is not always possible to release patches to end users. Without correct file management, teams would not be able to function. We are going to look at two keywords that help:

    Include

    IncBin

Include

Include allows the developer or a group of developers to split the tasks and avoid having all their code in one file. Let's take the Burger Place example from Chapter 9 (Figure 10-1).

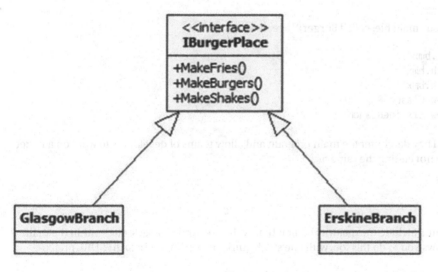

Figure 10-1. *Class diagram*

We are going to create a separate file for each of the classes, as follows:

IBurgerPlace.bmx:

```
Type IBurgerPlace Abstract
     Method MakeFries() Abstract
     Method MakeBurgers() Abstract
     Method MakeShakes() Abstract
End Type
```

```
    GlasgowBranch.bmx:
```

```
Type GlasgowBranch Extends IBurgerPlace
     Method MakeFries()
     End Method
     Method MakeBurgers()
     End Method
     Method MakeShakes()
     End Method
End Type
```

```
    ErskineBranch.bmx:
```

```
Type ErskineBranch Extends IBurgerPlace
     Method MakeFries()
     End Method
     Method MakeBurgers()
     End Method
     Method MakeShakes()
     End Method
End Type
```

And now we create our main file, called BurgerPlace.bmx.

```
Include "IBurgerPlace.bmx"
Include "GlasgowBranch.bmx"
Include "ErskineBranch.bmx"
gb:GlasgowBranch = New GlasgowBranch
eb:ErskineBranch = New ErskineBranch
```

Why use Includes? They de-clutter the main program and allow teams of developers to work on a larger project, because they are not editing the same file.

IncBin

Most professional programs include the majority of their binary data (sounds, images, etc.) within the main executable. BlitzMax allows you to do this too, with one small quirk, the use of the incbin:: URL prefix.

```
Incbin "images/tiger.png"
tiger = LoadImage("incbin::images/tiger.png")
```

We will see Include and IncBin used extensively from now on. Indeed, we started with the Tank Attack project.

CHAPTER 11

■ ■ ■

Graphics

The following built-in commands are available in BlitzMax, to allow us to display graphics on the screen:

AutoImageFlags	AutoMidHandle	Cls
CollideImage	CollideRect	CountGraphicsModes
CreateImage	DrawImage	DrawImageRect
DrawLine	DrawOval	DrawPixmap
DrawPoly	DrawRect	DrawText
EndGraphics	Flip	GetAlpha
GetBlend	GetClsColor	GetColor
GetGraphics	GetGraphicsMode	GetHandle
GetImageFont	GetLineWidth	GetMaskColor
GetOrigin	GetRotation	GetScale
GetViewport	GrabImage	GrabPixmap
Graphics	GraphicsHeight	GraphicsModeExists
GraphicsWidth	HideMouse	ImageHeight
ImagesCollide	ImagesCollide2	ImageWidth
LoadAnimImage	LoadImage	LoadImageFont
LockImage	MidHandleImage	Plot
ResetCollisions	SetAlpha	SetBlend
SetClsColor	SetColor	SetHandle
SetImageHandle	SetLineWidth	SetMaskColor
SetOrigin	SetRotation	SetScale
SetTransform	SetViewport	ShowMouse
TextHeight	TextWidth	TileImage
UnlockImage		

BlitzMax uses the OpenGL (www.opengl.org) API to draw graphics. Although OpenGL is known for producing 3D worlds, in this book, we only look at the production of 2D images. Blitz Research has called this Max2D, and although not three-dimensional, it allows us to use some special effects, such as blending and rotation.

© Sloan Kelly 2016
S. Kelly, *BlitzMax for Absolute Beginners*, DOI 10.1007/978-1-4842-2523-3_11

Graphics Modes

For each graphics card, there are a number of modes that it supports. Before we put the computer into graphics mode, we have to know that the mode exists. To access the list, BlitzMax has a number of commands.

```
CountGraphicsModes

GetGraphicsMode

GraphicsModeExists

Graphics

EndGraphics

GraphicsWidth

GraphicsHeight

GetGraphics
```

CountGraphicsModes

Used in conjunction with the GetGraphicsMode will list the modes available to the system.

```
Local ;
For i:Int = 0 To modes -1
    GetGraphicsMode(i, width, height, depth, hertz)
    Print width + "x" + height + " " + depth + "bit " + hertz + "hz"
Next
```

GraphicsModeExists(width, height, depth=0, hertz=0)

GraphicsModeExists returns Boolean True, if the graphics mode specified exists.

```
If GraphicsModeExists(640, 480)
    Print "680x480 exists!"
Else
    Print "Can't find 640x480 graphics mode"
End If
If GraphicsModeExists(640, 480, 48)
    Print "48bit color exists at 640x480"
Else
    Print "Don't be daft - 48bit color?!?"
End If
```

Graphics

Once we have our graphics mode, we can put the video card into graphics mode. We do this using the Graphics keyword, as follows:

```
Graphics 640, 480, 16, 75

While Not KeyHit(KEY_ESCAPE)
    DrawText("Hello, BlitzMax!", 0, 0)
    Flip
    Cls
Wend
```

The last two parameters—color depth and frequency—are optional and are defaulted to 16 and 60, respectively. However, as you have noticed, this Graphics keyword puts the video card in full-screen mode. What is we wanted to put it into windowed mode? Easy: just change the preceding Graphics line to

```
Graphics 640, 480
```

This creates a window with a 640×480 viewing area! Quite handy if a video mode is not available!

EndGraphics

Although not necessary, it is still good programming practice to end the graphics mode using the EndGraphics keyword. Note, though, that EndGraphics invalidates all images and image fonts. If you want to reuse these objects later, you will have to re-create them.

GraphicsWidth and GraphicsHeight

GraphicsWidth returns the width of the current graphics mode, and, likewise, GraphicsHeight returns the height of the current graphics mode. As in this example, it should be noted that it will also happily return the metrics of a windowed graphics mode.

```
Graphics 640, 480

While Not KeyHit(KEY_ESCAPE)
    DrawText("; + GraphicsWidth(), 0, 0)
    DrawText("Height: " + GraphicsHeight(), 0, 10)
    Flip
    Cls
Wend
```

GetGraphics

GetGraphics returns the metrics for the current graphics mode.

```
Graphics 800, 600, 16, 75
While Not KeyHit(KEY_ESCAPE)

    Local ;x" + height + ", " + depth + "bit color, " + hertz + "Hz", 0, 0)
    Flip
    Cls
Wend
```

If we ran similar code before putting the video card into graphics mode, we would get an entirely different answer. This is because although we are in a windowed environment, BlitzMax compiles to a shell window, in other words, a command line interpreter (such as Terminal/DOS prompt, bash).

```
Local ;
Print width + "x" + height + ", " + depth + "bit
color, " + hertz + "Hz"
```

Some Advice

Use a low-resolution (640×480) graphics mode to start your game to allow the user to choose the graphics mode they want to play the game at. Remember to check that the low-mode works before entering it!

Flip

Most modern video cards have two areas of memory. Both are used to display images to the user, but only one is shown at a time. This technique is called double buffering and is shown in the following diagram (Figure 11-1).

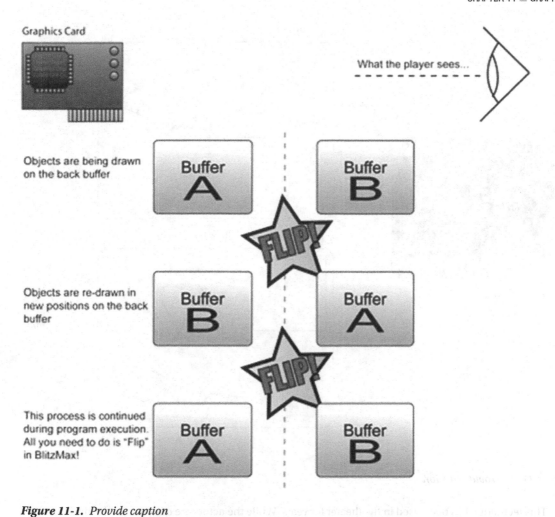

Figure 11-1. Provide caption

From the user's viewpoint, they see the items visible on the monitor, but behind the scenes, the program is drawing to the back buffer. With the flick of an electronic finger, the user is shown the images on the back buffer. The following diagram (Figure 11-2) shows what happens.

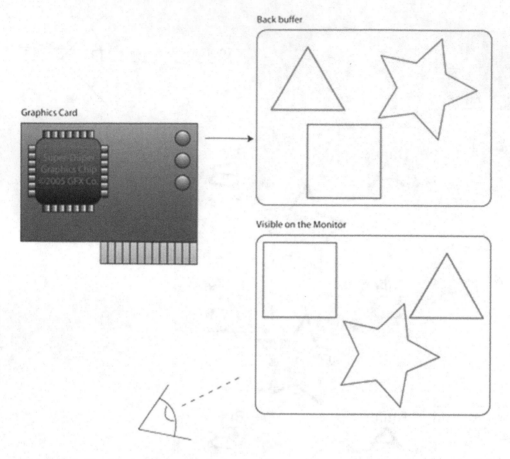

Figure 11-2. Provide caption

This technique has been used in the theater for years. While the actors are out on stage, behind the curtain, a new scene is being dressed. When the actors' scene is finished, the curtain opens, and the new scene is revealed.

All this happens in BlitzMax using two keywords: Cls and Flip.

Cls

The Cls keyword clears the back buffer of the video card, making it ready to draw on again. We have used this in all our graphic mode examples so far. Note that, for the most part, it is paired with the Flip command.

```
Flip
Cls
```

This means that all drawings on the back buffer are now on the front buffer, and the back buffer is once again ready to be drawn on.

Another common technique is to put the Cls after the update code in your main loop and then Flip just before the end—usually just before the Wend keyword. See the Tank Attack code for details. Either way will work.

SetClsColor

This sets the color Cls clears the screen to. In this example, pressing 1 will clear the screen to red, 2 to green, and 3 to blue. Key 0 will return the Cls color to black.

```
Graphics 640, 480

While Not KeyHit(KEY_ESCAPE)

    If KeyHit(KEY_1)
        SetClsColor(255, 0, 0)
    End If

    If KeyHit(KEY_2)
        SetClsColor(0, 255, 0)
    End If

    If KeyHit(KEY_3)
        SetClsColor(0, 0, 255)
    End If

    If KeyHit(KEY_0)
        SetClsColor(0, 0, 0)
    End If

    Flip
    Cls
Wend
```

GetClsColor

This returns the current color used to clear the screen with, as follows:

```
Graphics 640, 480

While Not KeyHit(KEY_ESCAPE)

    If KeyHit(KEY_1)
        SetClsColor(255, 0, 0)
    End If

    If KeyHit(KEY_2)
        SetClsColor(0, 255, 0)
    End If

    If KeyHit(KEY_3)
        SetClsColor(0, 0, 255)
    End If
```

```
    If KeyHit(KEY_0)
        SetClsColor(0, 0, 0)
    End If

    Local red:Int=0
    Local green:Int = 0
    Local blue:Int = 0

    GetClsColor(red, green, blue)
    DrawText("SetClsColor(" + red + "," + green + "," + blue + ")", 0, 0)

    Flip
    Cls
Wend
```

Drawing Simple Objects

BlitzMax allows the programmer to use some graphics primitives as well as more complex images. The primitives are

```
        Plot

        DrawRect

        DrawLine

        DrawOval

        DrawPoly

        DrawText
```

Plot

Plot draws a point on the graphics display.

```
Graphics 640, 480

While Not KeyHit(KEY_ESCAPE)

    Local red:Int = Rnd(255)
    Local green:Int = Rnd(255)
    Local blue:Int = Rnd(255)

    SetColor(red, green, blue)
    Plot Rnd(640), Rnd(480)
    Flip
Wend
```

DrawRect

DrawRect draws a rectangle at a given (x, y) coordinate with width and height.

```
Graphics 640, 480
While Not KeyHit(KEY_ESCAPE)

    Local red:Int = Rnd(255)
    Local green:Int = Rnd(255)
    Local blue:Int = Rnd(255)

    SetColor(red, green, blue)
    DrawRect (Rnd(640), Rnd(480), Rnd(640), Rnd(480))
    Flip
Wend
```

DrawLine

This draws a line from one (x, y) coordinate to another.

```
Graphics 640, 480
Local lastx:Int = 0
Local lasyy:Int = 0

While Not KeyHit(KEY_ESCAPE)
    Local red:Int = Rnd(255)
    Local green:Int = Rnd(255)
    Local blue:Int = Rnd(255)

    SetColor(red, green, blue)

    x = Rnd(640)
    y = Rnd(640)

    DrawLine(lastx, lasty, x, y)
    lastx = x
    lasty = y

    Flip
Wend
```

DrawOval

DrawOval draws an ellipse at the specified coordinates with two radii: one for the x axis and one for the y axis.

```
Graphics 640, 480
Local r:Int = 100
While Not KeyHit(KEY_ESCAPE)
    Cls
    DrawOval(320 - (r/2), 240 - (r/2), r, r)
    r = r - 1
```

```
    If r = 0
        r = 100
    End If

    Flip
Wend
```

DrawPoly

DrawPoly is slightly more complex than previous graphics, in that it requires an array of floats representing the coordinate groups. In this case, we are plotting the following points onscreen.

(50, 0), (100, 100), (0, 100)

This will draw a triangle at the top left of the screen.

```
Graphics 640,480
Local triangle#[]=[50.0,0.0,100.0,100.0,0.0,100.0]

While Not KeyHit(KEY_ESCAPE)
    Cls
    DrawPoly triangle
    Flip
Wend
```

DrawText

DrawText prints text in the current font at the specified x and y coordinates.

```
Graphics 640, 480
While Not KeyHit(KEY_ESCAPE)
    SetColor(Rnd(255),Rnd(255),Rnd(255))
    DrawText("BlitzMax", Rnd(640), Rnd(480))
    Flip
Wend
```

Images

Computer games need sprites to represent characters in the game world. A sprite is a small image manipulated by either the player directly or some logic programmed in. With BlitzMax, we have a wide range of commands to help us deal with images.

```
        LoadImage

        LoadAnimImage

        DrawImage

        DrawImageRect

        TileImage

        SetColor
```

As you can see from the list, that is quite a lot to get on with! Let's break this down into easy chunks of information. First, let's look at the image drawing.

Images and BlitzMax

For the most part, you will want to create images in a third-party product, such as the open source GIMP (GNU Image Manipulation Program) at www.gimp.org. GIMP is a professional-level graphics program on a par with Photoshop. If, like me, you have spent most of your professional life using Photoshop, you might find GIMP a bit frustrating to use at first. This is no fault of the application! Just relax, find your way around, and you'll be creating images like you did in Photoshop!

Any image creation program that allows you to generate BMP, PNG, and JPG images is fine. There is a list of these in the appendixes. If you are stuck with images, there are some (badly) drawn ones located on this book's web site (blitzmax.sloankelly.co.uk) to help you.

LoadImage

Before we can draw an image on the screen, we have to load it into memory. As we have seen in the Tank Attack project, this is done using the LoadImage keyword. The only required parameter is the path to the image file. In the following example, we are going to load a 16×16 picture with alternating 4-pixel wide blocks of yellow and blue. This will be displayed in the middle of the screen.

```
Graphics 640, 480
block:TImage = LoadImage("block.png")
While Not KeyHit(KEY_ESCAPE)
    DrawImage(block, 312, 232)
    Flip
    Cls
Wend
```

LoadAnimImage

An animated image is a block of images loaded as one graphic, and BlitzMax does all the hard work of splitting each individual block out into separate images. This can be used to load animated graphics or tiles for a platform game. The parameters for LoadAnimImage are:

> LoadAnimImage(path, width, height, first_index, image_count)

> path: Path to the image

> width: Width of the individual graphics

> height: Height of the individual graphics

> first_index: Always a zero

> image_count: Number of images in the larger block

In the following example, we load in a 32×16 image that has two 16×16 images on it.

```
Graphics 640, 480
Local block:TImage = LoadAnimImage("blockani.png",
16, 16, 0, 2)
Local tmr:Int = MilliSecs()
Local frame:Int=0
```

127

```
While Not KeyHit(KEY_ESCAPE)
    DrawImage(block, 312, 232, frame)
    If MilliSecs() > tmr + 450
        tmr = MilliSecs()
        frame:~1
    End If
    Flip
    Cls
Wend
```

DrawImage

As we have seen in the preceding two examples, DrawImage can be used to draw both static and animated images. The parameters for DrawImage are

```
DrawImage(image, x, y [, frame])
```

Note that the frame part is optional and must only be specified when you want to split up an image. Take a look at the following example:

```
Graphics 640, 480
Local block:TImage = LoadAnimImage("blockani.png",
16, 16, 0, 2)
Local tmr:Int = MilliSecs()
Local frame:Int=0

While Not KeyHit(KEY_ESCAPE)
    Cls
    DrawImage(block, 0, 0)
    DrawImage(block, 312, 232, frame)
    If MilliSecs() > tmr + 450
        tmr = MilliSecs()
        frame:~1
    End If
    Flip
Wend
```

What did you expect to see? Because BlitzMax defaults the frame parameter to zero, only the first image is shown.

TileImage

With DrawImage, we can display a single image on the screen once.

When we are working with a large area, we sometimes like to flood, that is, fill a backdrop with a single image. We can do this with TileImage.

The format for TileImage is: TileImage(image, x, y [, frame])

Again, the frame parameter is optional.

```
Graphics 640, 480
block:TImage = LoadImage("block.png")
```

```
While Not KeyHit(KEY_ESCAPE)
    TileImage(block, 0, 0)
    Flip
    Cls
Wend
```

SetViewport

SetViewport masks off an area of the screen that can be drawn to. Anything outside this area is not displayed. The format of SetViewport is

```
SetViewport(x, y, width, height)
```

In the following example, we use our animated image in the previous examples to simulate a ZX Spectrum loading:

```
Graphics 640, 480
Local block:TImage = LoadAnimImage("blockani.png",
16, 16, 0, 2)
Local tmr:Int = MilliSecs()
Local frame:Int=0

Local SPECTRUM_WIDTH = 256 * 2
Local SPECTRUM_HEIGHT = 192 * 2

Local SPECTRUM_LEFT = ((640 - SPECTRUM_WIDTH) / 2)
Local SPECTRUM_TOP = ((480 - SPECTRUM_HEIGHT) / 2)
Local msgx:Int = 640

While Not KeyHit(KEY_ESCAPE)
    If MilliSecs() > tmr + 450
        tmr = MilliSecs()
        frame:~1
    End If
    TileImage(block, 0, 0, frame)
    SetViewport(SPECTRUM_LEFT, SPECTRUM_TOP, SPECTRUM_WIDTH, SPECTRUM_HEIGHT)
    SetColor(0, 0, 0)
    DrawRect(SPECTRUM_LEFT, SPECTRUM_TOP, SPECTRUM_WIDTH, SPECTRUM_HEIGHT)

    SetColor(255, 255, 255)

    DrawText("BlitzMax!", msgx, 240)
    msgx:-2
    If msgx <= 0
        msgx = 640
    End If

    SetViewport(0, 0, 640, 480)

    Flip
    Cls
Wend
```

Those of you familiar with this wonderful machine will appreciate the retro ambience! For those of you who have never heard of a ZX Spectrum, it was an 8-bit computer from the early 1980s that (pretty much) kick-started bedroom coding in the United Kingdom.

GetViewport

GetViewport returns the metrics for the current viewport. The format of the command is

```
GetViewport(x, y, width, height)
```

See, for example, the following. Note that this is the same as the previous example, with a few extra lines to grab the viewport information.

```
Graphics 640, 480

Local block:TImage = LoadAnimImage("blockani.png",
16, 16, 0, 2)

Local tmr:Int = MilliSecs()
Local frame:Int=0
Local SPECTRUM_WIDTH = 256 * 2
Local SPECTRUM_HEIGHT = 192 * 2

Local SPECTRUM_LEFT = ((640 - SPECTRUM_WIDTH) / 2)
Local SPECTRUM_TOP = ((480 - SPECTRUM_HEIGHT) / 2)

Local msgx:Int = 640

While Not KeyHit(KEY_ESCAPE)
    If MilliSecs() > tmr + 450
        tmr = MilliSecs()
        frame:~1
    End If
    TileImage(block, 0, 0, frame)

    SetViewport(SPECTRUM_LEFT, SPECTRUM_TOP, SPECTRUM_WIDTH, SPECTRUM_HEIGHT)
    SetColor(0, 0, 0)
    DrawRect(SPECTRUM_LEFT, SPECTRUM_TOP,

    SPECTRUM_WIDTH, SPECTRUM_HEIGHT)

    SetColor(255, 255, 255)

    Local x:Int
    Local y:Int
    Local ;Current viewport is at " + x + "," +      y + " with dimensions " + width + " by
" + height, SPECTRUM_LEFT, SPECTRUM_TOP)

    DrawText("BlitzMax!", msgx, 240)
    msgx:-2
```

```
        If msgx <= 0
            msgx = 640
        End If
        SetViewport(0, 0, 640, 480)
        Flip
        Cls
Wend
```

Fonts

The BlitzMax system font is quite boring and can be livened up by loading your own fonts at runtime. BlitzMax can load TTF (TrueType Font) and FON files. TTF is standard across all three platforms now— Windows, Mac OS X, and Linux—and you should be able to locate some free distributable fonts for use in your applications. In the examples that follow, I will be using the Tahoma font, which is distributed with Windows and Office for Mac OS X. If you don't have this font, feel free to substitute it for another.

The following commands allow us to manipulate the fonts that can be used in our programs:

```
LoadImageFont

SetImageFont

GetImageFont
```

LoadImageFont

LoadImageFont requires two parameters and an optional third. The format of the keyword is shown following:

```
LoadImageFont:TImageFont(url:Object, size:Int, style:Int=SMOOTHFONT)

BOLDFONT = 1

ITALICFONT = 2

SMOOTHFONT = 4
```

SetImageFont

SetImageFont requires one parameter: the image font to use in subsequent DrawText() operations. If null is passed, the default font is used. The format of the keyword is shown following:

```
SetImageFont(font:TImageFont)
```

If null is passed, the default font is used.

GetImageFont

GetImageFont returns the current image font as an instance of TImageFont. It requires no parameters.

Example of Font Use in BlitzMax

For the example, to work, you will have to copy the Tahoma font to the same folder as your program. The example then loads in the font from size 8 to 48 in 8-pixel increments. It places all the fonts into a TList.

In the main loop, the fonts inside the TList fonts variable are cycled through, and the SetImageFont keyword is called. A message is displayed on the screen using the desired font. Notice that the y coordinate is incremented by the height of the letter *X* and 4 pixels. This gives a nice space between the last line and the next.

```
Graphics 800, 600
fonts:TList = CreateList()
For i = 8 To 48 Step 8
    font:TImageFont = LoadImageFont("tahoma.ttf", i, SMOOTHFONT)
    fonts.AddLast(font)
Next

While Not KeyHit(KEY_ESCAPE)

    y:Int = 0
    For f:TImageFont = EachIn fonts
        SetImageFont(f)
        DrawText("BlitzMax font handling!", 0, y)

        y = y + TextHeight("X") + 4
    Next
    Flip
    Cls
Wend
```

You can also be a little more adventurous. In the next example, I downloaded a font from dafont.com and placed it in the same folder as my .bmx file. I then used the incbin keyword to embed the font right into the executable, as follows:

```
Rem
    The font used in this program is called
    "PROMISES BROKEN DREAM" and was designed by Gersan Borge.
    It was retrieved from dafont.com on the 23rd May 2011
    http://www.dafont.com/promises-brokendream.font
    Gersan Borge's daFont page is:
    http://www.dafont.com/gersan-borge.d3068
EndRem

SuperStrict
Graphics 800, 600

Incbin "Promses Broken Dream1.ttf"
Local promises:TImageFont =
LoadImageFont("incbin::Promses Broken Dream1.ttf", 64)
SetImageFont promises
SetClsColor 0, 0, 192
```

```
While Not KeyHit(KEY_ESCAPE)
    Cls
    SetColor 0, 0, 0
    DrawText "1234567890ABCXYZ", 20, 50
    SetColor 255, 255, 0
    DrawText "1234567890ABCXYZ", 18, 48
    Flip
Wend
```

This displays the following on the screen (Figure 11-3).

Figure 11-3. *Provide figure caption*

CHAPTER 12

User Input

Because the operating systems that we are using are graphical in nature, the input method of choice is the mouse. There are several keywords available to the BlitzMax developer, including the following:

MouseX

MouseY

MouseZ

ShowMouse

HideMouse

MouseDown

MouseHit

MoveMouse

MouseX and MouseY

MouseX and MouseY return the current x and y coordinates of the mouse.

```
Graphics 640, 480
pointer:TImage = LoadImage("pointer.png")

While Not KeyHit(KEY_ESCAPE)

    Local x:Int = MouseX()
    Local y:Int = MouseY()

    DrawImage(pointer, x, y)
    Flip
    Cls

Wend
```

© Sloan Kelly 2016
S. Kelly, *BlitzMax for Absolute Beginners*, DOI 10.1007/978-1-4842-2523-3_12

Showing and Hiding the System Mouse

There is a problem, because, as you will have noticed after running the preceding code (you'll need a suitable image to use as a cursor), the operating system mouse is shown. We can get around this by executing the HideMouse keyword.

```
Graphics 640, 480

pointer:TImage = LoadImage("pointer.png")

While Not KeyHit(KEY_ESCAPE)

    If KeyHit(KEY_1)
        HideMouse()
    End If

    If KeyHit(KEY_2)
        ShowMouse()
    End If

    Local x:Int = MouseX()
    Local y:Int = MouseY()

    DrawImage(pointer, x, y)
    Flip
    Cls
Wend
```

By pressing 1 on the keyboard, you can hide the pointer. Pressing 2 will show the mouse pointer. At all times, the image is shown at the current mouse coordinates.

MouseZ

If your computer is suitably equipped with a scroll wheel, BlitzMax can use this to enhance the user experience.

```
Graphics 640, 480

pointer:TImage = LoadImage("pointer.png")

While Not KeyHit(KEY_ESCAPE)

    If KeyHit(KEY_1)
        HideMouse()
    End If

    If KeyHit(KEY_2)
        ShowMouse()
    End If
```

```
    Local x:Int = MouseX()
    Local y:Int = MouseY()
    Local z:Int = MouseZ()

    DrawText("Mouse Z= " + z, 0, 0)
    DrawImage(pointer, x, y)
    Flip
    Cls
Wend
```

On my system (IBM Thinkpad with a Microsoft Optical Trackball), a click on the mouse wheel represents an increment of 1 on the mouse z axis each time the mouse is scrolled away from me and a decrement of 1 each time the mouse is scrolled toward me.

MouseDown

In this example, I created a mouse image with four layers. The main layer has the mouse shape on it; the other layers have highlight colors (see Figure 12-1).

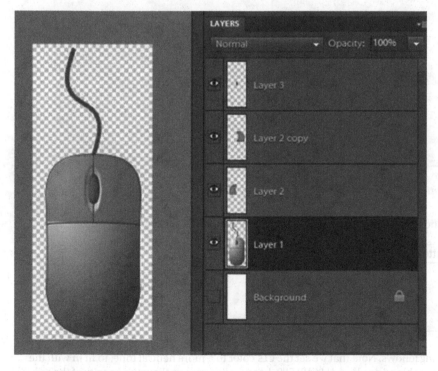

Figure 12-1. *Provide a caption*

When you press the mouse buttons, the corresponding images highlight which buttons were pressed. The output of the program with the left mouse button down is shown following (Figure 12-2).

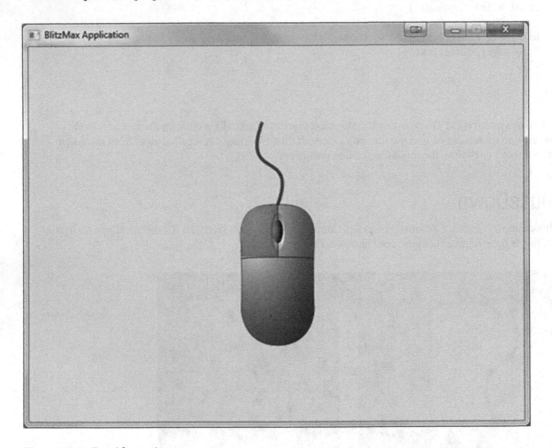

Figure 12-2. *Provide caption*

The MouseDown function takes one parameter: which mouse button to check.

Value	Mouse Button
1	Left
2	Right
3	Middle

The full program listing follows. Note that we set the Cls color to a more neutral tone, to fit in with the mouse image. We also set the blend mode to ALPHABLEND, because we want to show the opacity of the red overlays. Try taking the SetBlend line out to see what happens.

```
Graphics 640, 480

SetClsColor 224, 224, 224
SetBlend ALPHABLEND
```

```
mouse:TImage = LoadImage("mouse.png")
lmb:TImage = LoadImage("lmb.png")
rmb:TImage = LoadImage("rmb.png")
mmb:TImage = LoadImage("mmb.png")

x:Int = (640 - ImageWidth(mouse)) / 2
y:Int = (480 - ImageHeight(mouse)) / 2

While Not KeyHit(KEY_ESCAPE)
    Cls
    DrawImage(mouse, x, y)

    If MouseDown(1)
        DrawImage(lmb, x, y)
    End If

    If MouseDown(2)
        DrawImage(rmb, x, y)
    End If

    If MouseDown(3)
        DrawImage(mmb, x, y)
    End If

    Flip
Wend
```

MouseHit

MouseHit is slightly different, in that it only records if the mouse has been hit. It does not care if the mouse button is being held down.

This could be ideal for a click event on a button. The following example illustrates this best:

```
Graphics 640, 480
SetClsColor 224, 224, 224
SetBlend ALPHABLEND

mouse:TImage = LoadImage("mouse.png")
lmb:TImage = LoadImage("lmb.png")
rmb:TImage = LoadImage("rmb.png")
mmb:TImage = LoadImage("mmb.png")

x:Int = (640 - ImageWidth(mouse)) / 2
y:Int = (480 - ImageHeight(mouse)) / 2

While Not KeyHit(KEY_ESCAPE)
    Cls
```

```
        DrawImage(mouse, x, y)

        If MouseHit(1)
            DrawImage(lmb, x, y)
        End If

        If MouseHit(2)
            DrawImage(rmb, x, y)
        End If

        If MouseHit(3)
            DrawImage(mmb, x, y)
        End If

        Flip
Wend
```

WaitMouse

WaitMouse pauses the program and then returns which mouse button was clicked.

```
Graphics 640, 480
DrawText("Press any mouse button to exit", 0, 0)
Flip
WaitMouse()
```

MoveMouse

We can also move the mouse! The following example uses mathematical functions to move the cursor up and down the screen, plotting a nice ellipse:

```
Graphics 640, 480

Local angle:Float = 0
Local y:Int
Local x:Int
Local tmr:Int = MilliSecs()

While Not KeyHit(KEY_ESCAPE)

    y = Sin(angle) * 240
    x = Cos(angle) * 320

    If MilliSecs() > tmr + 150
        tmr = MilliSecs()
        angle = angle + 2
        If angle = 360
            angle = 0
        End If
```

```
    End If
    MoveMouse(320 + x, 240 + y)

    SetColor(255, 255, 255)
    Plot(320 + x, 240 + y)
    Flip

Wend
```

Adapt the preceding program to fill in the dots. Now add spokes to the wheel. Hint: The center is always 320, 240. And now, add random color each revolution.

CHAPTER 13

Keyboard Input

The second input device on a modern computer system is the keyboard. This is the most common keyboard input device and one that most people will use approximately 80% of the time. There are a number of ways to get information from the keyboard.

KeyDown

KeyHit

WaitKey

WaitChar

GetChar

KeyDown, KeyHit, and WaitKey all use the BlitzMax key code constants, listed in the appendixes. WaitChar and GetChar use the ASCII character set, again listed in the appendixes.

KeyDown

This is the simplest keyboard method and returns true if a key is being held down. In the following example, a rocket ship is taking off. Holding down the space bar will pump more fuel into the rocket. You will require a 64×64 pixel image of a rocket loaded as an animated image (128×4).

```
Graphics 640, 480

Const GRAVITY_VALUE:Float = .01

Local y:Float = GraphicsHeight() - 64
Local gravity:Float = GRAVITY_VALUE
Local frame:Int = 0
Local velocity:Float = 0

Local rocket:TImage = LoadAnimImage("spaceship.png", 64, 64, 0, 2)
SetBlend(ALPHABLEND)

HideMouse
While Not KeyHit(KEY_ESCAPE)
```

© Sloan Kelly 2016
S. Kelly, *BlitzMax for Absolute Beginners*, DOI 10.1007/978-1-4842-2523-3_13

```
    If KeyDown(KEY_SPACE)
         velocity = velocity + (GRAVITY_VALUE/2)
         frame = 1
         gravity=gravity-GRAVITY_VALUE
         If gravity <=0
             gravity = 0
         End If
    End If
    If Not KeyDown(KEY_SPACE)
         velo city = 0
         gravity = gravity + GRAVITY_VALUE
         If gravity > 9.81
             gravity = 9.81
         End If
         frame = 0
    End If

    y = y + gravity - velocity

    If y>= GraphicsHeight() - 64
         y = GraphicsHeight() - 64
    End If

    DrawImage(rocket, 320 - 32, y, frame)

    DrawText("Velocity:" + velocity + "m/s", 0, 0)
    DrawText("Gravity:" + gravity + "m/s", 0, 10)
    DrawText("Height: " + ((480-64) - y) + "m",0, 20)
    Flip
    Cls
Wend
```

KeyHit

We have used the KeyHit keyword on just about every example in this book to trap the Escape key being pressed. KeyHit is a one-off hit of a key and returns a Boolean True if the key has been hit.

```
Graphics 640, 480

While Not KeyHit(KEY_ESCAPE)

    If KeyHit(KEY_SPACE)

         SetColor(Rnd(255), Rnd(255), Rnd(255))
    End If

    DrawText("BlitzMax", Rnd(640), Rnd(480))
    Flip

Wend
```

Rewrite the rocket example with KeyHit and see how far you get up the screen! Rewrite the KeyHit example with KeyDown trapping the space bar being hit. What happens?

WaitKey

WaitKey halts all operations and waits until a key has been pressed. The following example shows an example of WaitKey, a retro text adventure input. But please be aware that this is not the perfect implementation. I'm getting to that!

```
Graphics 640, 480

Type TKeyInput

    Method GetMemo:String()

        memo:String = ""

        DrawText(">_", 0, 0)
        Flip
        ch:Int = WaitKey()

        While ch <> KEY_ENTER
            Select ch
                Case KEY_SPACE, KEY_A, KEY_B, KEY_C, KEY_D, KEY_E, KEY_F, KEY_G, KEY_H,
                KEY_I, KEY_J, KEY_K, KEY_L, KEY_M, KEY_N, KEY_O, KEY_P, KEY_Q, KEY_R,
                KEY_S, KEY_T, KEY_U, KEY_V, KEY_W, KEY_X, KEY_Y, KEY_Z
                    memo = memo + Chr(ch)
                Case KEY_DELETE, KEY_BACKSPACE

                    If memo <> ""
                        memo = Left(memo, Len(memo)-1)

                    End If
            End Select

            Cls
            DrawText(">" + memo + "_", 0, 0)
            Flip

            ch = WaitKey()
        Wend
        Return memo
    End Method
    Function Create:TKeyInput()
        o:TKeyInput = New TKeyInput
        Return o
    End Function
End Type
```

```
keyinput:TKeyInput = TKeyInput.Create()

s:String = keyinput.GetMemo()

Cls
Flip

FlushKeys()
DrawText("Input text:" + s, 0, 0)
Flip
WaitKey()
```

At the moment, only A–Z and space characters are allowed. Allow the user to enter numbers too.

WaitChar

Much like WaitKey, WaitChar pauses until a key is pressed. When it has been pressed, its ASCII representation is returned to the user. So, the preceding example can be rewritten as follows:

```
Graphics 640, 480

Type TKeyInput

    Method GetMemo:String()

        memo:String = ""

        DrawText(">_", 0, 0)
        Flip
        ch:Int = WaitChar()

        While ch <> 13
            If ch >="32" And ch <=127
                memo = memo + Chr(ch)
            End If
If ch = 8 And memo <> "" memo = Left(memo, Len(memo)-1)
            End If
            Cls
            DrawText(">" + memo + "_", 0, 0)
            Flip
            ch = WaitChar()
        Wend
        Return memo

    End Method

    Function Create:TKeyInput()
        o:TKeyInput = New TkeyInput
        Return o
    End Function
```

```
End Type
keyinput:TKeyInput = TKeyInput.Create()

s:String = keyinput.GetMemo()
Cls
Flip
FlushKeys()
DrawText("Input text:" + s, 0, 0)
Flip
WaitKey()
```

It is slightly more elegant, and it allows for a larger number of characters to be entered. For example, you can use a mixture of upper- and lowercase letters.

Don't allow the user to enter symbol characters. For a list of ASCII characters and codes, see the appendixes. Hint: The keyword Asc can be used to determine the ASCII value of any given character, for example, ASC("A") returns 65.

GetChar

Pausing a live game is a little severe, and BlitzMax addresses that by using the GetChar keyword. This means that we can have a flashing cursor! Rewriting the preceding examples, I have included a flashing cursor to show the user we are expecting input. Remember: This would not be possible if we were using WaitChar/WaitKey, because ALL PROCESSING is stopped for WaitChar/WaitKey.

```
Graphics 640, 480
Type TKeyInput
    Method GetMemo:String()

        memo:String = ""
        tmr:Int = MilliSecs()
        cursor:Int = 1

        DrawText(">_", 0, 0)
        Flip
    ch:Int = GetChar()

    While ch <> 13

            If ch >="32" And ch <=127
                memo = memo + Chr(ch)
            End If

            If ch = 8 And memo <> ""
                memo = Left(memo, Len(memo)-1)
            End If
            Cls
            If MilliSecs()>tmr+500
                tmr = MilliSecs()
                cursor:~1
            End If
```

```
                If cursor
                    DrawText(">" + memo + "_", 0, 0)

                Else
                    DrawText(">" + memo, 0, 0)
                End If

                Flip

                ch = GetChar()

        Wend
        Return memo

    End Method
    Function Create:TKeyInput()
        o:TKeyInput = New TkeyInput
        Return o
    End Function
End Type

keyinput:TKeyInput = TKeyInput.Create()

s:String = keyinput.GetMemo()

Cls
Flip

FlushKeys()
DrawText("Input text:" + s, 0, 0)
Flip
WaitKey()
```

Change the cursor to a solid block. Hint: Use the DrawRect and TextWidth keywords.

CHAPTER 14

■ ■ ■

Joystick

We've seen that BlitzMax can get input from keyboard and mouse, but the final piece of the puzzle is the joystick, or, as it's more commonly called now, the controller. BlitzMax offers a wide variety of functions to get input from this device.

JoyAxisCaps	JoyButtonCaps	JoyCount
JoyDown	JoyHat	JoyName
JoyPitch	JoyR	JoyRoll
JoyU	JoyV	JoyWheel
JoyX	JoyY	JoyYaw
JoyZ		

The joystick took a long time to be adopted by computer users who preferred the keyboard and mouse to move their onscreen avatar. This has all changed, and most gamers have either a joystick or a joypad with an easy-to-plug-in USB connection. I only have an inexpensive joypad to play with (Figure 14-1).

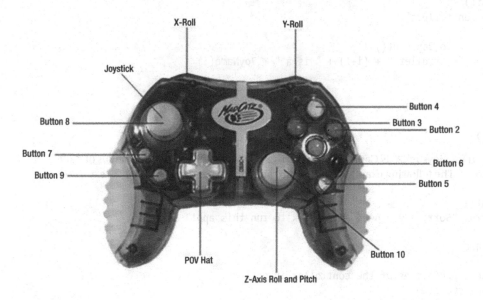

Figure 14-1. *Joypad*

© Sloan Kelly 2016
S. Kelly, *BlitzMax for Absolute Beginners*, DOI 10.1007/978-1-4842-2523-3_14

It's in the style of the PlayStation controller, with eight—count 'em—buttons. This will be my reference controller.

Joystick Information

We can get information on the various joysticks that are plugged into the system using the following keywords:

```
JoyCount

JoyName

JoyAxisCaps

JoyButtonCaps
```

JoyCount

JoyCount counts the number of game controllers you have connected to your system.

```
If Not JoyCount()
    Print "No controllers"
Else
    Print "You have " + JoyCount() + " game controllers connected to your system."
End If
```

JoyName

JoyName returns the name of the joystick on the selected port, as follows:

```
If Not JoyCount()
    Print "No controllers"
Else
    For i:Int = 0 To JoyCount()-1
        Print "Controller " + (i+1) + " is a " + JoyName(i)
    Next
End If
```

JoyAxisCaps

JoyAxisCaps, short for "Joystick Axis Capabilities," returns a bit field detailing the capabilities of the connected controller. The following example reads these capabilities and displays them as text:

```
If Not JoyCount()
    RuntimeError "Sorry - you need a joystick to run this app!"
End If
Graphics 640, 480

'' find out the capabilities of the controller in port 0
caps:Int = JoyAxisCaps(0)
```

150

```
'' string representing capabilities
capstring:String = "XYZYUVYPOHW"

While Not KeyHit(KEY_ESCAPE)
    '
    ' Loop through each of the capabilities
    '
    s:String = ""
    For i:Int = 0 To 10
        If caps And (2^i)
            s = s + Mid(capstring, i+1, 1)
        Else
            s = s + "-"
        End If
    Next
    '
    ' Draw the standard capabilities flags and the
    ' actuals reported from the controller
    '
    DrawText(capstring, 0, 0)
    DrawText(s, 0, 10)
    Flip
    Cls

Wend
```

The preceding program displays the axis capabilities of each joystick plugged into your PC. The program checks to see if you have at least one stick attached before proceeding.

The JoyAxisCaps keyword returns a bit-mapped representation of the capabilities of your joystick. This program splits out the bits and displays them as English words. The bitmap for these capabilities is

4	3	2	1	0
U	R	Z-Axis	Y-Axis	X-Axis

9	8	7	6	5
Hat	Roll	Pitch	Yaw	V

10
Wheel

JoyButtonCaps

JoyButtonCaps, short for "Joystick Button Capabilities," returns a bit field representing the number of buttons a joystick has. The following example returns this as a more meaningful number to the calling routine:

```
If Not JoyCount()
     RuntimeError "No joystick"
End If
Function JoyButtonCount:Int(buttoncaps:Int)
     s:String = Bin(buttoncaps)
     count:Int = 0
     For i:Int = 1 To Len(s)
          If Mid(s, i, 1) = "1"
               count:+1
          End If
     Next

     Return count
End Function

Print "There are " + JoyButtonCount(JoyButtonCaps(0)) + " buttons on the controller"
```

Getting Direction

Historically, PC joysticks have been analog in nature. This means that the change in direction is not a simple switch, as in modern controllers. Because this is the case, the values returned are between -1 and 1 in variable increments. The following example covers each of the values for the available axis:

> JoyX
>
> JoyY
>
> JoyZ
>
> JoyR
>
> JoyU
>
> JoyV
>
> JoyRoll
>
> JoyYaw
>
> JoyWheel

```
If Not JoyCount()
     RuntimeError "There is no joystick connected"
End If
Graphics 640, 480
Function DrawAxis(x:Int, y:Int, dir:Float, ishoriz:Int=True)
```

```
        Local w:Int
        Local h:Int

        SetColor(255, 192, 0)

        If ishoriz
            w = dir * 64
            h = 3
            If w < 0
                DrawRect(x+w-1, y-1, Abs(w), h)
            Else
                DrawRect(x-1, y+h-1, w, Abs(h))
            End If
        Else
            w = 3
            h = dir * 64 If h < 0
            if h < 0
                DrawRect(x-1, y-1, w, h)
            Else

                DrawRect(x-1, y-1, w, h)
            End If
        End If

        SetColor(255, 255, 255)

End Function

Function JoyButtonCount:Int(buttoncaps:Int)
    s:String = Bin(buttoncaps)
    count:Int = 0
    For i:Int = 1 To Len(s)
        If Mid(s, i, 1) = "1"
            count:+1
        End If
    Next
    Return count
End Function
While Not KeyHit(KEY_ESCAPE)

    SetColor(255, 255, 255)
    DrawLine(320, 240, 320+64, 240)
    DrawLine(320, 240, 320-64, 240)
    DrawLine(320, 240, 320, 240+64)
    DrawLine(320, 240, 320, 240-64)
    DrawAxis(320, 240, JoyX(), True)
    DrawAxis(320, 240, JoyY(), False)

    For i:Int = 0 To JoyButtonCount(JoyButtonCaps(0))-1
        If JoyDown(i)
            SetColor(228, 228, 228)
```

```
        Else
            SetColor(58, 58, 58)

        End If
        DrawOval(50 + (i * 16), 10, 10, 10)
    Next

    Flip
    Cls

Wend
```

Add lines for the R and U axis. Now what about Yaw and the Wheel? You will need a suitable joystick with these functions.

■ ■ ■

CHAPTER 15

Common Input Routine

I created a number of classes that allow movement by joystick or keyboard to be abstracted. The listing is in the appendixes and also available on the web site. Programs can then use these abstracted routines to move game characters around the screen. From this point, these classes will be used in the book to move playable objects around the screen.

This means that we can reuse these classes in all our projects, and we won't have to implement them over and over again.

The Classes

There are six classes, as listed following:

IController	An interface class that TStick and TKeyboard extend
IFire	An interface class that TStickFire and TKeyboardFire extend
TStick	Inherited from TController; handles joystick input
TKeyboard	Inherited from TController; handles keyboard input
TStickFire	Inherited from IFire; handles fire events from the joystick
TKeyFire	Inherited from IFire; handles fire events from the keyboard

IController

This is the base class for both TStick and TKeyboard. It contains a number of abstract methods that the child classes **must** implement. It also contains some fully formed Final methods that the classes will inherit. The abstract methods are as follows:

Dup: Returns Boolean True if the user presses the Up key

DDown: Returns Boolean True if the user presses the Down key

DLeft: Returns Boolean True if the user presses the Left key

DRight: Returns Boolean True if the user presses the Right key

IController contains two fields:

Name

FireMethods

© Sloan Kelly 2016
S. Kelly, *BlitzMax for Absolute Beginners*, DOI 10.1007/978-1-4842-2523-3_15

Name

The Name field can be used by the application to identify the controller, for example "Player1" or "Keyboard." This field is not used by the class but can be useful. See the sample application that follows below.

FireMethods

This is a collection of firing events that expose the IFire interface. At the moment this is just two classes: TkeyFire and TstickFire, for keyboard and joystick, respectively.

The three final methods contained within the abstract IController class are

> AddFire
>
> Fire
>
> ButtonCount

AddFire

AddFire passes in an IFire class to be added to the FireMethods list.

Fire

Fire takes in one integer parameter referencing the index of the button and returns a Boolean True, if the button has been pressed.

ButtonCount

ButtonCount returns the number of buttons in the abstract controller. Note that this is not the same as JoyButtonCaps. It is up to the developer to add all the joystick buttons to the class, as shown following:

```
For f:Int = 0 To 7
    jfire:TStickFire = TStickFire.Create(f, 0)
    stick.AddFire(jfire)
Next
```

This code would add eight buttons to the joystick (0 through 7 inclusive).

TStick and TKeyboard

TStick and TKeyboard abstract the game controller and keyboard, respectively. They both inherit from IController and use the interface that IController has defined to implement their own ways of capturing user input.

TStickFire and TKeyFire

TStickFire and TKeyFire abstract the firing events for the game controller and keyboard, respectively. They inherit from IFire and use the interface that IFire has defined to implement their own ways of capturing the user pressing a particular fire button.

156

Create a new class called TMouseFire that extends IFire. In this instance, we need to capture a mouse button being hit.

Sample Application Using Controller.bmx

This application is based on the joystick-only version referred to previously in this chapter. The F1 key toggles the input method. Note that the keyboard has one firing method (the spacebar), but that the keyboard has two (space and button zero). This shows that abstracting the controllers is good. We can have any mix of control that we need!

```
Include "Controller.bmx"
If Not JoyCount()
    RuntimeError "There is no joystick connected"
End If
Graphics 640, 480

Function DrawAxis(x:Int, y:Int, dir:Int, ishoriz:Int=True, isnegative:Int=True)

    Local w:Int
    Local h:Int

    SetColor(255, 192, 0)

    If ishoriz

        w = dir * 64
        h = 3
        If isnegative
            DrawRect(x-w-1, y-1, Abs(w), h)
        Else
            DrawRect(x-1, y-1, w, h)
        End If
    Else
        w = 3
        h = dir * 64
        If isnegative
            DrawRect(x-1, y-h-1, w, Abs(h))
        Else
            DrawRect(x-1, y-1, w, h)
        End If
    End If

    SetColor(255, 255, 255)

End Function

Function JoyButtonCount:Int(buttoncaps:Int)
    s:String = Bin(buttoncaps)
    count:Int = 0
    For i:Int = 1 To Len(s)
```

```
            If Mid(s, i, 1) = "1"
                count:+1
            End If
    Next

    Return count
End Function

stick:TStick = TStick.Create("Joystick", 0) keyboard:TKeyboard = TKeyboard.
Create("Keyboard", KEY_UP, KEY_DOWN, KEY_LEFT, KEY_RIGHT)

kfire:TKeyFire = TKeyFire.Create(KEY_SPACE) jfire:TStickFire = TStickFire.Create(0, 0)

keyboard.AddFire(kfire)

stick.AddFire(jfire)
stick.AddFire(kfire)

Local controller:IController = keyboard

While Not KeyHit(KEY_ESCAPE)

    SetColor(255, 255, 255)
    DrawLine(320, 240, 320+64, 240)
    DrawLine(320, 240, 320-64, 240)
    DrawLine(320, 240, 320, 240+64)
    DrawLine(320, 240, 320, 240-64)

    If KeyHit(KEY_F1)
            If controller.Name = "Keyboard"
                controller = stick
            Else
                controller = keyboard
            End If
    End If

    If controller.Name = "Keyboard"
            DrawText("Keyboard", 0, 25)
    Else
            DrawText("Joystick", 0, 25)
    End If

    DrawAxis(320, 240, controller.DLeft(), True, True)
    DrawAxis(320, 240, controller.DRight(), True, False)
    DrawAxis(320, 240, controller.DUp(), False, True)
    DrawAxis(320, 240, controller.DDown(), False, False)
```

```
      For i:Int = 0 To controller.ButtonCount()-1
          If controller.Fire(i)
              SetColor(228, 228, 228)
          Else

              SetColor(58, 58, 58)
          End If
          DrawOval(50 + (i * 16), 10, 10, 10)
      Next
      Flip
      Cls
Wend
```

■ ■ ■

CHAPTER 16

Collision Detection

Collision detection is the most important part of an action game. Without it, you would walk through walls, bullets...Wait! What am I saying? That would be great! Great, if we were cheating. This section takes us through what collision detection is.

Simple Collisions

In our game world, we must respect the laws of physics. We can bend them, if we like, but they should remain intact. To this end, there are some simple laws that we can apply.

- No object can occupy the same space and time as another object.

- A body is at rest until a force is applied to it.

- A body will maintain its motion until a force equal to it is applied.

The First Rule—Collision Detection

Because two physical objects cannot appear at the same space at the same time, we must be able to build that somehow into our game world. We can do this using the keyword ImagesCollide. For the following example, we will need two different images, both 32×32 pixels. One called a.png and the other called b.png. b.png will be controlled by the mouse, and a.png will remain static in the middle of the screen. When the two come into contact with each other (Figure 16-1), a message will be displayed ("Bang!").

© Sloan Kelly 2016
S. Kelly, *BlitzMax for Absolute Beginners*, DOI 10.1007/978-1-4842-2523-3_16

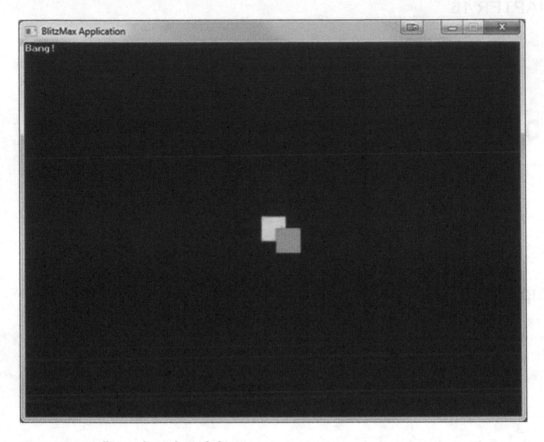

Figure 16-1. *Collision of two physical objects*

```
Graphics 640, 480
AutoMidHandle(True)
a:TImage = LoadImage("a.png")
b:TImage = LoadImage("b.png")
While Not KeyHit(KEY_ESCAPE)
    If ImagesCollide(a, 320, 240, 0, b, MouseX(), MouseY(), 0)
        DrawText("Bang!", 0, 0)
    End If

    DrawImage(a, 320, 240)
    DrawImage(b, MouseX(), MouseY())

    Flip
    Cls

Wend
```

Notice that, technically, we've broken the first rule. We can still move block B over block A (Figure 16-2). We can rewrite the preceding code to allow for solid collisions, as follows:

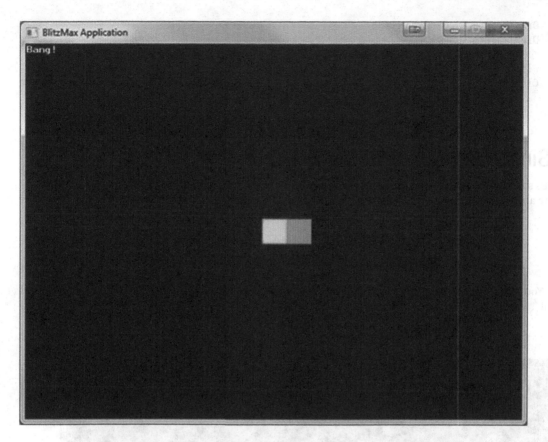

Figure 16-2. *Insert caption*

```
Graphics 640, 480
AutoMidHandle(True)
a:TImage = LoadImage("a.png")
b:TImage = LoadImage("b.png")
lastx:Int = MouseX()
lasty:Int = MouseY()

While Not KeyHit(KEY_ESCAPE)
    x = MouseX()

    y = MouseY()

    If ImagesCollide(a, 320, 240, 0, b, x, y, 0)
        DrawText("Bang!", 0, 0)
        x = lastx
        y = lasty
    Else

        lastx = x
        lasty = y
    End If
```

```
DrawImage(a, 320, 240).
DrawImage(b, x, y)

Flip
Cls
```

Wend

A Simple Game

In this simple game, you have to traverse the screen, starting at the top left and ending at the bottom right. There are a number of images to create—all at 16×16 pixels.

> Red: Red block will kill you (red.png)

> Blue: Blue block is impenetrable (blue.png)

> Yellow: End block (yellow.png)

You will also have to create a player (16×16 also) image (man.png) (Figure 16-3). Oh, and there is a time limit!

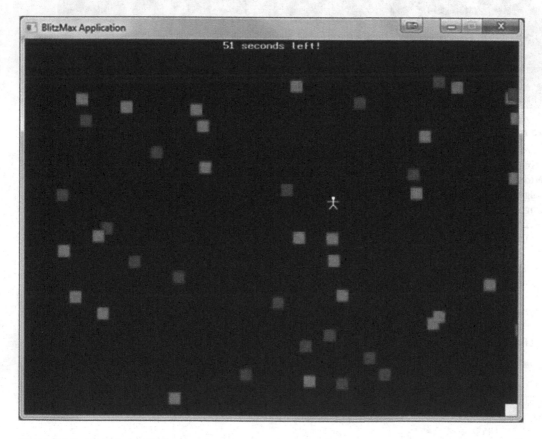

Figure 16-3. *Provide caption*

```
Rem

    Simple game
    Red - Avoid! They kill you and send you back to the start
    Blue - Can't get around them        Yellow - Your goal
End Rem
Graphics 640, 480
Incbin "red.png"
Incbin "blue.png"
Incbin "yellow.png"
Incbin "man.png"

Type TBlock
    Field X:Int
    Field Y:Int
    Field BlockType:Int

    Method Draw()
        Select BlockType
            Case 1
                DrawImage(red, X, Y)
            Case 2
                DrawImage(blue, X, Y)
        End Select
    End Method

    Function Create:TBlock()
        o:TBlock = New TBlock
        o.X = Rnd(600) + 40 ' buffer of 40 pixels around start
        o.Y = Rnd(440) + 40 ' and end markers
        o.BlockType = Rnd(2) + 1
        Return o
    End Function

End Type

Global red:TImage = LoadImage("red.png")
Global blue:TImage = LoadImage("blue.png")
Global yellow:TImage = LoadImage("yellow.png")
Global man:TImage = LoadImage("man.png")

Global blocks:TList = CreateList()

While Not KeyHit(KEY_SPACE)

    DrawText("This is a very simple game. Cursor keys move the man on-screen.", 0, 0)
    DrawText("Avoid the red blocks. The blue blocks just slow you down", 0, 10)
    DrawText("There is a time limit of 60 seconds. Each screen you go through", 0, 20)
    DrawText("your available time decreases by 5 seconds.", 0, 30)
    DrawText("Press SPACE to play", 0, 50)
```

```
        Flip
        Cls

Wend

#StartGame

Global counter:Int = 60000
Global blockcounter:Int = 40
exitgame:Int=False

#AnotherRound

tmr:Int = MilliSecs()
x:Int = 0
y:Int = 0
FlushKeys()
Rand(MilliSecs())
ClearList(blocks)

For i = 1 To blockcounter
    b:TBlock = TBlock.Create()
    blocks.AddLast(b)
Next

While MilliSecs() < (tmr + counter+1000) And Not exitgame

    allowmovement:Int = True

    If KeyHit(KEY_ESCAPE)
        exitgame=True
    End If

    If KeyDown(KEY_LEFT) And x > 0
        For b:Tblock = EachIn blocks
            If b.BlockType = 1
                If ImagesCollide(man, x-4, y, 0, red, b.X, b.Y, 0)

                    x = 0
                    y = 0
                End If
            Else

                If ImagesCollide(man, x-4, y, 0, blue, b.X, b.Y, 0)

                    allowmovement = False
                End If
            End If
        Next
```

```
        If allowmovement
            x = x -4
        End If
End If

allowmovement = True

If KeyDown(KEY_RIGHT) And x < 640 - 16
        For b:Tblock = EachIn blocks
            If b.BlockType = 1
                If ImagesCollide(man, x+4, y, 0, red, b.X, b.Y, 0)
                    x = 0
                    y = 0
                    allowmovement = False
                End If
            Else
                If ImagesCollide(man, x+4, y, 0, blue, b.X, b.Y, 0)
                    allowmovement = False
                    Exit
                End If
            End If
        Next

        If allowmovement
            x = x +4 End If
        End If
End If

allowmovement = True

If KeyDown(KEY_UP) And y > 0
        For b:Tblock = EachIn blocks
            If b.BlockType = 1
                If ImagesCollide(man, x, y-4, 0, red, b.X, b.Y, 0)
                    x = 0
                    y = 0
                    allowmovement = False
                End If
            Else
                If ImagesCollide(man, x+4, y, 0, blue, b.X, b.Y, 0)
                    allowmovement = False
                    Exit
                End If
            End If
        Next
        If allowmovement
            y = y -4
        End If
End If
allowmovement = True
```

167

```
        If KeyDown(KEY_DOWN) And y < 480 - 16
            For b:Tblock = EachIn blocks
                If b.BlockType = 1
                    If ImagesCollide(man, x, y+4, 0, red, b.X, b.Y, 0)
                        x = 0
                        y = 0
                        allowmovement = False
                    End If
                Else
                    If ImagesCollide(man, x, y+4, 0, blue, b.X, b.Y, 0)
                        allowmovement = False
                        Exit
                    End If
                End If
            Next

            If allowmovement
                y = y +4
            End If
        End If

        If ImagesCollide(man, x, y, 0, yellow, 640- 16, 480-16, 0)
            Goto EndGame
        End If

        secsleft:Float = (counter/1000) - ((MilliSecs() - tmr) / 1000)
        s:String = Int(secsleft) + " seconds left!" DrawText(s, (640 - TextWidth(s))/2, 0)
        For b:TBlock = EachIn blocks
            b.Draw()
        Next

        DrawImage(yellow, 640-16, 480-16)
        DrawImage(man, x, y)
        Flip
        Cls

        ResetCollisions()
        FlushMem()
Wend

#EndGame

FlushKeys()

If Int(secsleft) > 0 And Not exitgame

    counter = counter - 5000
    If counter < 10000
        counter = 10000
    End If
```

```
    While Not KeyHit(KEY_SPACE)
        DrawText("Congratulations you did that with only " + Int(secsleft) + " seconds
left!", 0, 10)
        DrawText("Press SPACE to start again -with only " + (Int(counter/1000)) + " on
the clock!", 0, 20)
            Flip
            Cls
    Wend
    blockcounter = blockcounter + 5
    Goto AnotherRound
Else If Int(secsleft) = 0
    While Not KeyHit(KEY_SPACE)
        DrawText("Bad luck! You ran out of time", 0, 10)
        DrawText("Press SPACE to start again!", 0, 20)
            Flip
            Cls
    Wend
    Goto AnotherRound
End If

DrawText("Want to play again? Y = Again", 0, 0)
Flip
Cls
kc = WaitKey()
If kc = KEY_Y
    Goto StartGame
End If
```

Rewrite the preceding simple game to allow the user to choose between a keyboard or joystick as controllers.

■ ■ ■

CHAPTER 17

OpenGL Special Effects

BlitzMax has access to the richness that the OpenGL API exposes. This also includes some neat screen-based effects.

Rotating Images

Images can be rotated in real time using SetRotation before you draw them. Note that unless you specify SetRotation(0), all images will be rotated.

SetRotation

Set rotation requires one parameter—the angle of rotation. BlitzMax then does all the hard calculations behind the scenes (Figure 17-1). The following example also uses GetRotation to obtain the angle of the current rotation:

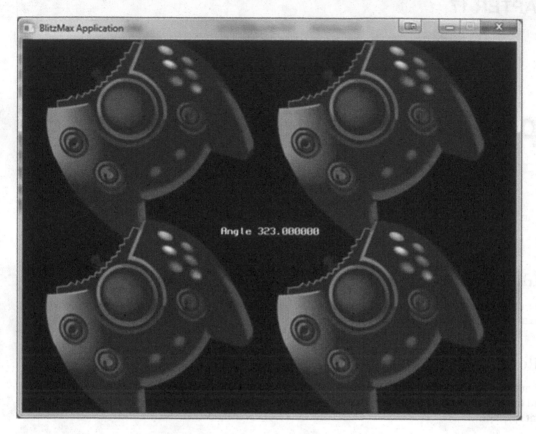

Figure 17-1. *BlitzMax rotating application*

```
Graphics 640, 480

Local stick:TImage = LoadImage("stick.png")
MidHandleImage(stick)

Local angle:Int = 0

While Not KeyHit(KEY_ESCAPE)

    SetRotation(angle)
    DrawImage(stick, 160, 120)
    DrawImage(stick, 460, 120)
    DrawImage(stick, 160, 360)
    DrawImage(stick, 460, 360)
    s:String = "Angle " + GetRotation()       SetRotation(0)
    DrawText(s, (640 - TextWidth(s))/2, 240)

    Flip
    Cls
```

```
angle = angle + 1

If angle=360
      angle = 0
End If
```

Wend

Notice that we have to call SetRotation(0) **after** we find out the current rotation.

What would happen if we removed SetRotation(0)? Alter the preceding program to only rotate the top-left and bottom-right images. Hint: Use SetRotation(0).

Scaling Images

Images can be scaled in BlitzMax just as easily as they can be rotated. The SetScale command is used to increase or decrease the scale of any objects drawn after its use, much as with the SetRotation keyword (Figure 17-2). The following program displays growing text, starting off very small and ending up ×3 scale:

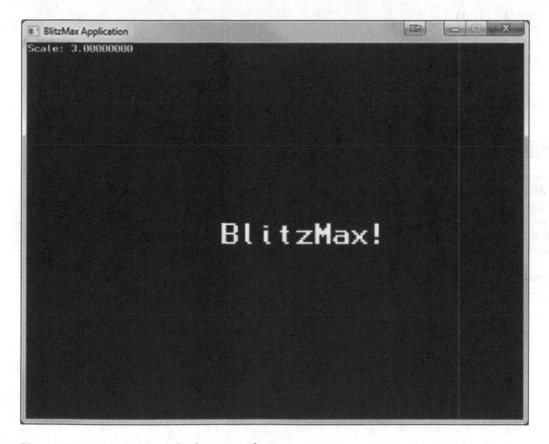

Figure 17-2. *Increasing the scale of text times three*

```
Graphics 640, 480

Local s:String = "BlitzMax!"
Local scale:Float = 0
Local x:Int = 0
Local y:Int = 0

While Not KeyHit(KEY_ESCAPE)
    SetScale(scale, scale)
    scale = scale + .05
    If scale > 3
        scale = 3
    End If

    x = (320 - TextWidth(s))
    y = (240 - TextHeight(s))

    DrawText(s, x, y)

    SetScale(1, 1)
    DrawText("Scale: " + scale, 0, 0)
    Flip
    Cls
Wend
```

Note that GetScale is used to display the current scale.

Collisions Revisited

The simple ImagesCollide keyword cannot be used with scaled or rotated images. There is another keyword that deals with images that have been rotated and/or scaled: the originally titled ImagesCollide2 keyword.

The parameters for ImagesCollide2 are

```
ImagesCollide(img1, x1, y1, frame1, angle1,  scalex1, scaley1, img2, x2, y2, frame2, angle2,
scalex2, scaley2)
```

The example below shows a rotating Xbox controller with our stick man from the simple game a few pages ago. When he touches the spinning controllers, "Man hits stick!" is displayed on the screen (Figure 17-3).

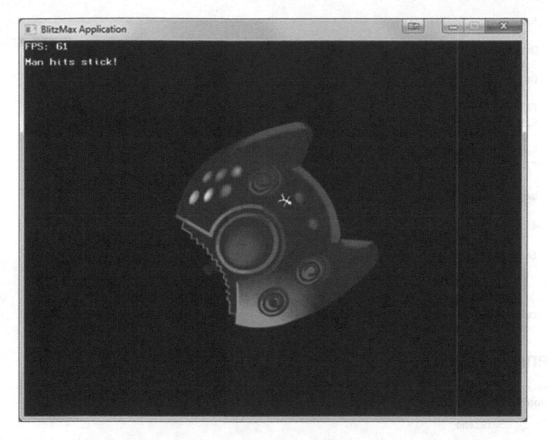

Figure 17-3. *Rotating Xbox controller colliding with stick man*

```
Graphics 640, 480

Local stick:TImage = LoadImage("stick.png")
Local man:TImage = LoadImage("man.png")
MidHandleImage(stick)
MidHandleImage(man)

Local angle:Int = 0

HideMouse
While Not KeyHit(KEY_ESCAPE)

    If ImagesCollide2(stick, 320, 240, 0, angle, 1, 1, man, MouseX(), MouseY(), 0, 0, 1, 1)
        SetRotation(0)
        DrawText("Man hits stick!", 0, 0)
    End If
```

```
        SetRotation(angle)

        DrawImage(stick, 320, 240)
        SetRotation(360 - angle)
        DrawImage(man, MouseX(), MouseY())

        Flip
        Cls

        ResetCollisions()
        FlushMem()

        angle = angle + 1

        If angle=360
                angle = 0
        End If

Wend
```

Scale the stick graphic from .5 to 2 as it rotates.

Blending Modes

BlitzMax allows you to control how pixels are combined with existing pixels in the back buffer. The two keywords that are used to set the blending modes are

```
        SetBlend
```

```
        SetAlpha
```

The SetBlend keyword controls the blend mode of how pixels are combined with the existing pixels in the back buffer. The effect values are shown in Table 17-1.

Table 17-1. *Blend Modes and Their Effects*

Blend mode	Effect
SOLIDBLEND	Pixels overwrite existing back buffer pixels.
MASKBLEND	Pixels are drawn only if their alpha component is greater than .5.
ALPHABLEND	Pixels are alpha blended with existing back buffer pixels.
LIGHTBLEND	Pixel colors are added to back buffer pixel colors, giving a "lightening" effect.
SHADEBLEND	Pixel colors are multiplied with back buffer pixel colors, giving a "shading" effect.

Blend Mode Effects

The following example uses the rotating Xbox controller graphic but adds a twist. By pressing the spacebar, the program toggles between all five modes (Figure 17-4).

Figure 17-4. *Using the spacebar to toggle between modes*

```
Graphics 640, 480

Local stick:TImage = LoadImage("stick.png")
Local flowers:TImage = LoadImage("flowers.jpg")
MidHandleImage(stick)

Local angle:Int = 0
Local blendmode:Int = ALPHABLEND
Local blendfordisplay:Int = 0

HideMouse
While Not KeyHit(KEY_ESCAPE)

    SetBlend(1)
    SetRotation(0)
    SetAlpha(1)
    DrawImage(flowers, 0, 0)

    DrawText("SOLID " + SOLIDBLEND + ".", 0, 0)
    DrawText("MASK " + MASKBLEND + ".", 0, 10)
    DrawText("ALPHABLEND " + ALPHABLEND, 0, 20)
```

```
    DrawText("LIGHTBLEND" + LIGHTBLEND,0 ,30)
    DrawText("SHADEBLEND" + SHADEBLEND, 0, 40)

    SetRotation(angle)

    If KeyHit(KEY_SPACE)

        blendmode = blendmode + 1
        If blendmode = 6
            blendmode = 1
        End If

        blendfordisplay = GetBlend()

    End If

    SetBlend(blendmode)
    If blendmode = ALPHABLEND
        SetAlpha(.5)
    Else
        SetAlpha(1)
    End If

    DrawImage(stick, 320, 240)
    Flip
    Cls
    angle = angle + 1

    If angle=360
        angle = 0
    End If
Wend
```

■ ■ ■

CHAPTER 18

Paratrooper: Retro Involved

Paratrooper is a game for one player. You control the gun turret at the bottom center of the screen (Figure 18-1). The idea is to protect your base from the descending paratroopers being flown in. Once 15 paratroopers have landed safely, it is game over.

Figure 18-1. The Paratrooper game screen

© Sloan Kelly 2016
S. Kelly, *BlitzMax for Absolute Beginners*, DOI 10.1007/978-1-4842-2523-3_18

It's a simple game concept that hides a number of intricate programming routines. For example, there is rotation in the gun barrel that is separate from the main turret block. Then the player fires the gun. We'll use a little math to send the bullet along the right trajectory.

We also look at some of the special effects covered in Chapter 17. You can, I hope, see the evolution of the games throughout the book and observe that, using BlitzMax, you can create some fantastic 2D games that are every bit as complex and fast as those made with machine code or C++. Not to mention the added bonus that all that is required to get it running across three platforms (PC , Mac, Linux) is a recompile!

Project Management

The project is split across multiple files. Each file contains either the main program or a supporting UDT definition. I have deliberately split up the files, to show that multiple developers can work on the same project at the same time.

The main `paratrooper.bmx` file contains all the code to instantiate the objects from the UDTs defined in the supporting files. There is no game code whatsoever in the `paratrooper.bmx` file! In fact, there is only code to control the menu system that we will employ on this project.

Game Dynamics

In order to keep the player interested, he or she can choose the level of difficulty before setting off to play the game. From the menu system, a player can choose from four options.

Lots of Options

Speaking of options, the player has the option to pause the game by pressing the F9 key. On doing so, the screen darkens, and the game freezes. This is a really simple but effective technique that will be explained in this chapter.

Graphics

There are a number of graphics associated with this project, and these are detailed below.

The Paratrooper

The paratrooper image is an animated image consisting of two frames. The first frame is a soldier at attention. The second is the paratrooper with his arms raised. This is the frame that is shown when the paratrooper is holding his parachute (Figure 18-2).

Figure 18-2. *Frame showing the paratrooper holding his parachute*

Each frame is 32×48, giving an overall size of 64×48.

The Gun Emplacement

The gun emplacement is split into two sections (Figure 18-3). The major part is the dome that measures 48×48 pixels.

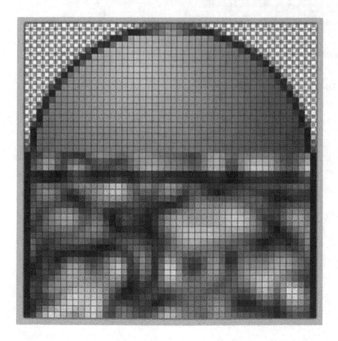

Figure 18-3. *The gun emplacement, split in two screens*

We cheat with the barrel of the emplacement. We're going to place the rotation handle for the barrel at the center of the image. This means that we also can make the barrel 48×48 pixels (Figure 18-4).

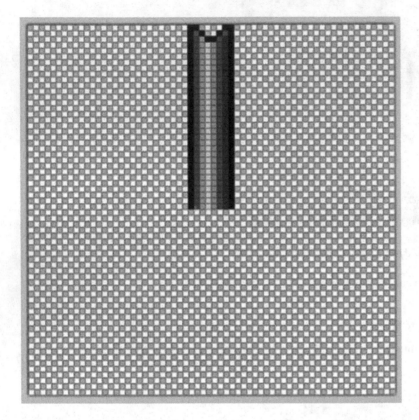

Figure 18-4. *The barrel of the gun emplacement*

The bullet is a simple 6×6 image (Figure 18-5).

Figure 18-5. *Image of the bullet*

Joystick vs. Keyboard?

Yes, it's true! You can use either the keyboard or joystick to play the game. Select the option you want from the main menu. There is no option for mouse—could you code one?

Sound FX

There are spot sound effects used throughout the game. I created them by making shooting noises and saying "Arrgh!" and generally making silly noises in Audacity.

On with the Game

As mentioned before, this game is based on the old Apple][game that's resurfaced on the iPod. It's always been good fun! Your job is to stop enemy troops from entering the base. When 15 troops have successfully landed, it's game over! Control the turret using the keyboard or joystick (left-right) and fire when ready. You can also use a joystick by changing the `playwithstick` variable to `True`. The control keys are left and right cursors and space fires. Good luck!

Paratroops.bmx

The `Paratroops.bmx` file contains the main program for our game. It controls the various options that can be set and how the game is started. The code is commented, so that we don't have to break up the code with explanatory text. The comment blocks contain the *why* rather than the *how* that the code provides.

```
Rem
        Paratroops! A game by Sloan Kelly

        This game is based upon the old Apple game that's resurfaced on the iPod. It's always
        good for a wee blast! Your job is to stop enemy troops entering the base. When 15
        troops have
        successfully landed, it's game over for you, m'laddy!

        Control the turret using the keyboard or joystick (left - right) and fire when ready.
        The control
        keys are left and right cursors and space fires. Good luck!

End Rem

Graphics 800, 600

'
' Some include files for classes
'
Include "Controller.bmx" ' this is the joystick /
keyboard abstract classes
Include "TParatroopGame.bmx" ' the actual game
itself is contained in this one file
'
' Include a few images in the executable
'

Incbin "images/dome.png"
Incbin "images/mountain.jpg"
Incbin "images/grass.png"
Incbin "images/bullet.png"
Incbin "images/barrel.png"
Incbin "images/paratrooper.png"
Incbin "images/parachute.png"

'
' some level constants
'
Const MOMMY:Int = 999
Const ADULT:Int = 995
Const FAST:Int = 990
Const DUDE:Int = 985

'
' Boolean: If we're using a game controller this is set to true
'
Global playwithstick:Int = False
'
' This is the percentage chance of another trooper being created in a
' game cycle. This is passed to the game engine
'
```

```
Global gamelevel:Int = 997

Rem

    Show the main menu from the list
End Rem
Function ShowMenu:Int()
    menuitems:TList = New Tlist
    menuitems.AddLast("Play Game")
    menuitems.AddLast("Help")
    If playwithstick
        menuitems.AddLast("Playing With Joystick")
    Else

        menuitems.AddLast("Playing With Keyboard")
    End If
    menuitems.AddLast("Set Difficulty")
    menuitems.AddLast("Exit")
    menu:TMenuScreen =TMenuScreen.Create("incbin::images/backdrop.png", "incbin::images/
    title.png", menuitems)
    item:Int = menu.Show()
    Return item
End Function

Rem

    Set the difficulty level of the game
End Rem
Function SetDifficulty:Int()
    Select gamelevel
        Case MOMMY
            itemsel = 0
        Case ADULT
            itemsel = 1
        Case FAST
            itemsel = 2
        Case DUDE
            itemsel = 3
    End Select

    menuitems:TList = New Tlist
    menuitems.AddLast("Please don't let mummy know I'm playing")
    menuitems.AddLast("It's OK - I'm an adult")
    menuitems.AddLast("2Fast 2Furious was for children!")
    menuitems.AddLast("Dude. That's just wrong...")
    menu:TMenuScreen = TMenuScreen.Create("incbin::images/backdrop.png",
    "incbin::images/title.png", menuitems, itemsel)
    item:Int = menu.Show()
    lvl:Int = 997
```

```
        Select item
              Case 0
                    lvl = MOMMY
              Case 1
                    lvl = ADULT
              Case 2
                    lvl = FAST
              Case 3
                    lvl = DUDE
        End Select

        Return lvl
End Function

Function ShowHelp()
     helplines:TList = New TList

     helplines.AddLast("Welcome to Paratroops!")
     helplines.AddLast("")
     helplines.AddLast("Move the cannon at the bottom of the screen to shoot down enemy
     paratroopers!")
     helplines.AddLast("")
     helplines.AddLast("Make sure you get all of them, because if 15 of them land it's game
     over!")
     helplines.AddLast("")
     helplines.AddLast("Use joystick or keys to move - cursor left/right and space is fire.
     F9 - Pause / Un-Pause")
     helplines.AddLast("")
     helplines.AddLast("You can select keyboard or joystick on the front menu.")
     helplines.AddLast("")
     helplines.AddLast("")
     helplines.AddLast("Press SPACE to return to the main menu.")

     help:THelpScreen = THelpScreen.Create("incbin::images/backdrop.png",. "incbin::images/
smalltitle.png",..helplines,.. 240)

     help.Show()
End Function

Function DoGame()
     '
     ' We're using the abstract IController from the previous section - see code in
appendices
     '
     Local controller:Icontroller
     Local stick:TStick = TStick.Create("Joystick", 0)
     Local keyboard:TKeyboard = TKeyboard.Create("Keyboard", KEY_UP, KEY_DOWN, KEY_LEFT,
     KEY_RIGHT)
     Local keyfire:TKeyFire = TKeyFire.Create(KEY_SPACE)
```

```
    For i:Int="0" To 7
        stickfire:TStickFire = TStickFire.Create(i)
        stick.AddFire(stickfire)
    Next

    keyboard.AddFire(keyfire)

    '
    ' Notice that the 'controller' variable is assigned
    ' a value depending on the 'playwithstick' boolean
    ' The 'controller' variable is then passed to the game
    ' engine. This abstraction means that we should be safe
    ' even If someone invents a New virtual reality glove to
    ' control game objects '
    If playwithstick
        controller = stick
    Else

        controller = keyboard
    End If
    '
    ' Setting up the game engine is a simple call to the create routine
    ' passing in the paths to the image files '
    game:TParatroopGame = TParatroopGame.Create(controller,..

"incbin::images/mountain.jpg",..

                            "incbin::images

"incbin::images/dome.png",..

"incbin::images/barrel.png",..

    "incbin::images/bullet.png",..

    "incbin::images/paratrooper.png",..

    "incbin::images/parachute.png",..

gamelevel)
    FlushKeys() '
    ' Start the game loop. This will run until the game is over (player loses)
    ' or the 'Quit' option is taken (player quits)
    '
    game.GameLoop()
    FlushKeys()
End Function

'
' This is the main program from this point.
'The mouse is hidden and the menu is shown.
```

```
' When the user selects an option, the respective ' function is called.
'
HideMouse()

#MainMenu
FlushKeys()
Select ShowMenu()
     Case 0
          DoGame() ' Play the game
     Case 1
          ShowHelp() ' Show the help screen
     Case 2
          playwithstick:~True ' Toggle between using the joystick and the keyboard
     Case 3
          gamelevel = SetDifficulty() ' set the difficulty of the game
     Case 4
          Goto Quitter
End Select
FlushKeys()
' There is an option on the main menu that allows the user to exit the game to the OS
' This functionality is missing in our game, so we're straight out to the OS when the
' user base is over run or they quit
''Goto MainMenu ' this has been commented out because the main menu isn't finished
'
' This is the end of the game. No more code to run, so the program exits
'
#Quitter
```

TMenuScreen.bmx

The menu screen gets its own class. Its purpose is to prompt the user with various options: play the game, change the input method, change the difficulty, request help, and quit to the OS. It does all that through the Show() method. It implements its own version of the outline draw. Could you re-code it to use a centrally available function?

```
Type TMenuScreen
     Field backdrop:Timage
     Field title:TImage
     Field current_item:Int = 0

     Field items:TList

     Method DrawOutline(str:String, x:Int, y:Int, r:Int, g:Int, b:Int)
          SetColor(0, 0, 0)
          DrawText(str, x, y)
          DrawText(str, x+1, y)
          DrawText(str, x-1, y)
          DrawText(str, x, y+1)
          DrawText(str, x, y-1)
          DrawText(str, x+1, y+1)
          DrawText(str, x+1, y-1)
```

```
            DrawText(str, x-1, y+1)
            DrawText(str, x-1, y-1)
            SetColor(r, g, b)
            DrawText(str, x, y)
            SetColor(255, 255, 255)
    End Method

Rem

        Show Method
        Displays the menu screen and does some basic animation You could spice this up
        somewhat...
End Rem
Method Show:Int()

            Local y:Int = 0
            Local count:Int = 0;
            Local last:Long = MilliSecs()

            SetBlend(ALPHABLEND)

            While Not KeyHit(KEY_SPACE) And Not KeyHit(KEY_ENTER)
                Cls
                DrawImage(backdrop, 0, 0)
                DrawImage(title, 0, 0)

                menu_y:Int = 388
                count:Int = 0;
                For s:String = EachIn items

                        If current_item = count DrawOutline(s, (800-
TextWidth(s))/2 , menu_y, 255, 255, 128)
                        Else
                        DrawOutline(s, (800- TextWidth(s))/2 , menu_y, 128, 128, 128)
                        End If
                        count = count + 1
                        menu_y = menu_y + 25
                Next
                Flip

                If KeyHit(KEY_DOWN)
                        current_item = current_item + 1
                End If

                If KeyHit(KEY_UP)
                        current_item = current_item - 1
                End If

                If current_item < 0
                        current_item = CountList(items)-1
                End If
```

189

```
            If current_item > CountList(items)-1
                current_item = 0
            End If

            Wend
            Return current_item '' return the currently selected item to the calling
            method

    End Method

    Rem

        Create Function
        Creates a copy of the TMenuScreen UDT and assigns
        two images and a list of menu options to it
    End Rem

    Function Create: TMenuScreen(backimg:String, titleimg:String, list:TList,
    itemsel:Int=0)
        o:TMenuScreen = New TmenuScreen
        o.backdrop = LoadImage(backimg)
        o.title = LoadImage(titleimg)
        o.items = list
        o.current_item = itemsel

        Return o
    End Function
End Type
```

Controller.bmx

`Controller.bmx` contains the abstraction for keyboard and joystick events (user turns right, user turns left, etc.) as well as starting the game itself. The code for this is in the appendixes at the end of the book.

TParatroopGame.bmx

This is the main game engine and controls all the aspects of the game while it is in play:

> User input
>
> Random trooper creation and placement
>
> Updating the existing troopers
>
> Pausing the game
>
> Quitting the game

It contains one function and nine methods. They are described following.

Create

This function creates an instance of TParatroopGame and assigns some default values before returning the instance to the calling routine (Paratrooper.bmx).

CheckCollisions

For each bullet fired, a check is made to see if it hits a falling trooper or his chute. If the trooper is hit, both the trooper and the chute are destroyed. If the chute is hit by the bullet, only the chute is destroyed, and the trooper's speed increases until he splats on the ground and is removed.

DrawScore

DrawScore draws the player's score onscreen. It uses scaling and a homemade routine to give an outline (see "DrawOutline").

DrawLanded

DrawLanded is similar to DrawScore in that it give the user feedback on his progress. In this case, a count of how many troops has landed on the ground. If there are ten or more, a further indication flashes, telling the user how many troops are required to overrun the base.

Draw

Draw cycles through all the displayable objects in the game and displays them. Note that objects drawn first are at the back. Later images are superimposed on these images in the back buffer.

Update

Update updates the player and adds more troops, if required. The trigger is set here if ten or more troops have landed to start the flashing sign (see "DrawLanded").

DoQuit

The background is dulled by making a call to SetColor. This is an important use of this keyword. You can create great effects just by changing the current drawing color. Try different colors!

DoGameOver

When all the troops have landed, a "Game Over" message is displayed.

DrawOutline

DrawOutline draws text in the system font with a black outline. It reminded me of Super Mario World on the SNES, and I liked the look.

GameLoop

The main game loop cycles through all the updates and screen draws in this order:

Update all the player nonplayer characters

Draw all the images

Flip the back buffer

Clear the back buffer

```
Include "TGameBackdrop.bmx"
Include "TDome.bmx"
Include "TParatrooper.bmx"

Type TParatroopGame

    Field back:TGameBackdrop = TGameBackdrop.Create()
    Field dome:TDome
    Field ctrl:Icontroller
    Field paused:Int = False
    Field quitgame:Int = False
    Field ChanceOfNewTrooper:Int = 997
    Field troops:TTroops

    Field flashlanded:Int=False
    Field flashtmr:Int = -1
    Field gametimer:Int = MilliSecs() '' every 10 seconds, your chances of more troops
    increase!

    Method DrawOutline(str:String, x:Int, y:Int, r:Int, g:Int, b:Int)
        SetColor(0, 0, 0)
        DrawText(str, x, y)
        DrawText(str, x+1, y)
        DrawText(str, x-1, y)
        DrawText(str, x, y+1)
        DrawText(str, x, y-1)
        DrawText(str, x+1, y+1)
        DrawText(str, x+1, y-1)
        DrawText(str, x-1, y+1)
        DrawText(str, x-1, y-1)
        SetColor(r, g, b)
        DrawText(str, x, y)
        SetColor(255, 255, 255)
    End Method

    Method CheckCollisions:Int(bulletlist:TList, trooperlist:TList)

        Local sc:Int = 0

        For b:TBullet = EachIn bulletlist
            For t:TParatrooper = EachIn trooperlist
```

```
                If Not t.Landed
                    If ImagesCollide(b.Image, b.X, b.Y, 0, t.Image, t.X, t.Y, 1)
                        b.Destroy = True
                        t.Destroy = True
                        sc = sc + 5
                    End If

                    If ImagesCollide(b.Image, b.X, b.Y, 0, t.ChuteImage, t.X-8,
                    t.Y-48, 0)
                        t.haschute = False
                        t.YSpeed:*1.5
                        sc = sc + 10
                    End If
                End If
            Next
        Next
        Return sc
End Method

Method DrawScore()
    s :String = "0000000" + dome.Score
    s = "Score " + Right(s, 5)
    SetScale(1.0, 2.0)
    DrawOutline(s, 4, 4, 255, 255, 0)
    SetScale(1.0, 1.0)
End Method

Method DrawLanded()
    s:String = "00" + troops.Landed()
    s = Right(s, 2) + " Landed!"
    s1:String = "00" + (15 - troops.Landed())
    s1 = "Watch out - " + Right(s1, 2) + " to go!"
    SetScale(1.0, 2.0)
    '
    ' this little bit of code flashes the "XX Landed!" text
    ' if the number landed >=10
    '
    If troops.Landed()>=10
        If MilliSecs() > flashtmr + 750
            flashtmr = MilliSecs()
            flashlanded = Not flashlanded
            End If
        If flashlanded
            DrawOutline(s, 794 - TextWidth(s), 4, 0, 255, 0)
            SetScale(2.0, 1.0)
            DrawOutline(s1, 400 - TextWidth(s)*2, 576, 0, 255, 0)
        Else
            DrawOutline(s, 794 -TextWidth(s), 4, 255, 0, 0)
            SetScale(2.0, 1.0)
            DrawOutline(s1, 400 - TextWidth(s)*2, 576, 255, 0, 0)
        End If
```

```
                Else
                        DrawOutline(s, 794 - TextWidth(s), 4, 0, 255, 0)
            End If
            SetScale(1.0, 1.0)
    End Method

    Method Draw()
            back.Draw(True) ' show backdrop scenery items
            dome.Draw()
            troops.Draw()
            back.Draw(False) ' show foreground scenery items
            DrawScore()
            DrawLanded()
    End Method
    Method Update()
            dome.Update(ctrl)
            dome.Score = dome.Score + CheckCollisions(dome.Bullets, troops.Troopers)
            troops.AddTrooper(ChanceOfNewTrooper)
            troops.Update()

            If troops.Landed() >= 10 And flashtmr = -1
                flashtmr = MilliSecs()
            End If

            If MilliSecs() > gametimer + 15000
                gametimer = MilliSecs()
                ChanceOfNewTrooper = ChanceOfNewTrooper - 1
            End If

    End Method

    Method DoQuit()
            SetColor(96, 96, 96)
            Draw()
            SetColor(255, 255, 255)
            DrawOutline("Quit Game? (Y - Quit, Any other key continues)",
            400-(TextWidth("Quit Game? (Y - Quit, Any other key continues)")/2), 298,
            255, 0, 0)
            Flip
            Cls
            ch = WaitKey()
            If ch = KEY_Y
                quitgame = True
            End If
    End Method

    Method DoGameOver()
            SetColor(96, 96, 96)
            Draw()
            SetColor(255, 255, 255)
```

```
    DrawOutline("G A M E O V E R - Y o u r b a s e w a s o v e r r u n !",
    400- (TextWidth("G A M E O V E R - Y o u r b a s e w a s o v e r r u n !")/2),
    298, 255, 0, 0)
    DrawOutline("Thank you for playing", 400-(TextWidth("Thank you for playing")/2),
    340, 255, 255, 255)
    Flip
    Cls
    tmr=MilliSecs()
    While MilliSecs() < tmr + 5000 ' wait five seconds
    Wend
    quitgame = True
End Method

Method GameLoop()
    While Not quitgame
        If KeyHit(KEY_ESCAPE) And Not paused

            DoQuit()
            'quitgame = True
            FlushMem()
            ResetCollisions()
        End If

        If troops.Landed() >=15
            DoGameOver()
        End If

        If Not quitgame
            If KeyHit(KEY_F9)
                paused:~True
            End If

            If Not paused
                Update()
                SetColor(255, 255, 255)
            Else
                SetColor(96, 96, 96) '' make everything 'dark'

            End If

            Draw()

            If paused
                SetColor(255, 255, 255)
                DrawOutline("G A M E P A U S E D", 400-(TextWidth("G A M E P A U
                S E D")/2), 298, 255, 255, 0)
            End If

            Flip
            Cls
            FlushMem()
```

```
                ResetCollisions()
            End If

        Wend
    End Method

    Function Create:TParatroopGame(controller:IController,..

background:String,..

    grass:String,..

domesrc:String,..

gunsrc:String,..

bullet:String,..

trooper:String,..

chute:String,..

chance:Int)
            o:TParatroopGame = New TparatroopGame
            o.ctrl = controller
            s:TScenery = TScenery.Create(background, False, 0, 0)
            g:TScenery = TScenery.Create(grass, True, 0, 568)
            o.back.AddImage(s)
            o.back.AddImage(g)
            o.Troops = TTroops.Create(trooper, chute)
            o.dome = TDome.Create(domesrc, gunsrc, bullet)
            o.ChanceOfNewTrooper = chance
            Return o
    End Function
End Type
```

TGameBackdrop.bmx

TGameBackdrop is a simple class to allow elaborate fore- and background objects to be drawn. I did it especially for this game, and it's not something that I would use all the time, but it's nice to have an extra class in there!

```
Type TScenery
    Field Image:TImage
    Field IsForeground:Int = False
    Field X:Int
    Field Y:Int
```

```
        Method Draw()
                DrawImage(Image, X, Y)
        End Method

        Function Create:TScenery(src:String, isFore:Int=False, x:Int, y:Int)
                o:TScenery = New Tscenery
                o.Image = LoadImage(src)
                o.IsForeground = isFore
                o.X = x
                o.Y = y
                Return o
        End Function
End Type

Type TGameBackdrop

        Field Images:TList = CreateList()
        Method Draw(backgroundOnly:Int=True)
                For s:TScenery = EachIn Images
                        If backgroundOnly = Not s.IsForeground
                                s.Draw()
                        End If
                Next
        End Method

        Method AddImage(s:TScenery)
                Images.AddLast(s)
        End Method

        Function Create:TGameBackdrop()
                o:TGameBackdrop = New TGameBackdrop

                Return o
        End Function

End Type
```

TParatrooper.bmx

The TParatrooper file contains two classes: TParatrooper and TTroops. TTroops is the container class for all the TParatrooper instances in the game.

TParatrooper

TParatrooper contains one function and two methods:

        Create

        Draw

        Update

Create

This creates an instance of the TParatrooper object.

Draw

When the trooper is in flight, his parachute is drawn, if he has landed, then the parachute is not drawn, and the standing trooper image is shown. If he has had his chute destroyed and is still falling, the chute is not displayed.

Update

This updates the position of the trooper, based upon its y axis speed. If the trooper lands without a parachute, he is destroyed—read removed from the game world.

```
Type Tparatrooper
    Field X:Float
    Field Y:Float
    Field Image:Timage
    Field ChuteImage:Timage
    Field YSpeed:Float
    Field Landed:Int = False
    Field haschute:Int = True
    Field Destroy:Int = False

    Method Update()
        If Not Landed
            Y = Y + Yspeed
            If Y >= 600-32
                Y = 600-32
                Landed = True
                YSpeed = 0
                If Not haschute ' get rid of the ones who fell to earth!
                    Destroy = True
                End If
            End If
        End If
    End Method

    Method Draw()
        If Landed
            DrawImage(Image, X, Y, 0)
        Else
            If haschute
                DrawImage(ChuteImage, X-8, Y- 48)
            End If
            DrawImage(Image, X, Y, 1)
        End If
    End Method
```

```
    Function Create:TParatrooper(x:Int,..
                                  y:Int=-64,..
                                  ys:Float=0.4,..
                                  trooper:String,..
                                  chute:String)
        o:TParatrooper = New TParatrooper
        o.X = x
        o.Y = y
        o.YSpeed = ys
        o.Image = LoadAnimImage(trooper, 32, 48, 0, 2)
        o.ChuteImage = LoadImage(chute)
        Return o
    End Function
End Type
```

TTroops

TTroops contains one function and three methods.

```
    Create

    Draw

    Update

    Landed
```

Create

This returns an instance of TTroops.

Draw

Draw cycles through all the TParatrooper instances within the Troopers field variable and draws them onscreen.

Update

This method cycles through all the TParatrooper instances within the Troopers field variable and updates them. Any that have their Destroy field set to True are removed from the list.

Landed

Landed returns the number of TParatrooper instances within the Troopers field variable that have their HasLanded flag set to True.

```
Type TTroops
    Field Image:String
    Field ChuteImage:String
    Field Troopers:TList = CreateList()
```

```
    Method Update()
        For t:TParatrooper = EachIn Troopers
            t.Update()
            If t.Destroy
                ListRemove(Troopers, t)
            End If
        Next
    End Method

    Method Landed:Int()
        c:Int = 0
        For t:TParatrooper = EachIn Troopers
            If t.Landed
                c:+1
            End If
        Next
        Return c
    End Method

    Method Draw()
        For t:TParatrooper = EachIn Troopers
            t.Draw()
        Next
    End Method

    Method AddTrooper(val:Int)

        If Rnd(1000) > val
            x:Int = Rnd(768) + 32
            y:Int = -64
            ys:Float = 2
            ''trooper = LoadAnimImage(Image, 32, 48, 0, 2)
            ''chute = LoadImage(ChuteImage)
            Rand(MilliSecs())
            t:TParatrooper = TParatrooper.Create(x, y, ys, Image, ChuteImage)
            Troopers.AddLast(t)
        End If

    End Method

    Function Create:TTroops(trooper:String, chute:String)
        o:TTroops = New Ttroops
        o.Image = trooper ''LoadAnimImage(trooper, 32, 48, 0, 2)
        o.ChuteImage = chute ''LoadImage(chute)
        Return o
    End Function
End Type
```

TDome.bmx

TDome.bmx contains two UDTs: TDome and TBullet.

TBullet

TBullet is the class containing information and methods about each and every bullet fired by the player. TBullet contains one function and two methods, as follows.

Create

Create returns an instance of the TBullet class.

Draw

Draw draws the image of the bullet onto the back buffer.

Update

Update adds the x and y speeds to move the bullet away from the gun barrel and toward the edges. If the bullet reaches the edges and has not hit a target, then it is destroyed.

```
Type TBullet
     Field X:Float
     Field Y:Float
     Field XSpeed:Float
     Field YSpeed:Float
     Field Destroy:Int = False
     Field Image:TImage

     Method Draw()
          DrawImage(Image, X, Y)
     End Method

     Method Update()
          x:+XSpeed
          y:+YSpeed

          If x < 0 Or x > 800
               Destroy = True
          End If

          If y < 0
               Destroy = True
          End If
     End Method
```

```
    Function Create:TBullet(x:Int, y:Int, xs:Float, ys:Float, img:TImage)
        o:TBullet = New TBullet
        o.X = x
      o.Y = y
        o.XSpeed = xs
        o.YSpeed = ys
        o.Image = img
        Return o
    End Function
End Type
```

TDome

TDome is the class that represents the player's gun installation at the foot of the screen. It contains seven fields, one function, and two methods.

The Fields

Dome: Shape of the dome

Gun: Shape of the gun

Bullet: Shape of the bullet

Rot: The current rotation (from -90 to +90) in degrees

LastFire: Timer used to count the last time the player fired. Although autofire is permitted, the user cannot fire in rapid succession, because there is a gap of 250ms between each shot.

Score: How well the player is doing

Bullets: List of TBullet instances

Create

Create returns an instance of the TDome class.

Draw

Draw cycles through all the bullets and draws them first. It then draws the gun at the current rotation and then draws the dome over the top.

Update

Update updates the position of the bullets and the rotation of the gun.

```
Rem
      Class    :  TDome
      Author   :  Sloan Kelly
      Purpose  :  Player object for Paratroops!
game
End Rem
Type TDome

      Const BULLET_SPEED:Float = 4.5

      Field Dome:TImage
      Field Gun:TImage
      Field Bullet:TImage
      Field Rot:Float = 0.0
      Field lastfire:Int
      Field Score:Int = 0

      Field Bullets:TList = CreateList()

      Method Draw()
            SetRotation(0)
            For b:TBullet = EachIn Bullets
                  b.Draw()
            Next
            SetRotation(Rot)
            DrawImage(Gun, 392, 576)
            SetRotation(0)
            DrawImage(Dome, 368, 555)
      End Method

      Method Update(controller:IController)
            For b:TBullet = EachIn Bullets
                  b.Update()
                  If b.Destroy
                        ListRemove(Bullets, b)
                  End If
            Next

            If controller.DLeft()
                  Rot = Rot - 5.0
                  If Rot <= -90.0
                        Rot = -90.0
                  End If
            End If
```

```
            If controller.DRight()
                Rot = Rot + 5.0
                If Rot >= 90.0
                    Rot = 90.0
                End If
            End If

        Local fired:Int = False

        If controller.Fire(0) And MilliSecs() > lastfire + 250 ' don't want them to fire
too quickly!
                lastfire = MilliSecs()
                bx:Int = 388 + (32 * Sin(Rot))
                by:Int = 574 - (32 * Cos(Rot))
                xs:Float = BULLET_SPEED * Sin(Rot)
                ys:Float = -BULLET_SPEED * Cos(Rot)
                b:TBullet = TBullet.Create(bx, by, xs, ys, Bullet)
                Bullets.AddLast(b)
        End If

    End Method

    Function Create:TDome(domesrc:String, gunsrc:String, bulletsrc:String)

        o:TDome = New TDome
        o.Dome = LoadImage(domesrc)
        o.Gun = LoadImage(gunsrc)
        o.Bullet = LoadImage(bulletsrc)
        MidHandleImage(o.Gun)
        Return o

    End Function
End Type
```

The image below (Figure 18-6) shows how the speed of the bullet is calculated. To get the bullet to move in the right direction, we have to employ a little bit of math.

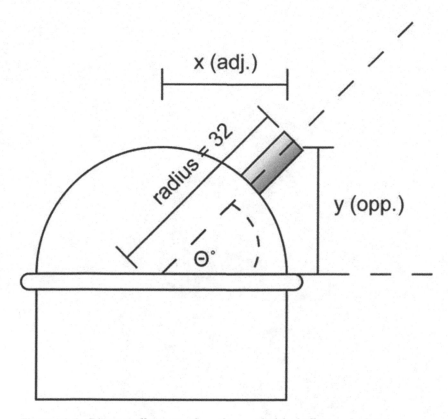

Figure 18-6. *Diagram illustrating how the speed of the bullet is calculated*

The x speed of the bullet is calculated by multiplying the radius of the barrel (32 pixels) by the sine of the barrel's angle.

The y speed of the bullet is calculated by multiplying the radius of the barrel (32 pixels) by the cosine of the barrel's angle.

This means that the bullet travels along the same path that the barrel is pointing. In the preceding example, the bullet would be fired out toward the top right of the screen.

Enter the code as listed previously in the files indicated. Save them all to the SAME folder. You will have to download images for these files. These images are available at www.blitzmaxbook.com.

Change the pause screen to show the background in a blue shade. Hint: Use SetColor(r, g, b), where r, g, and b are the red, green and blue elements.

CHAPTER 19

Sound Effects and Audio

There are a number of audio tools out there that will handle WAV and OGG files. The best I have come across so far, and one that is available on Mac, PC, and Linux, is Audacity. Visit the SourceForge web site for more details and download this great product. Best of all is that it's free!

Currently, BlitzMax can only play back two sound file formats: WAV and OGG.

WAV

Developed by IBM and Microsoft, this is a format for storing sound in files. Support for WAV files was built into Windows 95, making it the de facto standard for sound on PCs. WAV sound files end with a .wav extension and can be played by nearly all Windows applications that support sound.

OGG

Ogg Vorbis is an audio compression format, comparable to other MP3 or AAC used to store and play digital music, but differs in that it is free, open, and unpatented. The Ogg Vorbis specification is in the public domain and is freely available for commercial and/or noncommercial use. Ogg refers to the Ogg Project, which is an open source multimedia initiative, while Vorbis is the actual compression format.

BlitzMax and Sound

BlitzMax allows for a high degree of control over what sounds can be heard and where they are heard—left, right, or center to the listener. In this chapter, I will discuss the following keywords:

    LoadSound

    PlaySound

    SetChannelVolume

    PauseChannel

    ResumeChannel

© Sloan Kelly 2016
S. Kelly, *BlitzMax for Absolute Beginners*, DOI 10.1007/978-1-4842-2523-3_19

LoadSound

LoadSound loads a sound into memory to a TSound variable. The format for this keyword is

```
Variable:TSound = LoadSound(path:String
[,LoopSound:Int=False])
```

By default, any sound loaded into BlitzMax is not looped.

PlaySound

PlaySound returns a TChannel variable containing the channel the sound is being played on. We use this TChannel variable to control the sound later.

```
Channel:TChannel =
PlaySound(sound_variable:TSound)
```

SetChannelVolume

SetChannelVolume sets the volume for the specified channel. The format of the keyword is

```
SetChannelVolume(channel:TChannel, volume:Float)
```

where volume is between 0 and 1.0.

PauseChannel

PauseChannel pauses the playback of the sound on the specified channel. The format of this keyword is

```
PauseChannel(channel:TChannel)
```

ResumeChannel

ResumeChannel resumes the playback of the sound on the specified channel. The format of this keyword is

```
ResumeChannel(channel:TChannel)
```

BlitzMax Sound Example

The following example loads a sound—imaginatively called "music.ogg"—into memory and starts playing it.

```
Rem
      Example sound application
End Rem
Graphics 640, 480, 16, 75 ' put in graphics mode for KeyHit()

sound:TSound = LoadSound("music.ogg", True)
channel:TChannel = PlaySound(sound)
```

```
curvol:Float = 1
playing:Int = True

While Not KeyHit(KEY_ESCAPE)
    '
    ' Volume down...
    '
    If KeyHit(KEY_DOWN)
        curvol = curvol - 0.1
        If curvol < 0.0
            curvol = 0.0
        End If
        SetChannelVolume(channel, curvol)
    End If
    '
    ' Volume up...
    '
    If KeyHit(KEY_UP)
        curvol = curvol + 0.1
        If curvol > 1.0
            curvol = 1.0
        End If
        SetChannelVolume(channel, curvol)
    End If
    '
    ' Pause
    '
    If KeyHit(KEY_SPACE)
        If playing
            PauseChannel(channel)
        Else
            ResumeChannel(channel)
        End If
        playing:~True
    End If

    SetColor(255, 255, 255)
    DrawText("Vol: " + (curvol*10), 0, 0)
    If playing
        SetColor(0, 255, 0)
        DrawText("Play", 0, 10)
    Else
        SetColor(255, 0, 0)
        DrawText("Paused", 0, 10)
    End If
    Flip
    Cls

Wend
StopChannel(channel)
```

209

Installing Audacity

Launch a web browser and go to http://audacity.sourceforge.net/. Click the Download Audacity for Windows link. If you have a Mac or Linux, click Other Downloads.

Follow the links onscreen until you get to the Select a mirror page. Click the location nearest you. The file should download automatically. If you have a firewall or Microsoft Spyware filters, you may not be able to download the file without Ctrl+clicking the link.

When you have downloaded the installer, double-click it and follow the instructions. Audacity will be installed on your machine. Using Audacity, record the following three sounds.

Music.Ogg

Take an MP3 file that you own and load it into Audacity. To do this, click File ➤ Open from the menu bar along the top of the screen. Browse to the location where your file is located. Select it and click Open ➤ OK.

The file will load into Audacity, and the wave form will be displayed in the window. The file can be saved as an OGG file by clicking File ➤ Export as Ogg Vorbis...from the menu. Enter the name "music.ogg" and ensure that the location is the same folder as the Paratroops game. Click Save ➤ OK.

Argh.Ogg and Ugh.Ogg

For these two sounds, we're going to have a little fun! From the File menu in Audacity, select File ➤ New. This creates a new blank sound file. We're now going to populate it with our own voice! You will need a microphone connected to your computer for this to work.

Start recording by clicking the circular red Record button. Then, for the falling sound, say "Arghhhhh." Click the square yellow Stop button. You should have something like that shown in Figure 19-1.

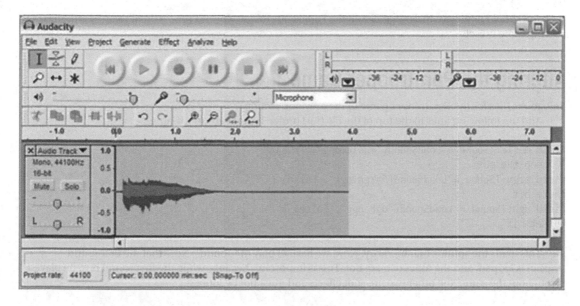

Figure 19-1. *What the "Arghhhhh" sound looks like in Audacity*

There will be a lot of space at either side of the actual sound. To get rid of this, highlight the quiet area by dragging the mouse over the quiet part of the wave (Figure 19-2).

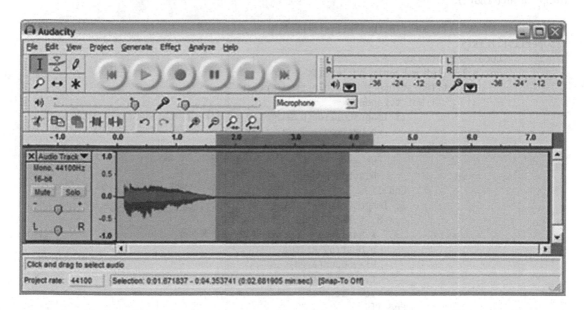

Figure 19-2. *Deleting whitespace*

With this area selected, press the Delete key. Repeat this process for the other side. Once you have a file you are happy with, export to Ogg Vorbis, as described in the preceding "Music.Ogg" section. Repeat this process for an "Ugh" sound.

You should now have three Ogg files in the Paratroops folder. Now it's time to load them in and start making some noise!

Altering the Paratrooper Game

Reload the files for the Paratrooper game in the previous section.

Add the following lines to the top of the file (just under Type TParatroopGame):

```
Field music:TSound = LoadSound("music.ogg", True)
'' loop the music
Field argh:TSound = LoadSound("argh.ogg", False) '
chute hit
Field ugh:TSound = LoadSound("ugh.ogg", False) '
bullet hit
```

This loads the sounds into memory. Now, we have to play the sounds. Note that the first sound (music) is looped, and the other two are not. This is important, because while the first sound is to be played throughout the game, the other two are spot effects and must not be looped.

Collisions

Alter the CheckCollisions() method to play a sound when either the parachute is hit ("Arghhhhh") or the trooper is hit ("Ugh!").

```
    Method CheckCollisions:Int(bulletlist:TList,
trooperlist:TList)
        Local sc:Int = 0
        For b:TBullet = EachIn bulletlist
            For t:TParatrooper = EachIn trooperlist
                If Not t.Landed
                    If ImagesCollide(b.Image, b.X, b.Y, 0, t.Image, t.X, t.Y, 1)
                        b.Destroy = True
                        t.Destroy = True
                        sc = sc + 5
                        PlaySound(ugh)
                    End If
                    If ImagesCollide(b.Image, b.X, b.Y, 0, t.ChuteImage,
                    t.X-8, t.Y-48, 0)
                        t.haschute = False
                        b.Destroy = True
                        PlaySound(argh)
                        t.YSpeed:*1.5
                        sc = sc + 10
                    End If
                End If
            Next
        Next
        Return sc
    End Method
```

Playing the Music

To play the music, add the PlaySound line to the GameLoop method, as follows:

```
Method GameLoop()
channel:TChannel = PlaySound(music)
     While Not quitgame
              :                    :
And at the bottom:
              :                    :

Wend
     StopChannel(channel)
End Method
```

And that's it! Music and sound added to the game!

The music still plays while the game is paused. Can you stop the music temporarily?

What about shooting? Can you make a suitable sound for the firing gun? Where would you load the sound? What event would play the sound?

CHAPTER 20

■ ■ ■

Putting It All Together

In this final chapter, we are going to look at designing a game from scratch and implementing and testing it. In order to do this, you have need to learn a little about the design process, as well as how to implement testing for each individual module. This chapter is divided into the following five sections:

> Game design
>
> Object-oriented design
>
> Implementing OOP in BlitzMax
>
> Testing modules
>
> Project management

We will be creating a game called Flood, starring Jasper, a bear. He has bred orchids on a remote island and must save them from the flood. Unfortunately, the island is inhabited by Badbears, who will stop at nothing to thwart our hero's quest!

The full code for the game, including the graphics and sound, is available to download from the companion web site: `www.blitzmaxbook.com/`.

© Sloan Kelly 2016
S. Kelly, *BlitzMax for Absolute Beginners*, DOI 10.1007/978-1-4842-2523-3_20

Putting it All Together

CHAPTER 21

Game Design

In this chapter, I discuss getting a game from an idea to storyboards. Once we have the storyboards, we can move onto taking that information and abstracting it. This is part of the object-oriented process that I will detail later.

What's the Big Idea?

Before we start to code our game, we have to have an idea. Ideas can be high-concept or low-concept. The definition of each concept depends on who you ask. We are going to use the Hollywood method.

High Concept

A high-concept idea can be expressed in one phrase: no more, no less. For example:

It's Pac-Man meets Doom

It's The Sims meets Mario with a twist of Ridge Racer

This is very similar to some companies adding radios to other devices, such as frying pans. Sometimes it's so quirky it might work. The last one in particular…

Low Concept

A low-concept idea, on the other hand, cannot be expressed in one phrase. It requires a great deal of text. Examples of these games include SimCity, WarCraft, etc.

So What Is Flood?

Flood is a collect-the-items-and-avoid-the-bad-guys game. This type of game has been popular since Donkey Kong. If you wanted a high-concept tag line, "It's Donkey Kong in the jungle, with bears and orchids." That pretty much sums up Flood!

© Sloan Kelly 2016
S. Kelly, *BlitzMax for Absolute Beginners*, DOI 10.1007/978-1-4842-2523-3_21

CHAPTER 22

■ ■ ■

Storyboarding

Before we start writing detailed ideas about the game, we should draw up some concepts first. For example, what will the screen look like? Where is the score lives text? Where will the platforms go? What about the bad guys? How will the wave work?

Figure 22-1 illustrates some concepts for the game that I roughed out of an evening.

Figure 22-1. *Some rough concepts for the game*

© Sloan Kelly 2016
S. Kelly, *BlitzMax for Absolute Beginners*, DOI 10.1007/978-1-4842-2523-3_22

I initially called it "Sinking Ship" and thought about global warming and ice caps...The mind does tend to wander. Once you play Flood, you'll realize that I changed the concept from sinking ship to flooding jungle. There was a very simple reason for that—graphics. The only graphics I could lay my hands on were for a jungle setting. This meant that the game's setting had to change. Other than that, though, the rough idea for the game remained. The right-hand column contains some notes about gravity and its effect on our main character—Jasper. The name "Baddie" appears later too. I also started to rough out the fields required for the objects.

Writing a Specification for a Game

When you write a specification for a game, you are defining the game world that your characters will inhabit. It should list all the events that can occur and what should be done when the event is triggered. Remember that it is possible that a nonplayer character can trigger an event. The sample specification below is for Flood.

Flood Game Specification

Introduction

Flood is a game for one player, using either the keyboard or joystick for movement. The object of the game is to collect the flashing orchids from around the screen. Two problems confront the player: roaming enemies on the platforms and a rising water level.

The roaming enemies cannot be damaged, and their touch sends the player's character spinning randomly about the screen and to his death. The player starts with five lives. When all five lives are exhausted, the game is over.

The water level rises from the bottom of the screen, and if the player's character goes beneath the level of the water, he is killed. Likewise, if an orchid falls beneath the level of the water, it is destroyed and cannot be collected.

To complete a level, the player must collect all the orchids on the screen and reach the end marker before the water level rises above the head of his/her character.

The Screen

The game screen is divided by platforms. The ground at the bottom is the main platform. The top platform has a gap, as if the middle platform sank at some point. The two side platforms are between the middle and ground platforms (Figure 22-2).

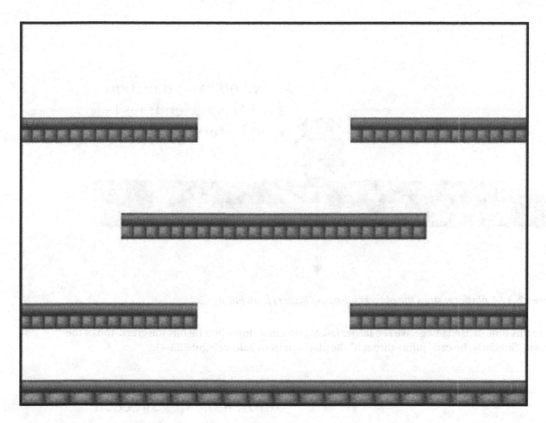

Figure 22-2. *Flood game screen*

The score will be displayed at the top left of the screen, and, at the top right, the number of lives remaining. It is possible to add branding to the lower right-hand area.

Main Actor—"Jasper"

The player character can move in two directions—left and right. He can jump onto platforms and over enemies. The player should not be hindered when jumping through a platform. It is only solid when the player lands on it. See the following diagram (Figure 22-3).

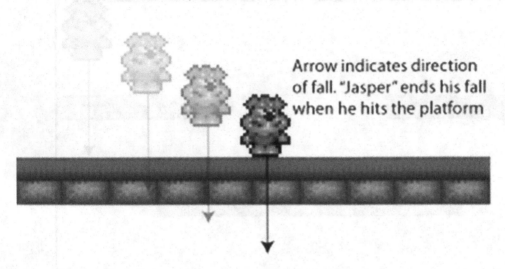

Figure 22-3. A platform stops the player character (Jasper) from falling

In this time-lapsed image, we see Jasper falling. He must stop when he hits the green-top of the platform. Similarly, he can "jump-through" the platform from below (Figure 22-4).

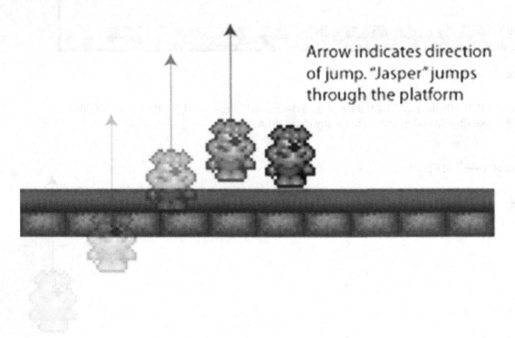

Figure 22-4. The player character (Jasper) can jump up through a platform

In this instance, Jasper jumps through the platform to land safely on top.

Enemies

There is only one enemy type in this game, and it patrols the following four platforms:

> Ground
>
> Left-bottom
>
> Right-bottom
>
> Middle

The patrol area for the enemy is limited to the length of the platform it patrols. The enemy can only move from left or right (Figure 22-5).

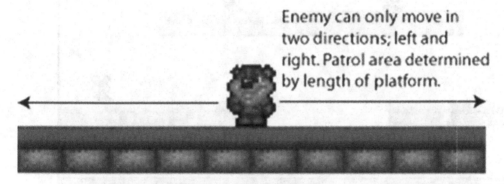

Figure 22-5. *The enemy can only move from left to right*

When an enemy touches Jasper, the player loses a life, and Jasper spins and moves around the screen randomly. This is nicknamed the "death rattle."

The Wave

The wave is initially configured by the user when he or she sets the level of difficulty. There are four levels of difficulty, and this equates to the number of milliseconds in which the wave rises up the screen by 1 pixel. The levels are

> 250ms
>
> 200ms
>
> 150ms
>
> 50ms

The Orchids

There are six orchids onscreen that the player must collect to complete the level. They are located as shown in the following diagram (Figure 22-6).

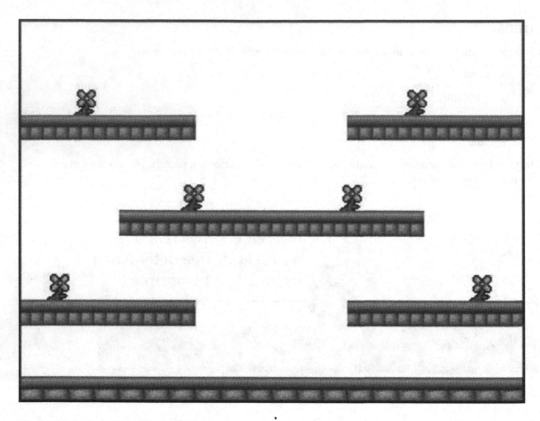

Figure 22-6. *Location of the orchids*

The player collects 100 points by collecting an orchid. This is achieved by running into it. Once an orchid has been collected, it is removed from the screen.

Entities

From this specification, we can determine that there are a number of entities. An entity is an element of the game, for example, the player character, enemy, orchid, etc. In Flood, the following entities have been identified:

> Player
>
> Enemy
>
> Platform
>
> Wave
>
> Orchid

Next Steps

The next step is to translate that specification into an abstract, using processes contained within the Unified Modeling Language (UML). The entities that are identified in the preceding section will be abstracted within the UML to create class diagrams. We may have to bring in other classes, such as our reusable `IController` class from before.

Object-Oriented Design

In this section, we will look at the role of object-oriented design in the context of video game development.

Introduction

In the early days of computing, people pretty much backed together solutions. These programs worked well enough but were virtually unmaintainable. There was no way you could go back to a program to try and fix a bug. It was, in fact, cheaper to scrap the code and start again.

As was mentioned in Chapter 9, reusability is important to software engineers and games programmers especially. With tighter and tighter deadlines being imposed, it is imperative to reuse code. This is where UML comes into play.

UML is the brainchild of the "Three Amigos": Grady Booch, James Rumbaugh, and Ivar Jacobson. They worked in separate organizations through the 1980s and 1990s, each devising his own methodology for object-oriented analysis and design. By the mid-1990s they decided to get together to create a unified modeling language.

UML is used by every major corporation, from Microsoft to IBM and Rational. In fact, the latter was bought by IBM because of its extensive ties to UML.

There are a number of components within UML, but we will be dealing with just two: use cases and class diagrams.

Use Cases

The specification that you get from a customer or an in-house designer may not be as complete as you would like. In order to go back to them and ask the question "Is this what you want?" we have to refine our ideas with documents called use case. Each use case represents a particular event that can occur within the system. So, for example:

> What happens when the player hits the boundaries of the screen?

> What happens when the player hits a platform?

> What happens when the player hits an enemy?

What Is a Use Case?

A use case document is a collection of scenarios, and each scenario is a sequence of steps. For each scenario, we want to show the following:

> A brief description of the scenario ("Player Boundaries")

> Assumptions for the scenario ("User can move in two directions and jump")

> The entity who initiates the use case ("Player")

225

Preconditions for the use case ("The player has moved")

Post-conditions for the use case ("Player is barred from moving left")

The format for a scenario is shown below:

UC-XXX Title of use case

Abstract:

Assumptions:

Actor:

Preconditions

Post-conditions:

Description:

The "XXX" represents a three-digit number, usually starting from 005 and going up in increments of five (005, 010, 015, etc.). You can group use cases together too, so, for example, all use cases referring to the Player might begin 1XX, the enemy 2XX, and so on.

The Title is fairly straightforward and can be used instead of the Abstract, so long as the Title is unambiguous and performs the same as the abstract.

The Abstract allows the author of the use case to give a brief overview of what is happening in the given scenario.

Assumptions allow the author to detail the items that are assumed to be correct. This is an important section, because assumptions can lead to complications later on. A programmer should read this section carefully!

An Actor in a use case is the same as an entity. It is a real-world object that can refer to the user, a (sub-) system or an external-to-the-system entity, such as a web server. The actor(s) supplied in this section are affected by the use case.

The Preconditions section lists all the conditions that must be met before the scenario can be stepped through.

The Post-conditions section lists all the conditions that will be met once the scenario has been stepped through.

The Description tells the programmer what must be done in a sequence of steps.

Sample Use Case

The following is a sample use case for the collision-detection system for the player. There are five scenarios:

UC-100 Player Movement

UC-105 Jumping

UC-110 Falling

UC-115 Enemy Collision

UC-120 Orchid Collision

The first (Player Movement) is shown in Figure 22-7.

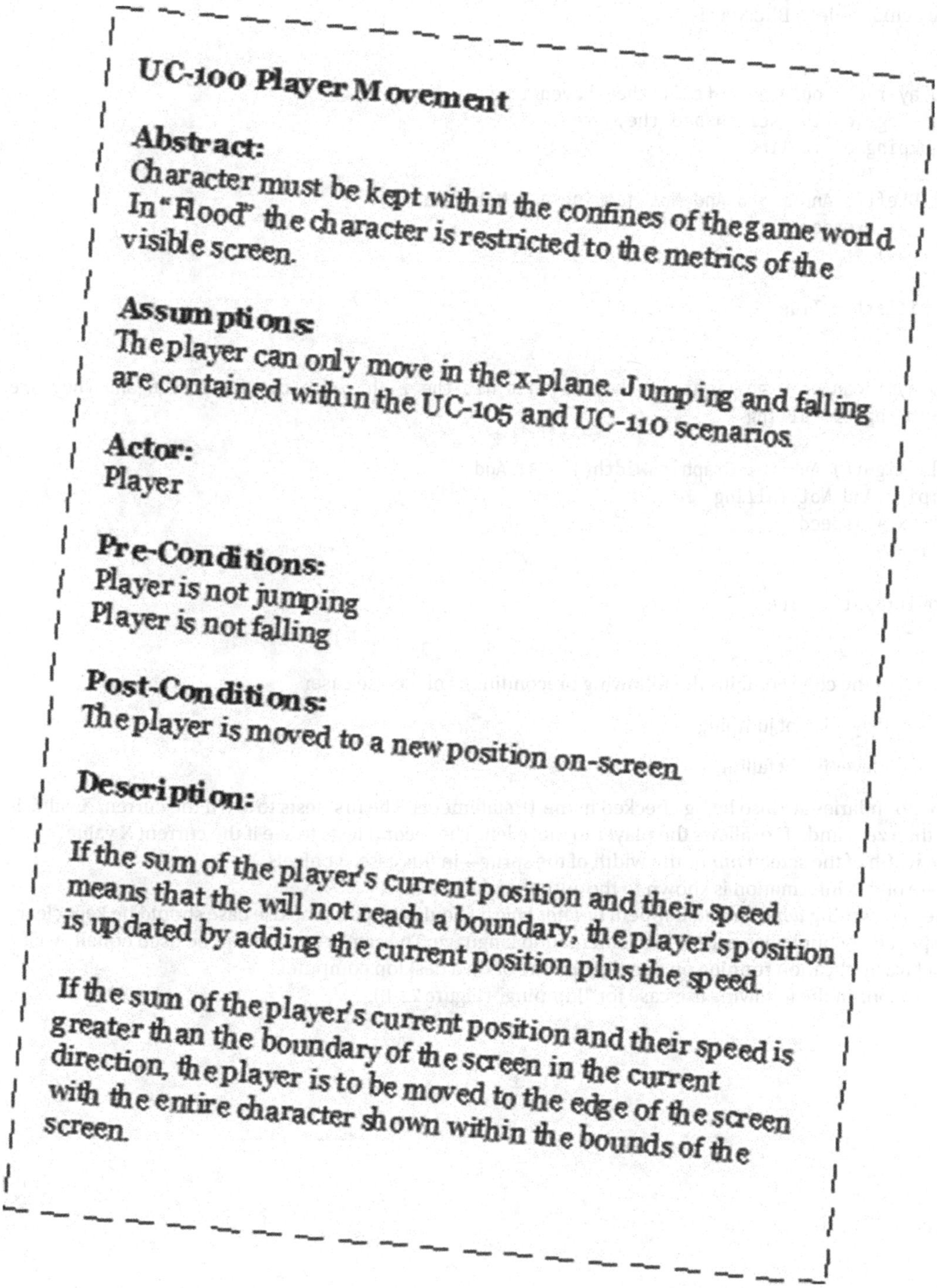

UC-100 Player Movement

Abstract:
Character must be kept within the confines of the game world. In "Flood" the character is restricted to the metrics of the visible screen.

Assumptions:
The player can only move in the x-plane. Jumping and falling are contained within the UC-105 and UC-110 scenarios.

Actor:
Player

Pre-Conditions:
Player is not jumping
Player is not falling

Post-Conditions:
The player is moved to a new position on-screen

Description:

If the sum of the player's current position and their speed means that the will not reach a boundary, the player's position is updated by adding the current position plus the speed.

If the sum of the player's current position and their speed is greater than the boundary of the screen in the current direction, the player is to be moved to the edge of the screen with the entire character shown within the bounds of the screen.

Figure 22-7. *My use case for Flood*

The actual code in BlitzMax is

```
'
' The player can only go left if they haven't hit
the left-edge of the screen and they are
' not jumping or falling
'
If ctrl.DLeft() And x > 0 And Not jumping And Not falling
    x = x - xspeed
    dir = 1
Else
    nohitleft = True
End If
'
' The player can only go right if they haven't hit the right-edge of the screen and they are
' not jumping or falling
'
If ctrl.DRight() And x < GraphicsWidth() - 34 And
Not jumping And Not falling
    x = x + xspeed
    dir = 2
Else
    nohitright = True
End If
```

Note that the code contains the following preconditions of the use case:

> Player is not jumping

> Player is not falling

The boundaries are also being checked in the IF statements. The first tests to see if the current X value is greater than zero and, if so, allows the player to move left. The second tests to see if the current X value is less than the width of the screen *minus* the width of the sprite—in this case, 34 pixels.

None of this information is known to the author of the use case.

They are writing *what* should happen, *but not how* it should happen. The use case should be kept clean with respect to technologies and/or implementation language. The same use case can be used equally well within a Java application running on a mobile phone or on a desktop computer.

Take a look at the following use case for "Jumping" (Figure 22-8):

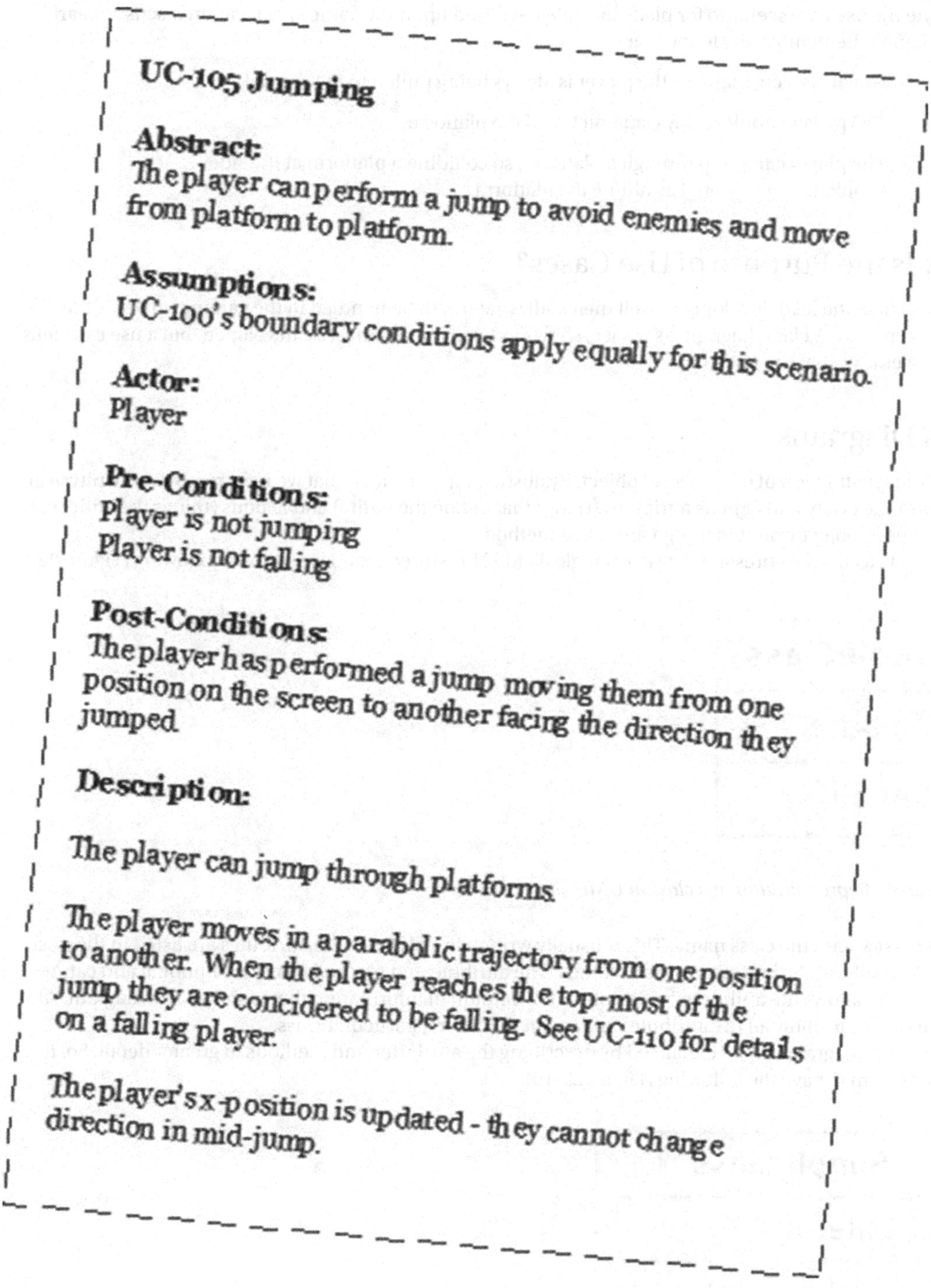

UC-105 Jumping

Abstract:
The player can perform a jump to avoid enemies and move from platform to platform.

Assumptions:
UC-100's boundary conditions apply equally for this scenario.

Actor:
Player

Pre-Conditions:
Player is not jumping
Player is not falling

Post-Conditions:
The player has performed a jump moving them from one position on the screen to another facing the direction they jumped.

Description:

The player can jump through platforms.

The player moves in a parabolic trajectory from one position to another. When the player reaches the top-most of the jump they are concidered to be falling. See UC-110 for details on a falling player.

The player's x-position is updated - they cannot change direction in mid-jump.

Figure 22-8. *Use case for "Jumping"*

Write the use case scenario for platform collision based upon the game specification discussed earlier in this chapter. Remember the following:

Gravity is a constant, so the player is always being pulled to the ground.

The player should always land on top of the platform.

The player can jump through a platform, so colliding a platform at the side should not be counted as hitting the platform.

What Is the Purpose of Use Cases?

Use cases allow the lead developers to tell their staff what has to be handled in the gaming universe the designers created. A class diagram, as we see, shows us what classes must be developed, but a use case tells us what events we have to code for.

Class Diagrams

A class is an abstraction of a real-world object. By abstraction, we mean that we have removed the physical portions of the entity and kept its attributes (things that define the entity) and actions (things the entity can do). Actions in object-oriented design are called methods.

In UML, a class is represented by a rectangle divided into three sections as shown following (Figure 22-9):

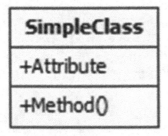

Figure 22-9. *Representation of a class in UML*

The first area is the class name. This is usually written in boldface. The attributes are listed in the next area, and, finally, at the bottom are the methods. The attribute and method boxes are optional and can be omitted. UML allows the author to be flexible in the amount of information that is shown in a diagram. Also, you do not have to show all the attributes and/or methods for a particular class.

The class diagram can be enhanced by describing the attributes and methods in greater detail. So, for example, you may have the following (Figure 22-10):

SimpleClass
+Attribute: int
+Method(type: int): string

Figure 22-10. *Enhanced class diagram*

Have you noticed that the types are separated from the attributes/methods by a colon? Isn't that similar to how BlitzMax makes you declare variables/fields/methods/functions? I think that Blitz Research spent a lot of time with these diagrams and decided to use them as a template when it came to defining the BlitzMax language.

The plus (+) and minus (-) signs indicate the scope of the attribute/method. A plus sign indicates that the item is exposed to anything outside of the class. A minus sign indicates that the item is internal to the class and is not visible outside. A class diagram is composed of the following:

- *Entity*: A real-world object

- *Class*: An abstraction of a real-world object

- *Attribute*: Something that describes the entity

- *Method*: Something that an action does

A DVD Recorder

A DVD recorder has a number of attributes—things that describe it—and a number of actions or methods that it can perform. These can be listed as:

- *Attributes*

    - Is Playing?

    - Is Recording?

    - Start Time of recording

    - End Time of recording

- *Methods*:

    - Eject disc

    - Play disc

    - Stop playback

    - Move to the next chapter

    - Move to the previous chapter

    - Show the menu

    - Record

In UML, this is drawn as a class diagram. A class diagram is a rectangle split into three areas. The top area is the name of the class (DVDRecorder); the middle area lists the attributes of the class; and the bottom area contains the list of methods. Note in this particular diagram there are plus (+) and minus (-) signs. This indicates the scope of the attributes and methods. A plus indicates that the attribute/method is public, and

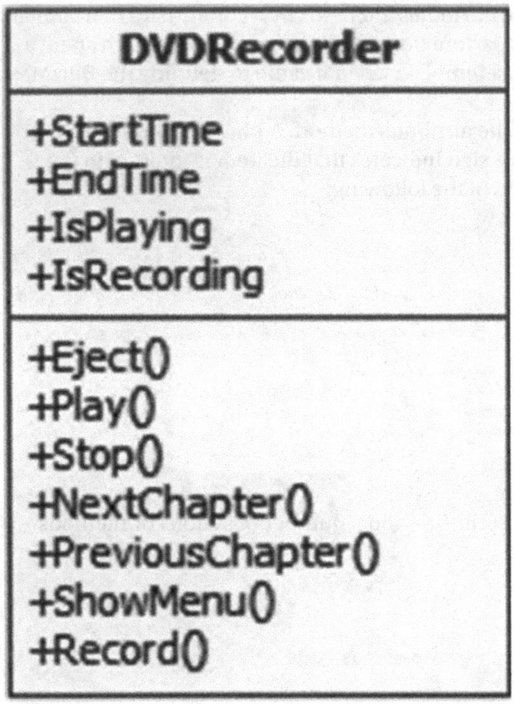

DVDRecorder
+StartTime +EndTime +IsPlaying +IsRecording
+Eject() +Play() +Stop() +NextChapter() +PreviousChapter() +ShowMenu() +Record()

Figure 22-11. *Class diagram for* DVDRecorder

the minus indicates that the attribute/method is private. In the following diagram (Figure 22-11), all the attributes are private.

What other attributes or methods do you think we could add to our DVD recorder? Should our recorder be able to record on an ad hoc basis too? What other method would be required?

Our Jasper character has the following attributes:

x

y

score

yspeed

xspeed

starty

lives

ctrl

These attributes describe the x and y coordinates, score, vertical speed, horizontal speed, the start y coordinate of the jump, number of lives, and controller used for the player character.

The main character has the following methods:

Reset

Update

```
    Draw

    Create
```

Draw the class diagram for the Jasper character. Call the class TPlayer and add the attributes and methods in the preceding list to it.

A class diagram only indicates a single entity, but in our object-oriented world, classes mix with each other. We need some way to show how each class relates to each other.

Class Relationships

We know that we can encapsulate other classes within each other and inherit classes from a parent class, using inheritance. We have seen this in BlitzMax. To show this in a class diagram, we draw lines between two classes representing the relationship.

Encapsulate "to contain within." Encapsulation is a fundamental part of object-oriented design. Attributes should not be accessible outside the method and should provide "getter" and "setter" methods to access them. This is not necessarily true in BlitzMax, however, because fields are by default visible outside the UDP-based Data Transfer (UDT).

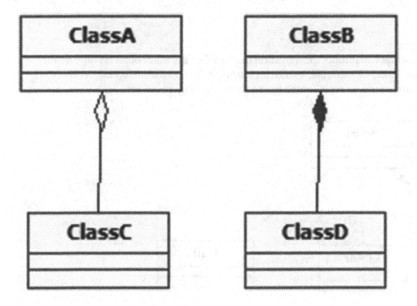

Figure 22-12. *Class diagram showing aggregation (left) and composition (right)*

Aggregation and Composition

Aggregation and composition occur when an instance of a class contains an attribute that is an instance of another object. The two types are shown following (Figure 22-12):

On the left is aggregation, with the white diamond representing the class containing the instance of the "partial class." The partial class, in this case, can be shared with any number of classes. On the right is composition, wherein the partial class can only be part of whole class.

Aggregation

Aggregation is represented by placing an outline diamond beside the aggregate class. Your computer system is an example of aggregation. It can contain a monitor, disk drives, CD-ROM drive, printer, keyboard and/or mouse. But these components can be shared with other computers too. For example, if you have a laptop, you can take your mouse with you on the go, and use it with the laptop. This can be represented in a class diagram, as follows (Figure 22-13):

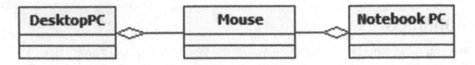

Figure 22-13. Class diagram of mouse aggregation with desktop and laptop

The Mouse class is contained within both the DesktopPC class and the NotebookPC class.

Aggregation is read as "Has a." So, "DesktopPC has a Mouse" and "NotebookPC has a Mouse" are valid statements. UML diagram relationships are bidirectional, unless arrowheads are used.

Composition

Composition is represented by a black diamond. Composition implies that the main object is only whole when composed of child classes. Take, for example, a shirt. It is comprised of two arms, a body, collar, and cuffs. In an object diagram, "Shirt" could be represented by the following (Figure 22-14):

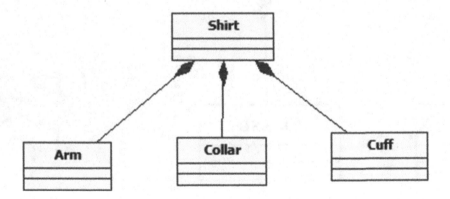

Figure 22-14. Class diagram for a hypothetical Shirt class

The diagram only shows that Shirt has to contain Arm, Collar, and Cuff. It does not show how many items of each are required. This is called multiplicity.

Multiplicity

Not only can we show the relationship between certain classes, but we can also show how many classes can be aggregated or composed with a particular class. This is shown by writing numbers and stars (*) and even two periods (..), to show the multiplicity of an aggregate or composite class. Taking another look at our Shirt example, we can use multiplicity to indicate the required number of each item that makes up our shirt (Figure 22-15).

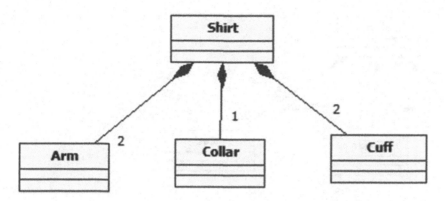

Figure 22-15. *Using multiplicity to indicate numbers of items in aggregated classes*

It is assumed for the time being that there is only one shirt, although we can explicitly place the value 1 beside the black diamond, if we desired. Other valid multiplicities are as follows (Figure 22-16):

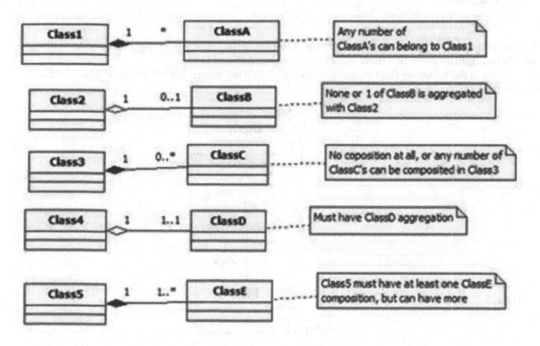

Figure 22-16. *Class diagram showing additional valid multiplicities*

In the preceding examples, I have included the diamond multiplicities, but they need not be included.

Naming the Attribute

It is also possible to name the attribute that the parent class calls the instance of the class it aggregates/ composes, as in the following illustration (Figure 22-17):

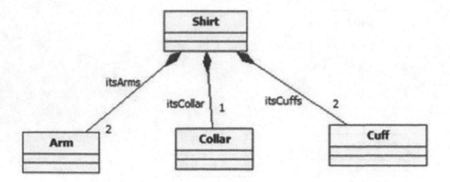

Figure 22-17. *Class diagram naming the attributes of the parent class*

From the preceding class diagram, we can see that the Shirt class contains three attributes:

itsArms

itsCollar

itsCuffs

We can also see that itsArms and itsCuffs include a list of the classes associated with the attributes, because the multiplicity states that there must be two each of Arm and Cuff.

Take a look at the following class diagram (Figure 22-18). It represents the old proverb "A bird in the hand is worth two in the bush."

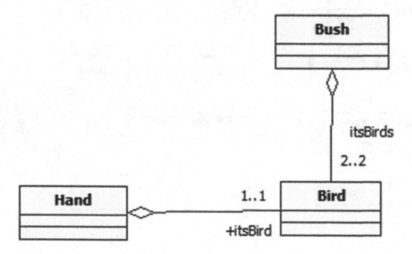

Figure 22-18. *Class diagram representing the proverb "A bird in the hand..."*

Draw a class diagram for each of the following:

"Every cloud has a silver lining"

"Cat of Nine Tails"

"Six of one, half a dozen of the other"

"Two's company; three's a crowd"

Inheritance

Inheritance is depicted by a triangular arrowhead. This arrowhead points to the base class. One or more lines proceed from the base class to the derived classes, as shown in the following diagram (Figure 22-19).

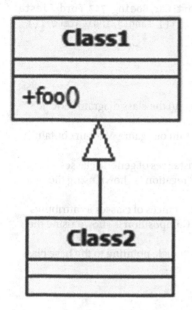

Figure 22-19. *Diagram depicting inheritance*

Although we do not explicitly place the foo() method in Class2, it is inherited from base Class1. We can also have detailed inheritance hierarchies, as expressed in the following diagram (Figure 22-20):

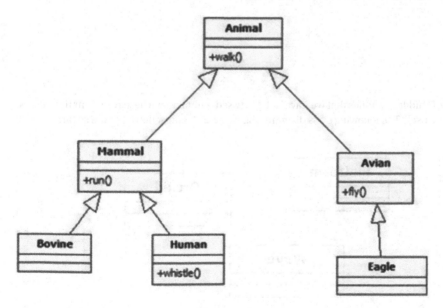

Figure 22-20. *Class diagram of detailed inheritance hierarchies*

237

The base class Animal is inherited by Mammal and Avian. Both classes inherit all the methods of Animal. In this case, the walk() method is inherited, so all their descendants also have this ability. The individual classes can either keep the method as is or redefine it, as required. **But:** They must implement some form of walk() method.

Draw inheritance diagrams for the following entities: Vehicle, Aircraft, Car, Boeing 747, Ford Fiesta.

Add the following methods, where appropriate: startEngine(), takeOff(), land(), indicateLeft(), indicateRight(), stopEngine().

Summary

Use cases allow us to tell the story for each and every event. These are fed into the class diagrams and become operations.

Class diagrams detail the relationship between each of the classes within our game. We can contain optional data too, such as attributes and operations (methods).

Aggregation is used in a class diagram to show classes that contain instances of generic classes as attributes. These classes are available for reuse within any other class. Aggregation is shown using the outline diamond and can include multiplicity metrics.

Composition is used in a class diagram to show classes that contain instances of classes as attributes. These classes that are contained in the parent cannot be used elsewhere. Composition is shown using the black diamond and can include multiplicity metrics.

Inheritance shows a class that has derived from a base class, using a triangle pointing to the base class and a line extending to the derived class.

Implementing OOP in BlitzMax

As we have discovered, there are only five entities in our game:

Player

Enemy

Platform

Wave

Orchid

There are a number of "hidden" entities that we have not discussed—until now. These represent the menus and the actual game engine itself. The following class diagram (Figure 22-21) represents our game so far:

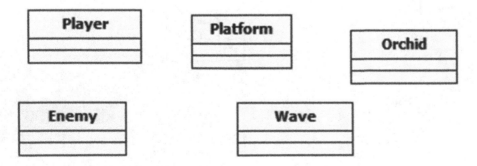

Figure 22-21. *Class diagram representing our game up to this point*

We will now examine these five classes and refine the requirements piece by piece until we are satisfied that we have defined all the classes that we require. Once this process has taken place, we will be in a position to convert the class diagram to UDTs.

Were Do We Get the Methods From?

The methods come from our previous work. Each playable object (either by the user or the computer) must be drawn, updated, reset, and created. I have included these operations in the class diagrams below.

Player

The Player class is fairly straightforward, and we will only be renaming this to fit in with BlitzMax convention. This means that the Player entity will become the TPlayer UDT (Figure 22-22).

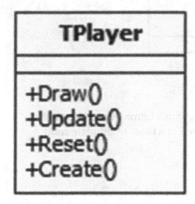

Figure 22-22. *Player class diagram*

Enemy

The Enemy class represents a single enemy's position. We will have several enemies onscreen at any one time, and this means that a single class will not do. We can use the Enemy class as a starting point. I also don't like the name "Enemy," so we are going to rename the classes that represent these as "Baddie" (Figure 22-23).

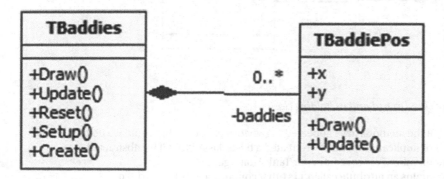

Figure 22-23. *Class diagrams for the "baddies" (enemies)*

CHAPTER 22 ■ STORYBOARDING

Now we have two classes. One represents each individual baddie (TBaddiePos), and the other is a container class, called TBaddies, that handles the creation, update, and drawing of each of the baddies.

Platform

The Platform class is much like the Enemy class, in that we require lists of these objects, not just single entities. I propose that we create a new class called TPlayScreen that handles the creation and drawing of these platforms (Figure 22-24).

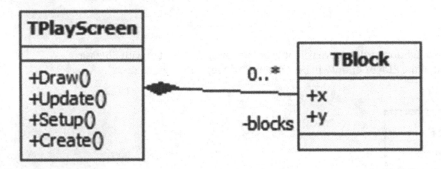

Figure 22-24. *Class diagram of the TPlayScreen class*

This is based on our knowing that the graphic artist has provided us with a bitmap containing a list of blocks. We will have to draw the blocks onscreen individually, one block at a time, to simulate solid platforms. This will be done using the Setup() method.

Orchid

The Orchid class like the Platform and Enemy classes requires a holding class. There is a distinct pattern forming here (Figure 22-25).

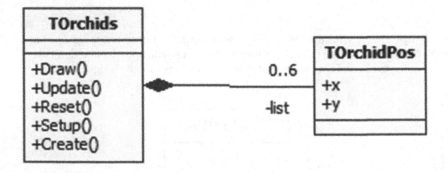

Figure 22-25. *Diagram of class Orchid and its holding class*

Note that some or all of the methods have appeared in previous classes. What could we do to marshal all that effort? There's a lot of duplication. What if we created a base class? What if we abstracted the positional information? Remember TVector2 from our Tank Attack game?

The TOrchids class contains an attribute called list that contains a list of TOrchidPos.

Wave

The Wave class is fairly simple and other than the name change, to Twave, we will not alter anything else (Figure 22-26).

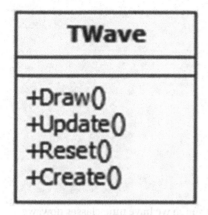

Figure 22-26. *TWave class diagram*

Putting It All Together

Putting all these classes together gives us a new class diagram (Figure 22-27). I have included another object called TFloodGame. This object will control our game.

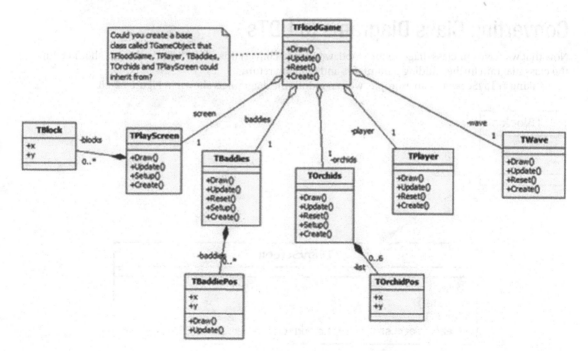

Figure 22-27. *Diagram of all the classes in the Flood game*

241

TFloodGame

We know from this diagram that TFloodGame contains the following methods:

Draw

Update

MainLoop

Create

TFloodGame also contains the following attributes:

Screen

Baddies

.Orchids

Wave

Player

Note that we still have five main classes! Isn't OOP wonderful? Although we have nine classes now, we still only have five main entities!

A main program is required to instantiate the TFloodGame class and to display menus/help screens, as we have done in previous projects.

We can see from this section so far that as we break the problem down into smaller chunks, we are making the program implementation (the coding) easier. This is because we are telling the developer what to code, what objects interact with other objects, etc.

Converting Class Diagrams to UDTs

Now that we have our class diagram for Flood, we have to convert this to UDT. To do this, we should refine the class diagram further, adding parameters and function returns.

Taking TPlayScreen as an example, we can redraw the diagram as shown in Figure 22-28.

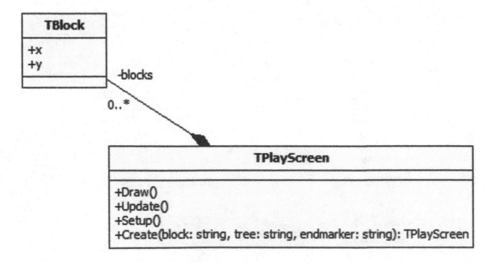

Figure 22-28. *Class diagram redrawn with new paramaters and functions*

The Create method has been underlined to indicate that it is part of a class definition and not part of an instance. In BlitzMax, this means that this operation is implemented as a function and not as a method.

An underlined operation (`SomeOperation()`) is implemented in BlitzMax as a function. All other operations (non-underlined) are implemented as methods in BlitzMax.

The parameters can be marked as in, out, or in/out. To implement out and in/out in BlitzMax, we use the Var keyword to indicate that a parameter is being passed by reference. Remember that by default, all parameters are passed by value.

See Chapter 6, on using functions, for details on the Var keyword. Again, I have taken some liberties here with the required parameters. We know that the screen requires blocks to display platforms and that an end marker is needed. We are assuming here that the path to these image files will be passed to the creation method. If we don't know the exact parameters at design time, we could use the following:

+Create() : TPlayScreen

This operation could be used if the parameters are unknown.

Stub Code for TFloodGame

I have included empty code for the TFloodGame annotated, to show the various attributes and methods. This is not the full implementation, as only the attributes, methods, and functions definitions are shown. There is no code between the blocks!

```
Type TFloodGame
    Field screen:TPlayScreen
    Field player:TPlayer
    Field baddies:TBaddies
    Field orchids:TOrchids
    Field wave:TWave
```

These are the instances of the classes in our class diagram. Note that there are no initial values set for these fields. We will implement this in the Create function later. Note also that these are the only fields that are listed in the class diagram.

```
Field background:TImage
```

The background field is used to store the jungle backdrop image that is placed behind all the platforms, baddies, orchids, and Jasper. We could have left it with a black background, but I thought that a backdrop would be nice.

```
Field wavespeed:Int = 275
Field levelid:Int = 0
Field doDeath:Int = False
Field endoflevel:Int = False
Field flushch:TChannel
Field flushplaying:Int = False
```

The preceding fields cover some housekeeping for our game engine. For example, we have to keep tabs on the current level (levelid), the speed of the wave rising (wavespeed), and whether the player is in the throws of death (doDeath).

```
Field ctrl:IController
```

The ctrl field holds an IController derived class for our controller—either joystick or keyboard. The IController class is from Chapter 17.

```
Method DrawOutline(str:String, x:Int, y:Int,
r:Int, g:Int, b:Int)
End Method
```

The DrawOutline method is used to draw text onscreen. It was used in our Paratrooper game to print text onscreen with a black outline. We have reused it here for the same effect.

```
Method DoLevelMessage(levelid:Int, top:Int)
End Method
```

A simple "Get Ready!" text excites the player and prepares him/her for the next level.

```
Method DoGameOver(top:Int)
End Method
```

DoGameOver displays the "Game Over!" message to the player.

```
Method Draw()
End Method
```

The Draw method is called by the MainLoop method. Draw calls all the objects' draw methods.

```
Method Update:Int()
End Method
```

The Update method is called by the MainLoop method. Update calls all the objects' update methods.

```
Method MainLoop()
End Method
```

The engine for this game is the MainLoop method. It is called by the main program after creating an instance of the object. Once called, the method initializes the variables and objects for the game and then falls into a loop to update the objects and display the characters and text onscreen.

```
Function Create:TFloodGame(flushsound:String,..
                        blocks:String, ..
                        tree:String, ..
                        endmarker:String,..
                        background:String,..
                        jasper:String, ..
                        jumpsound:String,..
                        baddies:String, ..
                        arghsound:String,..
                        orchid:String, ..
                        orchidsound:String, ..
                        wave:String, ..
                        ocean:String, ..
                        wavespeed:Int, ..
                        ctrl:IController)
End Function
```

244

The Create method is called by the main program to instantiate an instance of the TFloodGame class (UDT). The MainLoop method is then called, and the game begins on Level 1.

End Type

Testing Modules

The other advantage of structured design using OOP is that you can test modules on their own, without having to write the entire program first. The first module I wrote was TWave, to see what the flood wave would look like. The code for the module is shown following:

```
Rem
        UDT             :   TWave
        Author          :   Sloan Kelly
        Date            :   2005-08-31
        Description     :
```

UDT for the wave in the game "Flood". The wave moves up the screen at a predetermined rate 'speed'. The crest of the wave moves from left to right. It makes the wave look a little more realistic than a static pointy blue thing moving up the screen.

The start x-coordinate is offset to -64 (the width of the crest is 128). This is because we are using a little trick here. The x co-ordinate is increased until x = 0, we then reset it back to -64.

The user gets the appearance that the wave is moving from left to right.

```
End Rem
Type TWave
        Field crest:TImage                    ' Image file containing the crest of the wave
        Field ocean:TImage                    ' Image file containing the body of the wave
        Field crestx:Int = -64                ' Offset for the x-coordinate of the wave
        Field cresty:Int = GraphicsHeight()   ' Top of the wave - initially the bottom of the
                                                screen
        Field crestspeed:Int = 25             ' Speed in milliseconds for each increment of x-
        Field speed:Int = 250 ' in millisecs ' Speed of the wave, the increment of y-
        Field crestcount:Int = MilliSecs()    ' Counter for the crest movement (x-coord)
        Field speedcount:Int = MilliSecs()    ' Counter for the flood movement (y-coord)
        '
        ' Method        :   Reset
        ' Description    :   Resets the wave to the starting values. Used when a player dies or
        when a new level
        '                       is reached
        '
        Method Reset(newspeed:Int = 250)
                crestx = 0
                cresty = GraphicsHeight()
                crestspeed = 25
                speed = newspeed
```

```
        crestcount:Int = MilliSecs()
        speedcount:Int = MilliSecs()
End Method


'
' Method       : Update
' Description   : Updates the x- and ycoordinates based upon the speeds above. The wave
                can only get to
'                48 pixels from the top of the screen. The player would be killed by
                the wave by then
'
Method Update()
    '
    ' Update the crest - move it from left to right
    '
    If MilliSecs() > crestcount + crestspeed
        crestcount = MilliSecs()
        crestx = crestx + 1
        If crestx > 63
            crestx = -64
        End If
    End If
    '
    ' Update the y-coord of the flood
    '
    If MilliSecs() > speedcount + speed And cresty > 48
        speedcount = MilliSecs()
        cresty = cresty - 1
    End If

End Method


'
' Method       : StartFlush
' Description   : For future expansion
'
Method StartFlush()
    ' for future
    ' expansion
End Method


'
' Method       : FlushUpdate
' Description   : This is the alternative "Update" when the user completes a level, the
                water is flushed
'                out of the screen. This updates the position of the water level in the
                flood.
'
Method FlushUpdate:Int()
```

```
            If MilliSecs() > crestcount + crestspeed
                crestcount = MilliSecs()
                crestx = crestx + 1
                If crestx > 63
                    crestx = -64
                End If
            End If

            cresty = cresty + 1
            If cresty > GraphicsHeight()
                Return 1                     ' tell the calling routine we're finished
            Else
                Return 0                     ' tell the calling routine we're NOT finished
            End If
        End Method

        '
        ' Method       : TileOcean
        ' Description  : Fills in the rest of the screen with 'ocean'. I tried to use
        '                'TileImage' (in-built
        '                keyword) with no success.
Wrote this instead, it does exactly what TileImage should
        '                do!
        '
        Method TileOcean()
            For y:Int = cresty+32 To GraphicsHeight() + 32 Step 32 ' Height of crest is 32px,
            so draw below that on-screen
                For x:Int = 0 To GraphicsWidth() Step 32
                    DrawImage(ocean, x, y)
                Next
            Next
        End Method

        '
        ' Method       : Draw
        ' Description  : Draws the crest and ocean on-screen.
        '
        Method Draw()
            blend:Int = GetBlend() ' capture the blend mode
            SetBlend(ALPHABLEND)   ' only want to see a big thru the ocean
            SetAlpha(.6)           ' so 60% is ok
            For x:Int = crestx - 64 To GraphicsWidth() + 64 Step 64
                DrawImage(crest, x, cresty)
            Next
            TileOcean()
            SetBlend(blend)        ' reset the blend mode
            SetAlpha(1)            ' reset the alpha (should always be 1)
        End Method
```

```
'
' Function     : Create
' Description  : Creates a TWave object and passes it back to the calling routine
'
Function Create:TWave(crest:String, ocean:String, speed:Int)
     o:TWave = New TWave
     o.crest = LoadImage(crest)
     o.ocean = LoadImage(ocean)
     o.speed = speed
     Return o
End Function
```

```
End Type
```

Enter the code for TWave exactly as written and save it to your BlitzMax project folder Flood. Create Flood if you haven't done so already. Call the file TWave.bmx. We will use this file in the next section.

Testing the Code

A computer program is a complex machine. There are a number of moving parts in its construction, each of which must be tested before we start bolting them together. Because we have modularized the code by creating different classes (UDTs), we can test each one individually.

The code that we develop to test each module on its own is called stub code. Stub code will not form part of the completed program and is usually thrown away when development is completed.

Creating Stub Code

Stub code is a short program that will allow us to run through the functionality of any class or function, without having to place it into a larger program. This approach to software development leads to fewer headaches later because

> Each module/class can be tested as a single entity. This type of test is called a unit test.

> Small problems—bugs—can be spotted at an earlier stage of production. The earlier you catch a bug, the less it will cost to fix!

> Stub code can be seen as prototyping the main functionality.

The stub code for the TWave UDT is shown below:

```
Graphics 640, 480, 16, 75

Incbin "gfx/background.jpg"
Incbin "gfx/wave.png"
Incbin "gfx/ocean.png"

wave:TWave = TWave.Create("incbin::gfx/wave.png",
"incbin::gfx/ocean.png", 100)
background:TImage =
LoadImage("incbin::gfx/background.jpg")
```

```
While Not KeyHit(KEY_ESCAPE)
    wave.Update()
    DrawImage(background, 0, 0)
    wave.Draw()
    Flip
    Cls

Wend
```

I have highlighted the important lines in the code to show that you do not need a large amount of code to test modules/classes.

Open up the TWave.bmx file and enter the stub code at the bottom of the file. Save the file. When you run the application, you should see the wave traveling up the screen.

Using the TPlayScreen.bmx file, create stub code to display the play screen. Save the file.

CHAPTER 23

Project Management

So far, we have looked at programs that appear as one single file.

While this is suitable for the lone bedroom coder, it is not acceptable from a team-coding point of view. In BlitzMax, there is a way to write code in a team environment without everyone working on the same file.

Using the Include Keyword

The Include keyword allows you to bring in other people's code to be compiled with your project. In our case, we are working on a game called Flood that has a number of components (UDTs) that we can quite easily pass out to other developers. To bring the code back into our main program, we use the Include keyword.

Open the TWave.bmx file with the stub code attached to it. Take a copy of the stub code and create a new file. Paste the stub code into the new file and delete it from the TWave.bmx file. At the top of the new file, add the following line:

```
Include "TWave.bmx"
```

When including a file make sure you spell the name correctly and include its extension, ".bmx" in this case. You should have the following code in your new file:

```
Include "TWave.bmx"
Graphics 640, 480, 16, 75
Incbin "gfx/background.jpg"
Incbin "gfx/wave.png"
Incbin "gfx/ocean.png"
wave:TWave = TWave.Create("incbin::gfx/wave.png",
"incbin::gfx/ocean.png", 100)
background:TImage =
LoadImage("incbin::gfx/background.jpg")

While Not KeyHit(KEY_ESCAPE)
    wave.Update()
    DrawImage(background, 0, 0)
    wave.Draw()
    Flip
    Cls
Wend
```

Save the file as TWave_Stub.bmx and run the new file. You should get the same output as before: a wave slowly creeping up the screen. In the finished game, the main file is called FloodTheGame.bmx, and it contains the following lines:

```
Include "udts/TBlock.bmx"          ' The platform blocks
Include "udts/TWave.bmx"           ' The rising tide
Include "udts/TOrchidPos.bmx"      ' Orchid position
Include "udts/TOrchids.bmx"        ' All the orchids
Include "udts/TBaddiePos.bmx"      ' Baddie position
Include "udts/TBaddies.bmx"        ' All the baddies
Include "udts/TPlayScreen.bmx"     ' The actual screen - displays all the blocks
Include "udts/TPlayer.bmx"         ' Jasper - our hero
Include "udts/TFloodGame.bmx"      ' The game engine
Include "udts/TMenuScreen.bmx"     ' The menu
Include "udts/THelpScreen.bmx"     ' Help!
Include "udts/IController.bmx"     ' The infamous game controller
```

When the program is compiled, BlitzMax ensures that these files are compiled as if they were part of the program.

Be aware that if you mistakenly declare two items of the same name in two separate include files, you will have to track the problem down and change one of the item's names. You will get a compilation error if BlitzMax detects a variable being re-declared.

Advantages of Using the Include Keyword

The obvious advantage is that code can be developed by a number of programmers, and quick empty code can be used when there has yet to be code developed. It also makes your program easier to read, because you won't have to scroll past page after page of UDT definitions.

Embedding Binary Resources

As a BlitzMax developer, you can also embed binary resources, such as sound, image, and font files, to your executable. To do this, you use the IncBin keyword.

The IncBin Keyword

To embed a binary file into your executable, you use the IncBin keyword. The format of this keyword is

```
IncBin <path to file>
```

where <path to file> is a known path. This can be a relative path (using ../images/sprite.png) or an absolute path (such as C:\images\sprites\player1.png). So, for example, you could use the following:

```
Incbin "gfx/background.jpg"
Incbin "gfx/wave.png"
Incbin "gfx/ocean.png"
wave:TWave = TWave.Create("incbin::gfx/wave.png",
```

```
"incbin::gfx/ocean.png", 100)
background:TImage =
LoadImage("incbin::gfx/background.jpg")
```

When we reference the file later, we put `incbin::` in front of the path to the file. This ensures that we are referencing the copy contained within our executable, as follows:

```
background:TImage =
LoadImage("incbin::gfx/background.jpg")
```

APPENDIX A

■ ■ ■

Web Site Addresses

All code and graphics used within this book are available for download from www.blitzmaxbook.com/ (Figure A-1).

Figure A-1. BlitzMax web site (Blitz Research Limited © 2011)

© Sloan Kelly 2016
S. Kelly, *BlitzMax for Absolute Beginners*, DOI 10.1007/978-1-4842-2523-3

To order a copy of BlitzMax, or to join the BlitzMax development community, visit www.blitzmax.com/ (Figure A-2).

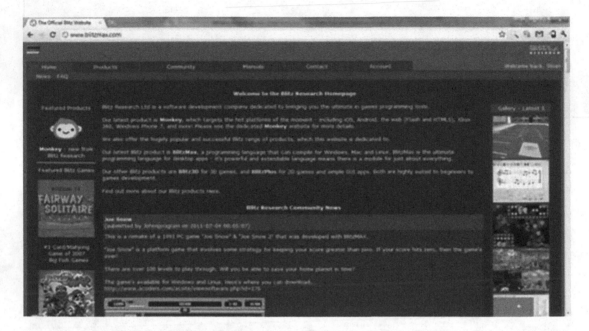

Figure A-2. *BlitzMax web site (Blitz Research Limited © 2011)*

APPENDIX B

■ ■ ■

BlitzMax Key Codes

For use with KeyHit, KeyDown, etc.

Table B-1. *Key Codes in BlitzMax*

Key	Value	Key	Value
Backspace	KEY_BACKSPACE	V	KEY_V
Tab	KEY_TAB	W	KEY_W
Clear	KEY_CLEAR	X	KEY_X
Return	KEY_RETURN	Y	KEY_Y
Enter	KEY_ENTER	Z	KEY_Z
Pause	KEY_PAUSE	Sys key (Left)	KEY_LSYS
Escape	KEY_ESCAPE	Sys key (Right)	KEY_RSYS
Space	KEY_SPACE	Numpad 0	KEY_NUM0
Page Up	KEY_PAGEUP	Numpad 1	KEY_NUM1
Page Down	KEY_PAGEDOWN	Numpad 2	KEY_NUM2
End	KEY_END	Numpad 3	KEY_NUM3
Home	KEY_HOME	Numpad 4	KEY_NUM4
Cursor (Left)	KEY_LEFT	Numpad 5	KEY_NUM5
Cursor (Up)	KEY_UP	Numpad 6	KEY_NUM6
Cursor (Right)	KEY_RIGHT	Numpad 7	KEY_NUM7
Cursor (Down)	KEY_DOWN	Numpad 8	KEY_NUM8
Select	KEY_SELECT	Numpad 9	KEY_NUM9
Print	KEY_PRINT	Numpad *	KEY_NUMMULTIP
Execute	KEY_EXECUTE	Numpad +	KEY_NUMADD
Screen	KEY_SCREEN	Numpad -	KEY_NUMSUBTRA
Insert	KEY_INSERT	Numpad .	KEY_NUMDECIMA
Delete	KEY_DELETE	Numpad /	KEY_NUMDIVIDE
Help	KEY_HELP	F1	KEY_F1

(continued)

© Sloan Kelly 2016

S. Kelly, *BlitzMax for Absolute Beginners*, DOI 10.1007/978-1-4842-2523-3

Table B-1. (*continued*)

Key	Value	Key	Value
0	KEY_0	F2	KEY_F2
1	KEY_1	F3	KEY_F3
2	KEY_2	F4	KEY_F4
3	KEY_3	F5	KEY_F5
4	KEY_4	F6	KEY_F6
5	KEY_5	F7	KEY_F7
6	KEY_6	F8	KEY_F8
7	KEY_7	F9	KEY_F9
8	KEY_8	F10	KEY_F10
9	KEY_9	F11	KEY_F11
A	KEY_A	F12	KEY_F12
B	KEY_B	Num Lock	KEY_NUMLOCK
C	KEY_C	Scroll Lock	KEY_SCROLL
D	KEY_D	Shift (Left)	KEY_LSHIFT
E	KEY_E	Shift (Right)	KEY_RSHIFT
F	KEY_F	Control (Left)	KEY_LCONTROL
G	KEY_G	Control (Right)	KEY_RCONTROL
H	KEY_H	Alt key (Left)	KEY_LALT
I	KEY_I	Alt key (Right)	KEY_RALT
J	KEY_J	Tilde	KEY_TILDE
K	KEY_K	Minus	KEY_MINUS
L	KEY_L	Equals	KEY_EQUALS
M	KEY_M	Bracket (Open)	KEY_OPENBRACK
N	KEY_N	Bracket (Close)	KEY_CLOSEBRAC
O	KEY_O	Backslash	KEY_BACKSLASH
P	KEY_P	Semicolon	KEY_SEMICOLON
Q	KEY_Q	Quote	KEY_QUOTES
R	KEY_R	Comma	KEY_COMMA
S	KEY_S	Period	KEY_PERIOD
T	KEY_T	Slash	KEY_SLASH
U	KEY_U		

APPENDIX C

■ ■ ■

ASCII Table

Table C-1. *AACII Table*

Dec.	Hex.	Meaning / Symbol	Dec.	Hex.	Meaning/Symbol
0	0	null	64	40	@
1	1	start of heading	65	41	A
2	2	start of text	66	42	B
3	3	end of text	67	43	C
4	4	end of transmission	68	44	D
5	5	enquiry	69	45	E
6	6	acknowledge	70	46	F
7	7	bell	71	47	G
8	8	backspace	72	48	H
9	9	horizontal tab	73	49	I
10	A	new line	74	4A	J
11	B	vertical tab	75	4B	K
12	C	new page	76	4C	L
13	D	carriage return	77	4D	M
14	E	shift out	78	4E	N
15	F	shift in	79	4F	O
16	10	data link escape	80	50	P
17	11	device control 1	81	51	Q
18	12	device control 2	82	52	R
19	13	device control 3	83	53	S
20	14	device control 4	84	54	T
21	15	negative acknowledge	85	55	U
22	16	synchronous idle	86	56	V

(continued)

© Sloan Kelly 2016
S. Kelly, *BlitzMax for Absolute Beginners*, DOI 10.1007/978-1-4842-2523-3

Table C-1. (*continued*)

Dec.	Hex.	Meaning / Symbol	Dec.	Hex.	Meaning/Symbol
23	17	end of trans. block	87	57	W
24	18	cancel	88	58	X
25	19	end of medium	89	59	Y
26	1A	substitute	90	5A	Z
27	1B	escape	91	5B	[
28	1C	file separator	92	5C	\
29	1D	group separator	93	5D	]
30	1E	record separator	94	5E	^
31	1F	unit separator	95	5F	_
32	20	space	96	60	`
33	21	!	97	61	a
34	22	"	98	62	b
35	23	#	99	63	c
36	24	$	100	64	d
37	25	%	101	65	e
38	26	&	102	66	f
39	27	'	103	67	g
40	28	(	104	68	h
41	29	)	105	69	i
42	2A	*	106	6A	j
43	2B	+	107	6B	k
44	2C	,	108	6C	l
45	2D	-	109	6D	m
46	2E	.	110	6E	n
47	2F	/	111	6F	o
48	30	0	112	70	p
49	31	1	113	71	q
50	32	2	114	72	r
51	33	3	115	73	s
52	34	4	116	74	t
53	35	5	117	75	u
54	36	6	118	76	v
55	37	7	119	77	w

(*continued*)

Table C-1. (*continued*)

Dec.	Hex.	Meaning / Symbol	Dec.	Hex.	Meaning/Symbol
56	38	8	120	78	x
57	39	9	121	79	y
58	3A	:	122	7A	z
59	3B	;	123	7B	{
60	3C	<	124	7C	|
61	3D	=	125	7D	}
62	3E	>	126	7E	~
63	3F	?	127	7F	DEL

Controller Abstraction Classes

```
Rem
    File       : Controller.bmx
    Author     : Sloan Kelly
    Purpose    : Controller abstraction classes to allow game code to be free from multiple
                 controller code.
Keeping the game engine pure, if you will
End Rem

Rem
    Class       : IFire
    Author      : Sloan Kelly
    Description : Abstract firing mechanism.
Contained within the IController
                class is a list of firing mechanisms. It's possible to extend
                this list over time to other input devices. For example a mouse
                button etc.
End Rem

Type IFire Abstract

    Field Item:Int

    Method FireDown:Int() Abstract
    Method FireHit:Int() Abstract

End Type

Rem
    Class      : IController
    Author     : Sloan Kelly
    Purpose    : Abstraction of controller method. Useful if you want your game to be
                 played with people who want to use either keyboard or joysticks.
                 Contains a number of abstract methods that are implemented in the
                 child classes that inherit. Contains three final methods that are
                 used by all child-controller classes.
End Rem
Type IController Abstract
```

© Sloan Kelly 2016

S. Kelly, *BlitzMax for Absolute Beginners*, DOI 10.1007/978-1-4842-2523-3

```
    Field FireMethods:TList = CreateList() ' List of ways user can press fire / jump
    / dash ...
    Field
Name:String                              ' Name of controller ("Keyboard", "Mouse",
"Joystick")

' can be used within the program to identify the controller

' implementation to the coder
    Method DUp:Int()
Abstract                                 ' User presses
Up
    Method DDown:Int()
Abstract                                 ' User
presses Down
    Method DLeft:Int()
Abstract                                 ' User
presses Left
    Method DRight:Int()
Abstract                              ' User presses Right

    '
    ' Adds an IFire method to the list of available
    ' methods. Notice that this is an INTERFACE that
    ' is required, so any object that inherits this
    ' interface can be used too. This method is built-in
    ' to all classes that inherit IController
    '
    Method AddFire(fire:IFire) Final
         FireMethods.AddLast(fire)
    End Method

    '
    ' Checks to see that fire 'index' has been hit and
    ' returns a boolean True if it has. Like AddFire, this
    ' method is inherited by all children of IController
    '
    Method Fire:Int(index:Int) Final
         rtn:Int = False
         i:Int = 0
         For f:IFire = EachIn FireMethods
              If i = index
                   If f.FireDown()
                         rtn = True
                   End If
              End If
              i = i + 1
         Next
         Return rtn
    End Method
```

```
'
' Returns the number of buttons a particular controller has
'
    Method ButtonCount:Int() Final
        Return CountList(FireMethods)
    End Method

End Type

Rem
    Class           : TStick
    Author          : Sloan Kelly
    Purpose         : Implementation of the
IController interface. This is the code for a joystick or similar game controller
End Rem
Type TStick Extends IController

    Field Port:Int

    Method DUp:Int()
        Return JoyY(Port) = -1
    End Method

    Method DDown:Int()
        Return JoyY(port) = 1
    End Method

    Method DLeft:Int()
        Return JoyX(Port) = -1
    End Method

    Method DRight:Int()
        Return JoyX(Port) = 1
    End Method

    Function Create:TStick(Name:String, Port:Int)
        o:TStick = New TStick
        o.Name = Name
        o.Port = Port
        Return o
    End Function

End Type

Rem
    Class           : TKeyboard
    Author          : Sloan Kelly
    Purpose         : Implementation of the IController interface. This is the code for a
                      keyboard
End Rem
Type TKeyboard Extends IController
```

```
        Field kcUp:Int
        Field kcDown:Int
        Field kcLeft:Int
        Field kcRight:Int

        Method DUp:Int()
            Return KeyDown(kcUp)
        End Method

        Method DDown:Int()
            Return KeyDown(kcDown)
        End Method

        Method DLeft:Int()
            Return KeyDown(kcLeft)
        End Method

        Method DRight:Int()
            Return KeyDown(kcRight)
        End Method

        Function Create:TKeyboard(Name:String, up:Int, dwn:Int, lft:Int, rght:Int)
            o:TKeyboard = New TKeyboard
            o.Name = Name
            o.kcUp = up
            o.kcDown = dwn
            o.kcLeft = lft
            o.kcRight = rght
            Return o
        End Function

End Type

Rem
        Class          : TKeyFire
        Author         : Sloan Kelly
        Purpose        : Inherits from the IFire interface. This class traps keyboard
events.
End Rem
Type TKeyFire Extends IFire
        Field Item:Int

        Method FireDown:Int()
            Return KeyDown(Item)
        End Method

        Method FireHit:Int()
            Return KeyHit(Item)
        End Method
```

```
    Function Create:TKeyFire(kc:Int)
        o:TKeyFire = New TKeyFire
        o.Item = kc
        Return o
    End Function

End Type

Rem
    Class           : TStickFire
    Author          : Sloan Kelly
    Purpose         : Inherits from the IFire interface. This class traps joystick button
                      events.
End Rem
Type TStickFire Extends IFire
    Field Item:Int
    Field Port:Int

    Method FireDown:Int()
        Return JoyDown(Item, Port)
    End Method

    Method FireHit:Int()
        Return JoyDown(Item, Port)
    End Method

    Function Create:TStickFire(Item:Int, Port:Int)
        o:TStickFire = New TStickFire
        o.Item = Item
        o.Port = Port
        Return o
    End Function
End Type
```

APPENDIX E

Compiler Directives

Compiler directives are statements that are not converted into actual code but control the compiler's operation. BlitzMax supports the following compiler directives:

> Strict
>
> Operating-system-specific code
>
> Processor-specific code
>
> Endian-specific code
>
> Debug mode code

Strict

Usually, if BlitzMax encounters an identifier (variable name) in your code that has not already been declared, it assumes that it is an integer variable.

In the following code example, as myVar has not been declared, the compiler will create a new integer and set its value to 0.

```
Print(myVar)
```

This can cause problems if you misspell a variable name, as instead of giving an error, the compiler will think that the misspelled variable is actually a different variable altogether.

To avoid this, place the Strict compiler directive at the top of the code.

```
Strict
Local myVar=42
Print(myVar)
```

This gives an error, because myVaar has not been declared.

```
Print(myVaar)
```

© Sloan Kelly 2016

S. Kelly, *BlitzMax for Absolute Beginners*, DOI 10.1007/978-1-4842-2523-3

When in Strict mode, all variables must be declared using the Local or Global keywords (unless they are fields inside types or parameters inside a function). You can go one step further and use the SuperStrict keyword, to ensure that you explicitly set your data types too.

```
SuperStrict
Local i:Int = 5
Print i
```

By default, BlitzMax assumes the Integer (Int) data type. With SuperStrict mode, you must *explicitly* indicate that the variable is an integer.

Operating-System-Specific Code

In BlitzMax, you can specify that a certain block of code should only be included when the code is compiled on a certain operating system (OS). This is useful if you want a module to have one function that actually runs different code on different operating systems. To start an OS-specific block, use the statement ?Linux, ?MacOS, or ?Win32. To switch back to non-OS-specific mode, just use a question mark (?).

```
?Linux
 'this block of code will only be compiled under Linux
?Win32
 'this block of code will only be compiled under Windows.
?MacOS
 'this block of code will only be compiled under Mac.
?
 'this block of code will be compiled on all platforms.
```

Processor-Specific Code

Use these if you must know which processor the code is being compiled for. It comes in handy if you are using an assembler.

```
?PPC
 'this block of code will only be compiled on a PowerPC system.
?x86
 'this block of code will only be compiled on a x86 (Intel, AMD etc) system.
?
 'all code from this point on will be compiled on all systems.
```

Endian-Specific Code

Sometimes, you only have to know the endianness of the target platform. The following directives can help.

```
?LittleEndian
 'this block of code will only be compiled on platforms that use the little endian format.
?BigEndian
 'this block of code will only be compiled on platforms that use the big endian format.
?
 'all code from this point on will be compiled on all platforms.
```

Debug Mode Code

This works in a similar way to OS-specific code, except that it allows the program to specify that code will only be compiled when the project is built in debug mode.

```
?Debug
 'this block of code will only be compiled in debug mode.
?
 'all code from this point on will be compiled in debug and release modes.
```

Index

Get the eBook for only $4.99!

Why limit yourself?

Now you can take the weightless companion with you wherever you go and access your content on your PC, phone, tablet, or reader.

Since you've purchased this print book, we are happy to offer you the eBook for just $4.99.

Convenient and fully searchable, the PDF version enables you to easily find and copy code—or perform examples by quickly toggling between instructions and applications.

To learn more, go to http://www.apress.com/us/shop/companion or contact support@apress.com.

All Apress eBooks are subject to copyright. All rights are reserved by the Publisher, whether the whole or part of the material is concerned, specifically the rights of translation, reprinting, reuse of illustrations, recitation, broadcasting, reproduction on microfilms or in any other physical way, and transmission or information storage and retrieval, electronic adaptation, computer software, or by similar or dissimilar methodology now known or hereafter developed. Exempted from this legal reservation are brief excerpts in connection with reviews or scholarly analysis or material supplied specifically for the purpose of being entered and executed on a computer system, for exclusive use by the purchaser of the work. Duplication of this publication or parts thereof is permitted only under the provisions of the Copyright Law of the Publisher's location, in its current version, and permission for use must always be obtained from Springer. Permissions for use may be obtained through RightsLink at the Copyright Clearance Center. Violations are liable to prosecution under the respective Copyright Law.

Get the eBook for only $4.99!

Why limit yourself?

Now you can take the weight of knowledge with you wherever you go and access your content on your PC, phone, tablet, or reader.

Since you purchased this print book, we're happy to offer you the eBook for just $4.99.

Convenient and fully searchable, the PDF version enables you to easily find and copy code—or perform examples by quickly toggling between instructions and applications.

To learn more, go to http://www.apress.com/shop/companion or contact support@apress.com.

Apress®
THE EXPERT'S VOICE®

Printed in the United States
by Bookmasters

Printed in the United States
By Bookmasters